DOUGLASS C. NORTH, Professor of Economics and
Director of the Institute for Economic Research at the
University of Washington, is the author of *The Economic Growth of the United States, 1790-1860* (published in 1961) and *Growth and Welfare in the American Past: A New Economic History* (to be published
the end of 1965). He has served as the Review Editor
of the Foreign Trade Section, revision of *Historical
Statistics,* and continues to serve as co-editor of *The
Journal of Economic History* and as a Trustee of the
Economic History Association. He was one of the in-
vited lecturers to present a portion of the national tele-
vision course "The American Economy" in 1962.

Douglass C. North
University of Washington

THE ECONOMIC GROWTH
of the
UNITED STATES
1790-1860

The Norton Library
W · W · NORTON & COMPANY · INC ·
NEW YORK

First published in the Norton Library 1966
by arrangement with Prentice-Hall, Inc.

Published simultaneously in Canada
by George J. McLeod Limited
Toronto

To

Lois and Edie

and

Adelaide and Cess
with affection and respect

SBN 393-00346-9

PRINTED IN THE UNITED STATES OF AMERICA

5 6 7 8 9 0

PREFACE

On the eve of the Civil War the United States had already achieved rapid and sustained economic expansion. We had filled out our territorial boundaries, and the frontier was already encroaching upon the parched lands in the lee of the Rocky Mountains and moving east of the Sierra Nevadas. Territorial acquisition had preceded the frontiersman, but the rapid pace of his westward movement had been a continuous goad. We were an industrial nation second only to Britain in manufacturing.[1] Our expansion had been matched by an acceleration in economic well-being.[2] The obstacles to American economic growth had been removed before the Civil War took place. That war was a costly and bitter interruption.

---

[1] *Twelfth Census of the United States, Manufactures,* Part I, Vol. VII, IV (Washington: Government Printing Office, 1902) quotes Mulhall's *Industries and Wealth of Nations* to the effect that the United States in 1860 was fourth in manufacturing in terms of value as follows:

United Kingdom	$2,808,000,000
France	2,092,000,000
Germany	1,995,000,000
United States	1,907,000,000

On the same page these figures are criticized, and indeed the weight of evidence suggests that the U.S. had already passed all other countries but Britain. In *Industrialization and Foreign Trade* (New York: League of Nations, 1945) the 1870 figures for percentage distribution of world manufacturing output are as follows:

United Kingdom	31.8%
United States	23.3%
Germany	13.2%
France	10.3%

The statistical data used for these figures were far more comprehensive and reliable than those of Mulhall. It is simply inconceivable in the light of the slower growth of the economy which occurred during the decade 1860-1870 that the distribution of world manufacturing output could have changed so radically that Mulhall's relative figures could be correct for the earlier decade.

[2] Professor Raymond Goldsmith provides evidence that an acceleration in the growth of per capita real income took place some time before 1839. U.S. Congress, Joint Economic Committee, 86th Congress, 1st Session, *Hearings,* Part 2, "Historical and Comparative Rates of Production, Productivity and Prices," p. 278.

We have been accustomed to look at this country from 1865 on-ward to search out the sources of its economic success, or even to see the Civil War as the force which broke the shackles on our potential expansion. Yet the truth is that the critical period in this country's economic development had already passed by that time. Both the westward expansion, which gave us unrivaled natural resources, and the conditions necessary to sustained indus-trial growth were accomplished. This study is therefore both an essay in American economic history and a study in economic growth. Its objective is to shed light upon the determinants of the pace and character of American growth between the years 1790 and 1860, and to examine the interrelationships involved in this economic expansion.

As economic history this essay deliberately breaks with the tra-ditional treatments of America's economic past. For the most part American economic historians have been preoccupied with de-scription and institutional change, and have only incidentally fo-cussed on the process of economic growth. As a result there is no comprehensive, integrated analysis of United States develop-ment. Textbooks in the field illustrate this difficulty. Typically they provide separate treatments of the various sectors in the economy, agriculture, manufacturing, banking, the international economy, etc., with only superficial linkages between them.

The United States is a classic case of a society in which social structure and sanctions have provided a hospitable setting for in-dividual pursuit of economic gain. Whatever strictures existed in the theocratic atmosphere of early New England or in the social and political disorganization of the Confederation had been over-come by 1790. Even the frontiersman became an important influ-ence on our economic development only after he could supply goods to existing markets. As long as he lived a self-sufficient ex-istence on the land with little or no production for the market, he exerted only a peripheral influence on American economic growth.[3] Though production for the market occupied a far smaller

---

[3] The classic article by Guy S. Callender, "The Early Transportation and Banking Enterprises of the States in Relation to the Growth of the Corpora-tion," *Quarterly Journal of Economics* XVII (1930), 111-62, not only supports this argument but, along with the other writings of Callender, presents many valuable insights into U.S. economic growth during this period. I am in his debt.

percentage of the population than it does today, the spread of the market economy was a strategic influence on the character of economic growth. It exerted a continual pull on productive factors, attracting an increasing percentage of resources into production for the market and out of pioneer self-sufficiency. And the size of the market was the most important determinant of manufacturing development and increasing economic efficiency.

This study is based on the proposition that U. S. growth was the evolution of a market economy where the behavior of prices of goods, services and productive factors was the major element in any explanation of economic change. Institutional and political policies have certainly been influential. They have acted to accelerate or retard growth on many occasions in our past, primarily by affecting the behavior of the prices of goods, services or productive factors either directly or indirectly. But they have modified rather than replaced the underlying forces of a market economy.

Originally the study was to cover the years 1815 to 1860, on the hypothesis that this had been the critical period in the economy's development. As work progressed it became clear that the previous era of warfare (and particularly the years 1793 to 1808) had played an important role in the country's development, and accordingly the study was extended back to 1790. Part I covers the early period and Part II the years after 1815. This division is made because the sources of expansion in the two periods are clearly different.

The scope of this monograph inevitably limits the depth of analysis in exploring the implications of the process of American economic growth. It is in effect an extended argument with supporting statistical and qualitative evidence rather than an economic history of the period. The objective here is to build a *skeletal framework* of the disparate parts which constitute American economic history today. The flesh and blood (not to mention the clothing) are available to complete the frame, since our discipline is already rich in description of the several parts that are here joined together.

I am indebted to many people. Professor M. M. Knight of the University of California first showed me what an exciting field of research economic history is. Professor Arthur H. Cole of Harvard University has provided assistance and encouragement over the past decade in addition to the direct assistance I have received from the pioneering studies he has written, collaborated upon, or encouraged. The National Bureau of Economic Research provided me with a year as Research Associate during which part of the statistical data was organized; Dr. Solomon Fabricant, Director of Research, went out of his way to provide me with every assistance. Professors Moses Abramovitz, Milton Friedman, and Simon Kuznets have all contributed generously of their time in discussing the study or in reading earlier drafts of the manuscript. Finally, my colleagues at the University of Washington have been a continuous source of advice and critical review. Professor Donald F. Gordon, in particular, has done his best to improve my education as an economist.

Richard Beyer, John Bowman, Donald Farness, and Keith Phillips have all provided valuable research assistance in organizing the statistics for this study. The development of the export and import price indices was a particularly laborious task, and I am very much in their debt for the painstaking care with which the data were gathered and organized. Finally, Mrs. Ralph B. Anderson and Mrs. Robert O. Beale have toiled over this manuscript to a degree that puts me very much in their debt.

D. C. N.

TABLE OF CONTENTS

Tables in Appendix I

INTERNATIONAL ECONOMIC RELATIONS: STATISTICAL DATA

Tables in Appendix I

EXPORT AND IMPORT PRICE INDICES, 1790-1860

I

THE ANALYTICAL FRAMEWORK

The analytical framework of this study is a composite of several propositions, the most important of which was a cornerstone of *The Wealth of Nations*. Taken together they reflect certain underlying features of economic behavior which have characterized the development of market economies over the past several centuries. These propositions emerged in the course of the give and take between some initial hypotheses about economic development,[1] the subsequent organization of statistical data and qualitative information to test these hypotheses, and their modification [2] in the light of this evidence. The gist of the argument is that the timing and pace of an economy's development has been determined by: (1) the success of its export sector, and (2) the characteristics of the export industry and the disposition of the income received from the export sector.

I

The expanding international economy of the past two centuries has provided the avenue by which one economy after another has

---

[1] Cf. Douglass C. North, "Location Theory and Regional Economic Growth," *Journal of Political Economy* LXII, No. 3 (June 1955), 243-58, and subsequent exchange with Charles Tiebout in the same journal, LXIV, No. 2 (April 1956), 160-69.

[2] Douglass C. North, "Agriculture and Regional Economic Growth," paper delivered before the American Farm Economics Association, Cornell, August 1959, and subsequently published in American Farm Economics Association, *Proceedings* XLI, No. 5 (December 1959), 943-51. This argument would require some modification for countries with population "pressure." Cf. Harvey Leibenstein's *Economic Backwardness and Economic Growth* (New York: Wiley and Sons, 1957), Chapter 10.

accelerated its rate of growth.[3] There are few exceptions to the essential initiating role of a successful export sector in the early stages of accelerated growth of market economies. The reason is that the domestic market has been small and scattered. These economies have been predominantly rural, with a high degree of individual self-sufficiency. Reflecting this aspect of the market, specialization and division of labor have been limited and rudimentary. An expanding external market has provided the means for an increase in the size of the domestic market, growth in money income, and the spread of specialization and division of labor. Under the favorable conditions outlined below (with respect to the disposition of income from the export sector), it has set in motion a chain of consequences leading to sustained growth. Before examining these factors it is important to explore in more detail the conditions underlying successful production of goods and services for export.

Credits earned from the exportation of goods and services can be seen from the country's balance of payments, but an explanation lies in the character of the demand for the export and in the nature of the supply function. The analysis must explore the determinants of the demand and shifts in demand as well as the shape of the supply function and shifts in supply. The supply response to a change in price plays an important role in the analysis. It is a central part of the argument with respect to long swings in prices and other economic activity that supply shifts in response to price changes proceeded irregularly, and, in conjunction with the speculative behavior which accompanied the latter phases of periods of accelerated growth, were important in the explanation of long swings in economic activity which characterized the United States development after 1815.

While export and import prices constructed into indices provide a measure of the net barter terms of trade, the significance of movements in these terms of trade is frequently ambiguous. During at least one period of this study, 1793–1807, the change in relative prices of exports versus imports clearly played a vital part in the growth and well-being of the economy and its people.

---

[3] Cf. A. J. Youngson, *Possibilities of Economic Progress* (Cambridge: The University Press, 1959), the case studies in Part II and the Conclusions in Chapter XII.

II

The first step in the analysis is an exploration of the determinants of the export sector of the economy. The next is an examination of the characteristics of the export sector and the disposition of the income received from outside the economy or region.[4] Certainly one of the perplexing problems in the study of economic growth has been the varying progress of different economies as a result of an increment to income from the export sector. Why does one area remain tied to a single export staple while another diversifies its production and becomes an urbanized, industrialized economy? Regions or nations which remain tied to a single export commodity almost inevitably fail to achieve sustained expansion. Not only will there be a slowing down in the rate of growth of the export good or service which adversely affects development, but the fact that the economy remains tied to a single industry will mean that specialization and division of labor outside that industry are limited. Historically, it has meant that a large share of the populace has remained outside the market economy, the development of more effective factor markets has been limited, and inflow of additional productive factors has usually been confined to capital flowing into the export industry. The factors which appear to be most important in the sustained development of economies subsequent to expansion of the export sector can be subsumed under three headings: [5]

1. The natural endowments of the region (at any given level of technology),
2. The character of the export industry, and
3. Changes in technology and transfer costs.

It is worthwhile to examine each of these in turn.

---

[4] This discussion is equally applicable to a nation or a region where either can be delineated in terms of a particular pattern of areal specialization resulting from the unequal distribution of the quantity and quality of productive factors. While the United States is undifferentiated in this study before 1815, after that date the pattern of regional specialization which emerges is central to the overall argument.

[5] North, "Agricultural and Regional Economic Growth," *loc. cit.*

The natural endowments of a region dictate its initial export commodities. If these endowments result in a tremendous comparative advantage in one commodity over any other, the immediate consequence will be for resources to concentrate on its production. But if the region has broad production possibilities such that the rate of return on the production of a number of goods and services is not too much less than on the initial export commodity, with the growth of the region and accompanying changes in factor proportions such production is likely to be a simple process.

The character of the export commodity's influence on regional growth is more complicated. A number of important consequences stem from the technological nature of the production function. If the export commodity is a *plantation* type which is relatively labor intensive, with significant increasing returns to scale, then its development will be in marked contrast to one where the export commodity may be most efficiently produced on a family-size farm with relatively smaller absolute amounts of labor required.[6] In the first case, extremely unequal distribution of income will tend to result, with the bulk of the population devoting most of its income to foodstuffs and simple necessities (much of which may be self-sufficient production). At the other end of the income scale, the plantation owners will tend to spend most of their income on imported luxury goods. There will be slight encouragement of residentiary types of economic activity. With more equitable distribution of incomes, there is a demand for a broad range of goods and services, part of which will be residentiary, thus inducing investment in other types of economic activities. Trading centers will tend to develop to provide these goods and services, in contrast to the plantation economy, which will merely develop a few urban areas devoted to export of the staple commodity and distribution of imports.

A natural consequence of these divergent patterns will be the attitude towards investment in knowledge.[7] Under the plantation system, with its marked inequality of incomes, the planter will be

---

[6] Cf. R. E. Baldwin, "Patterns of Development in Newly Settled Regions," *The Manchester School of Economic and Social Studies* XXIV, No. 2 (May 1956), 161-79.

[7] I am in Professor Theodore Schultz's debt for focussing my attention on this problem.

reluctant to devote his tax monies to expenditures for education or research other than that related to the staple commodity. In contrast, the region with more equitable income distribution will be aware of the stake in improving its comparative position through education and research, and be willing to devote public expenditures in these directions. This will improve its relative position in a variety of types of economic activity and broaden the resultant economic base. This does not imply that equal income distribution will produce optimum investment of this kind, but only that the distribution of income should not be extremely skewed, as in the plantation type economy.

Equally important is the investment induced by the export commodity or service. If the export requires substantial investment in transport, warehousing, port facilities and other types of social overhead investment, external economies are created which facilitate the development of other exports. If the export industry encourages the growth of complementary and subsidiary industries, and if technology, transport costs and resource endowments permit these to be locally produced, further development will be induced. In both social overhead investment and investment in complementary and subsidiary industry, urbanization and increased specialization are promoted, and additional residentiary activity geared to the increasing local demand for consumption goods and services develops. At the other extreme is the export industry, which requires only the immediate development of a few centers for collection and export and develops little subsidiary industry, or develops such subsidiary industry and marketing facilities, even though they are of a nature to be most efficiently imported.[8]

Changes in technology and transport may completely alter the region's comparative advantage.[9] Technological change may increase the potential rate of return from the production of other goods and services, and lead to exploitation of new resources and a shift away from the old export industry. The initial development of transportation facilities to implement the export industry tends to reinforce dependence upon it and inhibit more diversified eco-

---

[8] Therefore, the development of subsidiary industry depends, at least in part, on the first point discussed above, the natural endowments of the region.

[9] North, "Location Theory and Regional Economic Growth," *loc. cit.*, pp. 254-56.

nomic activity. The early development of transport typically (under competitive conditions) leads to a rapid fall in the transport rate, increasing the comparative advantage of the export commodity.[10] Moreover, with newly settled regions the outward shipment of a bulky product has no counterpart in the inward voyage, which must be made mostly empty or in ballast. Inward freights are consequently low and can compete with locally produced goods. Local industries which had been protected by high transport costs, or which might develop if high transport costs continued, face effective competition from imports.[11]

The disposition of income earned from the export industry plays a decisive role in the growth of the region. Related to this argument is the region's propensity to import. To the extent that a region's income directly flows out in the purchase of goods and services rather than having a regional multiplier-accelerator effect,[12] it is inducing growth elsewhere but reaping few of the benefits of increased income from the export sector itself. The *successful* economy grows because the initial developments from the export industry lead to a widening of the export base and growth in the size of the domestic market. Growing demand in the domestic sector leads to an ever widening variety of residentiary industries. These industries (and services) producing for the local market vary in character. They range from those which must by necessity be residentiary (retail trade, some services, etc.) to those which— as the size of the market permits firms to achieve efficient scale of operations—become substitutes for some imports. In response to profitable opportunities in the economy, there is an inflow of labor and capital to augment the domestic increase. Changing factor proportions, along with the cost reducing consequences of social overhead investments and the improved skills, training and

---

[10] Douglass C. North, "Ocean Freight Rates and Economic Development 1750-1913," *Journal of Economic History* XVII, No. 4 (December 1958), 537-55.

[11] The early hopes of Gallatin and Tench Coxe which rested upon the burgeoning development of manufacturing during the Embargo as reported in the 1810 census were in good part for the local market, which was completely unable to compete with imports following the end of the second war with England.

[12] Cf. J. S. Dusenberry, "Some Aspects of the Theory of Economic Development," *Explorations in Entrepreneurial History* III, No. 2 (December 1950), 63-102.

knowledge that come from diversion of capital into investment in education, lead to a broadening of the export base. This usually occurs first in the processing of a wider variety of raw materials and then in the fabrication of goods, typically entailing a greater use of capital and skills. Some of this manufacturing may develop initially for the export market, while other forms of manufacturing may be initially oriented to the expanding domestic market.

In the *unsuccessful* economy, the increment to income from expansion of the export industry leads to an increase in the supply of that export commodity, but not to broadening of the export base nor growth in the size of the domestic market. Income flows out of the area with little more than expansion of the export industry as a result.

III

The argument has thus far been aimed at what may be called the *extensive* growth of an economy. Growth in income from the export sector and its favorable disposition along the lines of the above arguments leads to an increase in the supply of productive factors from both domestic sources and immigration, the inflow of capital and entrepreneurial talent, and frequently from the acquisition of land. It leads to an increase in aggregate income, but the analysis has not been focussed directly on the increased efficiency of productive factors which is necessary to rising per capita real income.

To what extent were the productivity increases resulting from technological innovations, investment in research, training and education, and improved organization of economic activity simply a consequence of the activities of an acquisitive society in the context of the favorable conditions for extensive growth described above?

In the case of technological change we were followers in the process of industrialization and in the more fundamental beginnings of scientific development which underlay the rapid advances of the nineteenth century. Accompanying the economic expansion of the Western World was the development of science. This development provided a reservoir of knowledge that could be tapped to produce new techniques required by more pressing economic needs.

This is not the place for the theory of societal change which would be necessary to support such an argument, but several specific points should be made:

1. There was available to us a reservoir of technological information as a result of the prior development in England, and to a lesser degree other western European countries, of these scientific innovations. Under the competitive market conditions which characterized our economy, the rewards awaiting the entrepreneur who successfully adapted these innovations to the American scene were sufficient incentive. Throughout this era, beginning with Samuel Slater, such adaptations were made as it became profitable to do so.

2. In the case of indigenous innovations, the most striking aspect of many of them was that they emerged in the context of a mounting problem, reflecting the search for alternative uses of existing sunk capital or the rising price of a resource or productive factor, especially labor. Whether it was Eli Whitney's cotton gin—certainly the major domestic innovation for the economy's growth during the period—or the labor saving devices which impressed British investigators of American manufacturing in the 1850's, they clearly owed their origins to the deliberate search for solutions to economic problems, particularly in the export sector.

If the argument of the preceding paragraphs is accepted, it follows that productivity changes stemming from technological innovations are, in part at least, a nearly automatic response to successful expansion of industries in an acquisitive society under competitive market conditions. Not only was there available a reservoir of technological improvements, but the structure of a competitive market provided important rewards for successful innovation in a society whose value system prized such activity. This is not a complete explanation of technological change in America during this period. The role of the entrepreneur and innovator is an important one, but I would downgrade its significance for the study of growth in economies which: (1) followed in the process of industrial development, and (2) were acquisitively oriented under competitive market conditions.

Investment in knowledge represents a deliberate decision by a society to divert resources from more immediately productive pursuits. Implicitly or explicitly, a society makes assumptions about the returns on such investment which affect the level of expenditure of tax monies. The amount of capital diverted into investment in knowledge will depend upon the structure of political power and the attitudes of that group in a society which is in a position to enact legislation regarding taxes and public expenditure. Where extremely unequal income distribution is paralleled by unequal distribution of political power, the development of broadly based public education is less likely, since there are no obvious gains to those who must provide the bulk of the tax monies for such an investment. Such investment is likely to be a larger proportion of income under conditions of more equal income distribution, since the broader distribution of costs will be matched by an equally expanded distribution of benefits. Very unequal income distribution, *per se,* will only be a reinforcing factor in the unwillingness to invest in human capital where it is not obvious to the dominant political-economic group that such an investment will yield a high return to them. However, a substantial degree of income inequality is compatible with a relatively large investment in knowledge when the range of production possibilities may be enhanced and profitable opportunities increased by a better educated populace. It was not only the western farmer and mechanic in an atmosphere of egalitarianism who espoused educational investment, but also the eastern entrepreneur and employer who equally recognized the importance of such investment.[13] The striking difference between educational investment in the South and in the other two regions during the period 1815–1860 is explainable in terms of this argument. There is abundant contemporary evidence that Westerners and residents of the Northeast set a high value on such investment compared to the southern planter, who saw little return to himself from a better educated populace. Investment in knowledge partially reflected the economic structure of the region.

The most important *proximate* cause of increasing productivity

---

[13] While incomes were certainly unequal in the North, political representation was of course far broader in the North than in the South, and the added pressure from lower income groups (and particularly immigrants) was a further impetus to educational investment in the North.

of the economy during this period came from improved organization of economic activity. By this I mean the consequences of
increasing specialization and division of labor which were responsible not only for growing efficiency in agriculture and transport,
but which determined the pace, timing, and character of manufacturing development as well. The cause of increasing specialization
was, of course, the size of the market, which permitted individual
specialization of function in the productive process and specialization of the firm in the form of vertical dis-integration, and also
encouraged the adoption of technological processes. It should not
be necessary here to argue the cause of Adam Smith's theorem,
but it is necessary to elaborate on a modern day restatement of the
theorem, which has widespread implications for economic growth.
I am referring to the article by George J. Stigler which uses Smith's
proposition as its title.[14] Stigler elaborates a case of external economies which provides the essential connecting link between extensive expansion and consequent growth in the size of the market,
and increasing efficiency. He argues that a firm performs a number
of functions, some subject to diminishing returns, other subject to
increasing returns. With a limited market the firm necessarily performs all of these functions, from recruiting its labor force and
constructing its machinery to marketing its product. With expansion in the size of the market some of these functions with increasing returns split off from the firm and realize decreasing costs
with expansion in their output. A cotton textile firm, which initially
had to perform all the functions from machinery construction to
retailing, gradually divests itself from all functions but spinning
and weaving. Specialized textile machinery and retailing establishments develop as the market attains sufficient size. These new
specialized firms, subject to increasing returns, effectively realize
and pass on, under competitive conditions, the lower costs of
machinery or retailing. This process of specialization of function
with growth of the market size was one of the most striking features
of industrialization in this country. The size of the market, of
course, was basically a function of the success of the export sector
and the disposition of income from this sector.

---

[14] "The Division of Labor is Limited by the Extent of the Market," *Journal
of Political Economy* LIX, No. 3 (June 1951), 185-93.

The answer to the question about the relationship between factors making for improved efficiency and those promoting extensive growth of the economy is that they stemmed in large part from the same causes.

IV

The temporal divisions in this study, as in any historical work, inevitably do violence to the continuity of change. For the period before 1815, the choice is easily made on the basis of external events or non-economic decisions which were paramount in shaping the economy's development. After the second war with England, the chronological breakdown must be in terms of the internal operations of the economy, domestic or international, rather than non-economic events. The business cycle is a poor framework for the analysis of economic growth. The shortness of the period, monetary disturbances, and speculative excesses combine to conceal rather than expose the underlying factors in the long-run growth of the economy. While business cycles must be integrated into the analysis, their proper position is as an inherent feature of a market economy in which underlying factors shape the proximate events and timing of cyclical activity.

A more promising temporal framework is the long cycle in economic activity which characterized the economy after 1815. Its pervasiveness in most of the time series for the period,[15] and the coincidence of most of the major turning points of these series with other evidence of important changes in the economy, makes it a useful chronological framework. No attempt is made here to offer a complete theory of long swings,[16] although the evidence suggests that this cycle is intimately connected with capital investments of a relatively long gestation period, such as transportation and construction. We do know that the growth of the economy

[15] See Moses Abramovitz, "Long Swings in United States Economic Growth," *38th Annual Report* of the National Bureau of Economic Research (New York: National Bureau of Economic Research, 1958), pp. 47-56, which presents 24 series showing long cycles for the pre-1860 period.

[16] Abramovitz prefers the name "long swings" to describe these movements, although they are also sometimes referred to as secondary secular movements and trend cycles.

has proceeded in a series of surges followed by periods of slower growth, and that the length of these swings has usually been between eighteen and twenty years.[17] These periods of acceleration and retardation are strikingly evident after 1815, and each complete long swing provides the temporal limits for the chapters which examine the economy's growth.[18]

The chronology of long swings during this period is as follows. The trough of each cycle coincided with the trough of a serious depression. From this trough, the initial expansion was gradual. The substantial growth of capacity during the previous boom resulted in several years of depressed prices, modest profit expectations and only gradual reabsorption of unemployed or underemployed resources into production. As demand for the commodities in the export sector increased, existing capacity was finally utilized. It was not until prices began to rise that there began a significant redirection of productive factors into the export sector to increase supply. Initial redirection of productive factors was primarily within the region. At first it was a reabsorption of unemployed or underemployed (as in the case of self-sufficient farmers) factors. With increasing profit expectations, there was both an interregional and an international flow of labor and capital. The pace of expansion accelerated, and the boom was under way. It is during such periods that the real growth rate of the economy was greatest, because of both the addition of real resources to economic activity and increases of productivity. The latter resulted from the more efficient uses of productive factors in the export sector, or social overhead investment related to the export sector, as compared to their use in locally oriented or self-sufficient economic activity.

Each surge of expansion during this period consisted of extensive movement into new territory, with all the concomitant internal migration and investment in transportation and construction which accompanied the opening up, settlement, and integration of the

[17] An excellent summary of the evidence on long swings is contained in Moses Abramovitz's testimony before the Joint Economic Committee. 86th Congress, 1st Session, *Hearings,* Part 2, "Historical and Comparative Rates of Production," pp. 411-33.

[18] The dating of long swings in this study is different from the peak and trough years of Abramovitz for reasons which are discussed in the appropriate chapters.

area into the economy. In the new area itself there was induced growth in all the necessary residentiary industry and services, while in older areas there was increasing demand for consumer and capital goods for the new area.

An important part of the argument is that there is a lag in production as a result of the lengthy gestation period required to produce substantial increases in supply. Transportation developments in the West to open up new land and increased cotton production in the South were time consuming processes. In the interim, with full employment achieved, prices rose, reflecting both the diversion of productive factors from consumer goods and increased demand with rising income. The capital imports which directed resources into the export sector or into social overhead investment financed a high level of consumption goods imports, which mitigated the inflationary pressures.

The actual growth rate of the economy in the latter part of the periods of expansion was slower. With fully employed resources, growth in real output was limited to productivity increases. Productivity changes themselves occurred at a slower rate than during the earlier period, when productive factors were shifting into industries of higher productivity than those from which they had moved.

Two factors combined to bring a boom to a close, and since they did not necessarily coincide in their timing it was possible to have a sharp recession and brief revival, as in 1837–1839, before both coincided to end the period of expansion. Although both resulted in a decline in investment, one was primarily monetary and acted through the money supply, and the other was real and related to the realization of increases in capacity which had been under way.

There is no intention in this differentiation between monetary and real factors to imply that the two are not intimately related. The former, whether from political policies within the economy or from without, is more susceptible to exogenous influences, reacting upon the domestic money supply through exchange rates and specie flows.

The gold standard, which served as the most immediate sensitive tie in our international economic relations, resulted in changes in the domestic money supply. In each boom, a growing disparity between domestic and foreign price levels inevitably set in motion a domestic readjustment process to bring prices in line. United States prices rose relative to foreign prices as a result of the expansion and price effects described above. While specific domestic and foreign economic policies were proximately related to the contractions in the money supply, the more general reason lay in the price *distortions* from the boom itself.

While monetary effects were proximate forces in the downturn, factors resulting from the expansion in capacity during the boom are most important in the lengthy period of decline and readjustment which ensued. Construction, transportation and the integration of new areas into the economy all involved lengthy commitments of resources before substantial increases in supply resulted. The increase, when it did come about, typically resulted in such a substantial increment to capacity that supply increased disproportionately relative to the growth in demand. The result was not only a fall in the price of the commodity but a long period of depressed prices until demand had shifted to the right sufficiently to *catch up* with this capacity.

The drastic drop in the prices of leading export commodities was paralleled by declining prices in general. Downward price flexibility was a characteristic of the economy during this period. The fall in prices was rapid, and was followed by several years of depressed activity with only slight further declines in prices. The painful readjustment and re-valuation of assets that followed was extended by the very large increase in capacity of the previous boom until the trough was reached at the very bottom of the business cycle.

This brief chronology of long swings will be elaborated in Chapter VII, where it is specifically applied to the United States economy between 1815 and 1860. But before 1815 there was a twenty-five year period dominated by revolution and war in the Western World. We begin in 1790.

PART ONE

1790-1814

II

THE UNITED STATES ECONOMY IN 1790

The years following the achievement of independence were difficult ones for the new American nation. Bickering among the states and groping for a viable political structure were paralleled by difficult economic readjustments. By 1790 the political crisis had been resolved and the economy enjoyed a measure of prosperity. Given political stability, an energetic populace, and an abundance of resources, the country's long run economic growth would appear assured. Yet there was little prospect of rapid growth on the horizon, and available information about the economy from 1789 through 1792 provides incomplete but convincing evidence that the prospects of the economy in the foreseeable future were limited by the size of the domestic market and an inability to expand the foreign market.

The population of the United States in 1790 was approximately 3.9 million, of which almost 700,000 were slaves. The population was almost evenly divided between North and South, with a little more than 200,000 west of the Allegheny mountains.[1] Only 201,555 people, in twenty-four places, were listed as urban. There were no cities of 50,000, two between 25,000 and 50,000 whose total population was 61,653, and three between 10,000 and 25,000 with an aggregate population of 48,182. There were seven places with over 5,000 and twelve with over 2,500. The remaining population of 3.7 million was rural.[2]

It would be erroneous to conclude that the domestic market was

---

[1] There were 109,000 in Kentucky and the area northwest of the Ohio and approximately another 100,000 in western Virginia and Pennsylvania. See Appendix II, Table A-II.

[2] Population figures from U.S. Census Bureau, *Historical Statistics of the United States, 1789-1945* (Washington: Government Printing Office, 1949), p. 29. Hereafter cited as *Historical Statistics*.

limited to the urban population and that the rural populace were all self-sufficient farmers. There is no way to tell with any degree of precision what percentage of the rural population was producing for the market, and were themselves a regular part of the domestic market. Clearly a large percentage did not regularly engage in market production. For a still larger number, the contribution to market production was peripheral and an irregular supplement to a way of life largely self-sufficient. Relatively high value commodities like whiskey, ginseng and furs or occasional movements of livestock to tidewater markets provided small, irregular cash incomes. The high cost of land transportation restricted to short distances the movement of bulky goods of lower value. Only those locations near navigable waterways could market foodstuffs and raw materials.

Whatever proportion of the rural population is assumed to have been part of the domestic market, it is impossible to escape the conclusion that this market was small and not heavily concentrated. Since a small fraction of the population constituted a market for commercial production, it is not surprising that the domestic demand for goods and services did not result in a rapid shift of people into the market, nor did the market exist on a scale that made possible any but household manufacturing.[3] Had the United States of 1790 been a closed system, the possibilities for growth would have been limited indeed.

If the outlook for rapid growth from domestically induced expansion did not appear promising, the prospects of increasing foreign demand for our goods and services were hardly more favorable. Trade with Great Britain, our leading customer, was less in 1790 than it had been at the beginning of the Revolution. During the six years prior to 1774, our exports to Great Britain averaged £1,752,142.[4] After the Revolution, they were as follows: [5]

---

[3] The correspondence of Alexander Hamilton leading up to the *Report on Manufactures* reveals very clearly the vicissitudes of the early manufacturer. Cf. Arthur H. Cole, Ed., *Industrial and Commercial Correspondence of Alexander Hamilton, Anticipating his Report on Manufactures* (Chicago: A. W. Shaw & Co., 1928).

[4] Timothy Pitkin, *A Statistical View of the Commerce of the United States: Including also an Account of Banks, Manufactures and Internal Trade* (New Haven: Durrie and Peck, 1835). Hereafter cited as *A Statistical View.*

[5] *Ibid.*, p. 30.

1784	£ 749,395
1785	£ 893,594
1786	£ 843,119
1787	£ 893,637
1788	£ 1,023,789
1789	£ 1,050,198
1790	£ 1,191,071

The explanation of our failure to prosper in foreign trade reflected two factors:

1. As an independent nation we no longer received favored treatment from Great Britain, and were subject to the restrictive measures which characterized the international trade policies of most western European countries. Patterned to some degree after the British Navigation Acts, they effectively limited the American carrying trade to direct trade with the countries concerned. We were excluded from the lucrative West Indies trade, as well as that of the North American colonies, and subjected to all the discriminatory duties leveled against foreign bottoms in our direct trade with other countries. As a result, foreign tonnage carried 45.6 per cent of our foreign trade in 1789 and 41.4 per cent in 1790.[6]

2. If prospects for expanding the carrying trade were circumscribed by foreign commercial policies, the prospects for expansion of our export trade appeared equally dark. The demand for staple exports, which was the basis of colonial well-being, was no longer expanding. Tobacco, which accounted for approximately one-third of the value of colonial exports, amounted to about 85,000 hogsheads before the Revolution, and did not exceed that figure in the post-Revolutionary period.[7] Rice exports actually declined between 1770 and 1791.[8] The exports of wheat and flour varied substantially from year to year but showed no tendency toward sustained expansion. In 1770 the colonies exported 751,240 bushels of wheat and 458,868 barrels of flour. I know of no figures for the years of the Confederacy. Wheat and flour exports were high in 1791 and 1793, while during the rest of the

---

[6] *Ibid.,* p. 363.
[7] *Ibid.,* p. 107.
[8] *Ibid.,* p. 100.

decade they were in the aggregate less than in 1770.[9] The problem of United States foreign economic relationships in 1790 was that, in those goods and services where it enjoyed a distinct comparative advantage, the commercial policies of England and Europe effectively prevented U. S. competition. In other major exports, predominantly agricultural, the advantage was not sufficient to overcome high transport costs and assure an expanding market in a Europe at peace, still largely agricultural and self-sufficient in most primary products.

The years following the Revolutionary War were difficult for the economies of the Confederated States. The want of a central government with power to support commercial expansion, or at the very least to retaliate against foreign discrimination as a weapon to force concessions, was keenly felt. While Congress made commercial treaties with France, Holland, Sweden and Prussia, they were of little effect, since Congress was powerless to regulate commerce effectively or to impose import duties. The British government refused to make any commercial treaty with the United States; its commercial regulations with the new nation were regulated by proclamations of the Privy Council.[10] British port charges, tonnage duties, discriminatory insurance rates, and enforcement of navigation laws all operated to favor the British carrying trade. With the establishment of the Constitution, the United States went far toward removing the disadvantages imposed by the lack of a centralized commercial policy. By an act of July 20, 1789, discriminatory tonnage duties were imposed on foreign bottoms, and a ten per cent rebate of duties on imports in American ships was put into effect.

While there is no doubt that the Constitution and subsequent legislation passed by Congress favoring our carrying trade (including the exclusion of foreign ships from our coastwise trade) and our foreign commerce were beneficial to the economy, the years 1790–92 reflected no significant alteration in the position of our

---

9 *Ibid.*, p. 96.

10 The United States did enjoy some advantages in these regulations as compared with other countries. See Emory R. Johnson *et al.*, *History of Domestic and Foreign Commerce of the United States* (Washington: The Carnegie Institution of Washington, publication no. 215-A, 1915), p. 129. Hereafter cited as *History*.

carrying trade and exports. The proportion of United States ships in our foreign trade increased from fifty-nine per cent in 1790 to sixty-three per cent in 1792. Domestic exports were less in 1791 and 1792 than in 1790, and only an increase in the re-export trade in 1792 made exports a little higher that year than in the two preceding ones. It is worth quoting Thomas Jefferson at some length on the obstacles to our foreign commerce:

First. In Europe, our bread stuff is at most times under prohibitory duties in England, and considerably dutied on reexportation from Spain to her colonies.

Our tobaccos are heavily dutied in England, Sweden, France, and prohibited in Spain and Portugal.

Our rice is heavily dutied in England and Sweden, and prohibited in Portugal.

Our fish and salted provisions are prohibited in England, and under prohibitory duties in France.

Our whale oils are prohibited in England and Portugal. And our vessels are denied naturalization in England, and of late, in France.

Second. In the West Indies—All intercourse is prohibited with the possessions of Spain and Portugal.

Our salted provisions and fish are prohibited by England.

Our salted pork and bread stuff (except maise) are received under temporary laws only in the dominions of France, and our salted fish pays there a weighty duty.

Third. In the article of navigation—our own carriage of our own tobacco is heavily dutied in Sweden, and lately in France. We can carry no article, not of our own production, to the British ports in Europe. Nor even our own produce to her American possessions. Our ships, though purchased and navigated by their own subjects, are not permitted to be used, even in their trade with us. While the vessels of other nations are secured by standing laws, which cannot be altered but by the concurrent will of the three branches of the British Legislature, in carrying thither any produce or manufacture of the country to which they belong, which may be lawfully carried in any vessels, ours, with the same prohibition of what is foreign, are further prohibited by a standing law (12 Car. 2, 18, Sec. 3) from carrying thither all and any of our own domestic productions and manufactures. A subsequent act, indeed, has authorized their Executive to permit the carriage of our own productions in our own bottoms *at its sole discretion;* and the permission has been given, from year to year, by proclamation, but subject every moment to be withdrawn *on that single will,* in which event our vessels, having anything on board, stand interdicted from entry of all British ports. The disadvantage of a tenure which may be so suddenly discontinued was experienced by our merchants on a late occasion (April 12, 1792) when an official notification, that this law would be strictly enforced, gave them just apprehensions for the fate of their vessels and cargoes dispatched or destined to the ports of Great Britain. The Minister of that Court, indeed, frankly expressed his personal conviction, that the words of the order went further than was intended, and so he afterwards officially informed us; but the embarrassments of the moment were real and great, and the possibility of their renewal lays our commerce to that country under the same species of discouragement as to other countries, where it is regulated by a single legislator; and the distinction is too remarkable not to be noticed, that *our navigation is excluded from the security of fixed laws*, while that security is given *to the navigation of others*.

Our vessels pay in their ports, 1*s*. 9*d*. sterling per ton, light and trinity dues, more than is paid by British ships, except in the port of London, where they pay the same as British.

The greater part of what they receive from us is reexported to other countries, under the useless charges of an intermediate deposite, and double voyage.[11]

The obstacles to rapid economic growth of the new nation, therefore, were a small and scattered domestic market and a foreign market which gave little indication of expansion. The outspoken views of the Earl of Sheffield appeared justified.[12] The comparative advantage of the United States was confined, with a few exceptions of which shipbuilding and shipping were the most significant, to the production of primary goods. The relatively high costs of capital and labor and the size of the market were formidable obstacles encountered by the many societies which were formed to

---

11 William W. Bates, *American Navigation; the Political History of its Rise and Ruin and the Proper Means for its Encouragement* (Boston and New York: Houghton Mifflin & Co., 1902), pp. 83-84. Hereafter cited as *American Navigation.*

12 ". . . Great Britain will lose few of the advantages she possessed before these States became independent, and with prudent management she will have as much of their trade as it will be her interest to wish for, without any expense for civil establishment or protection. The States will suffer—they have lost much by separation. We shall regret the money that has been squandered, but it is certainly not probable our commerce will be much hurt, and it is certain the means of employing and adding to our seamen will be greatly increased, if we do not throw away the opportunity." John Baker Holroyd, 1st Earl of Sheffield, *Observations on the Commerce of the American States,* as quoted in Guy S. Callender, *Selections from the Economic History of the United States, 1765-1860* (Boston: Ginn & Co., 1909), p. 210. Hereafter cited as *Economic History.*

promote manufacturing. Not only was the price of capital high, but domestic financial intermediaries were limited to three banking institutions in Philadelphia, New York, and Boston, which catered to the existing internal and foreign trade of the country. While Great Britain continued to provide mercantile credit which facilitated our foreign trade, there were no organized international financial intermediaries to span the Atlantic and provide a partial substitute for a domestic long-term capital market. In addition to the foreign debt, some of our domestic federal debt had found its way abroad, but no organized channels for such transfers existed.

Population growth was rapid. The astonishingly high birth rate, 55 per 1000 in 1800, reflected the agricultural structure of an economy where large families were an asset. Yet, for the immediate future, the low absolute level of population meant that, even with such a birth rate compounded over generations, relative scarcity of labor would continue to be characteristic of the society. Restrictions on emigration from the Old World and recurrent wars rendered substantial additions from this source unlikely.

The relative scarcity of labor and capital was not likely to be ameliorated in the near future, nor did prospects for expanding markets appear imminent. It remained for external events to alter these prospects and initiate a period of rapid, if hectic, growth.

III

THE ECONOMY—1790-1814

The Statistical Evidence

Government revenues derived from external trade and the international orientation of the American economy during this period have resulted in a greater wealth of statistical materials relating to our external relations than to internal movements. The primary reason for this was the primitive state of internal trade, arising both from the prohibitively high cost of land transportation and the diversified character of production in different parts of the country. The high degree of sectional specialization which was to develop during this period was in embryonic form in 1790. Even the southern states, with a heritage of specialized production of staples for export, were self-sufficient for most foodstuffs.[1] As a result, the price currents of the period and the statistics gathered by the government were concerned mostly with our foreign trade.

I

Even in the area of international economic relations the figures leave a great deal to be desired. It was not until 1820 that import values were collected; official figures for the years before 1820 were estimated in 1835. Primary data relevant to our other credits

---

[1] Jedidiah Mills, in his *Statistics of South Carolina*, wrote in 1826, "For domestic use, maize, wheat, rye, barley, tobacco, potatoes (the sweet and Irish), indigo, hemp, flour, madder, and a variety of smaller articles are raised. Indian corn, wheat, barley, tobacco, hemp, flax, and indigo were formerly exported from this state, but they have all given place to cotton and rice." (p. 153). Cited in Callender, *Economic History*, p. 290 and footnote 1 thereto.

and debits are equally sparse, and immigration was not even re-corded before 1820. The trade figures presented here represent a revision of the official figures, and other elements of the balance of payments have been constructed from the fragmentary data avail-able, so the figures are not as reliable as for the later period. This is particularly true of the absolute level of two important items, the value of imports and earnings of the carrying trade. While this absolute level is subject to error, the movements of these items from year to year and their rates of change are more reliable, and the subsequent analysis rests upon the latter, not on precise ab-solute values.[2]

Two items completely dominated the credits in our balance of payments during this period,[3] exports and earnings from the carry-ing trade. Both exhibited little change until 1793, but grew there-after with striking rapidity. Between 1793 and 1801 there was almost a five-fold increase in the value of exports and in net[4] earnings from the carrying trade. 1807 was a peak year, with ex-ports of $108.3 million as compared to $20.2 million in 1790, and net earnings for the carrying trade of $42.1 million as compared to $5.9 million in 1790.

The expansion of our exports was primarily a result of the rapid development of the re-export trade. While domestic exports doubled between 1790 and 1807, re-exports grew from $300,000 in 1790 to $59,643,558 during the same period and actually exceeded by $11 million the value of domestic exports.[5] Chart I-III shows the growth

---

[2] Cf. Douglass C. North, "The United States Balance of Payments, 1790-1860," *Trends in the American Economy in the Nineteenth Century*, Studies in Income and Wealth, Vol. 24 (Princeton: Princeton University Press for the National Bureau of Economic Research, 1960). Hereafter cited as "Balance of Payments." Unless otherwise stated, figures in this chapter are from this study.

[3] See Appendix I, Table A-III for the complete balance of payments state-ment. The sale of ships (here separated from commodity exports) was another small but persistent credit item.

[4] The difference between net and gross earnings consists of subtracting any debits accruing to foreigners in the carrying trade from credits accruing to us. See Douglass North, "Balance of Payments," *loc. cit.*, Appendix B, for an elaboration of the elements making up debits and credits in shipping earnings.

[5] The absolute figure is in agreement with contemporary accounts of earnings in the carrying trade. Adam Seybert, *Statistical Annals: Embracing Views of the Population, Commerce, Navigation . . . of the United States of America* (Philadelphia: Thomas Dobson & Son, 1818). Hereafter cited as *Statistical Annals*.

of re-exports and total exports during the years 1790–1815. As noteworthy as the substantial growth of exports until 1807 was their sharp break in earnings in 1802–1803, preceded by a lesser drop in 1797, and decline after 1807, interrupted only by the brief

CHART I-III

Value of Exports and Re-exports from the U.S. 1790–1815

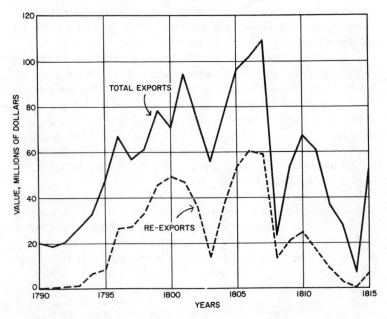

Source: Appendix I, Table B-III.

resurgence of 1809–1810. To what extent was the increased value of exports a function of price increases rather than volume? Chart II-III illustrates the way in which price movements influenced the value of exports.[6] Quite clearly price increases were an important part of the growth in the value of the export trade.

---

[6] The limitations of data during this period do not make possible the construction of an export or import prior index of the quality which has been done for the period 1815-60.

Earnings from the carrying trade, illustrated in Chart III-III, show a pattern similar to that of re-exports. The major difference

CHART II-III

Export Price Index: 1790–1815
Base 1790

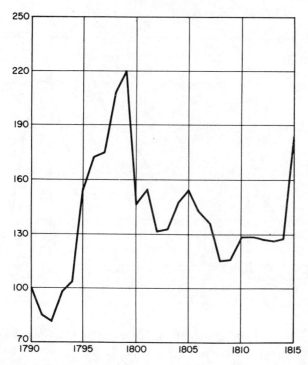

Source: Appendix I, Table C-III.

was in the sharper revival of earnings in 1810–1811 before the collapse of 1812–1814. Gross registered tonnage in foreign trade little more than doubled during these years, so the seven-fold increase in earnings is to be accounted for partly from increased utilization of ships but primarily from the very substantial rise in ocean freight rates. Chart IV-III illustrates the movement of freight rates on a number of commodity routes for this period and shows that they more than doubled during this period.

The debit side of our international balance of payments included payments for insurance and commissions, and interest upon our

CHART III-III

Net Freight Earnings of U.S. Carrying Trade: 1790–1815

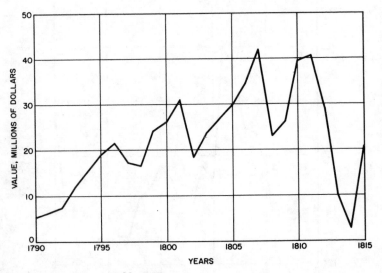

Source: Appendix II, Table A-III.

indebtedness,[7] with imports the single overwhelming item. Imports expanded even faster than exports, producing an import balance of commodity trade in every year except 1811 and 1813. While part of this increase was imports for re-export, imports for consumption in 1807 were almost four times what they had been in 1790.[8] Chart V-III shows the total value of imports and the value of imports for consumption. Chart VI-III shows the prices of im-

---

[7] See Table A-III, Appendix I, for the figures on these items.
[8] The figures are $23.5 million in 1790 and $81.8 million in 1807.

ports. The sharp rises in import prices in 1803 and 1812–1815 are particularly noteworthy.

With the data limitations of the export and import price indices, the terms of trade are necessarily a rather rough indication of price movements, but Chart VII-III does provide a general outline. With only a minor interruption in 1797, they become increas-

CHART IV-III

Freight Rates of a Number of Commodities on Different Routes: 1790–1815
(Actual Data Expressed as Relatives to the Base 1790)

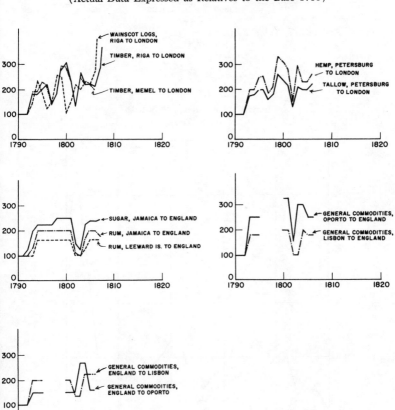

Source: Appendix I, Table D-III

CHART V-III

Value of Imports and Value of Imports for Consumption: 1790–1815

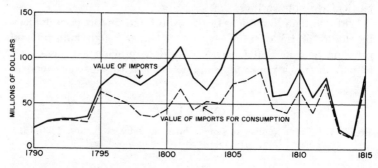

Source: Appendix I, Table E-III.

CHART VI-III

Import Price Index: 1790–1815
Base 1790

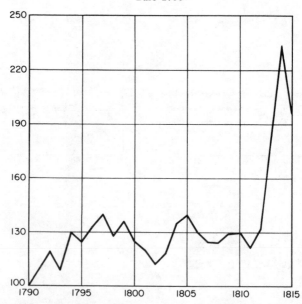

Source: Appendix I, Table F-III.

ingly favorable until 1799–1800, and then decline. They drop sharply in 1808 and again in 1813–1814. If the price of shipping is included, as it should be in the light of its significant proportion of total credits, the terms of trade would be much more favorable, reflecting the far greater rise in freight rates than in other prices in the international market.

CHART VII-III

United States Terms of Trade: 1790–1815
Base 1790

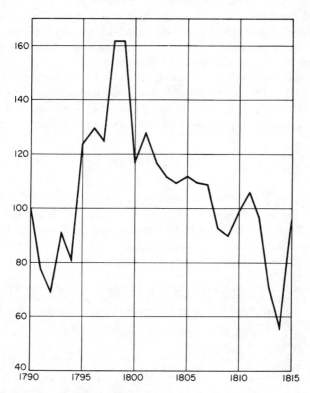

Source: Appendix I, Table G-III.

The period in general is characterized by the fact that the value of exports plus earnings in the carrying trade almost equalled imports. Specie movements were not large, and moved fairly consistently with the price of foreign exchange.[9]

The international movement of productive factors was not very large during this period. While we maintained a revolving credit with Great Britain that financed a good part of our external trade, the net changes were less significant. There was some increase in indebtedness from 1795–1799, 1805–1808 and in 1815, with a decline in our foreign debt in 1800–1805 and 1809–1811.[10]

There are no figures for immigration during the period. Seybert [11] estimated it at about 6000 annually, and Blodget [12] cites a figure of 4000 for the years 1790–1803. There was a general agreement among contemporaries that immigration was not large during the period, and consequently did not exert a significant influence upon the size of the population and labor force.

Certainly the most important contribution to the supply of productive factors from our international economic relations was the acquisition of land, specifically the purchase of Louisiana in 1803, which approximately doubled the land area of the United States.

II

The internal trade of the period was preponderantly local, connecting the major seaports with the hinterland. Philadelphia was both the major market and collection point for the Delaware River and Bay, Baltimore for the Chesapeake, and New York for the Hudson River and Long Island. Few figures exist to provide con-

---

[9] Walter B. Smith and Arthur H. Cole, *Fluctuations in American Business, 1790-1860.* Harvard Economic Studies L (Cambridge: Harvard University Press, 1935), Part I, Chapter VI for movement of foreign exchange rate. Hereafter cited as *Fluctuations.*

[10] See North, "Balance of Payments," *loc. cit.*, Table 2, for the changes in indebtedness.

[11] Seybert, *Statistical Annals.* Seybert's figure was for 1790-1810, with the notation that there were 10,000 immigrants in 1794.

[12] Samuel Blodget, *Economica: A Statistical Manual for the United States of America* . . . (Washington: Printed for the author, 1806). This figure included slaves. The figure for 1804 is given as 9,500, which may include that into the new Louisiana Territory. Hereafter cited as *Economica.*

crete evidence of the growth of this trade, although they would be important to the argument advanced in the following chapters. One fragmentary piece of evidence is the volume of goods passing through locks on the Potomac; this is indicated in Chart VIII-III. Unquestionably the spread of turnpikes during this period ex-

CHART VIII-III

Tonnage Passing Through Locks on Potomac

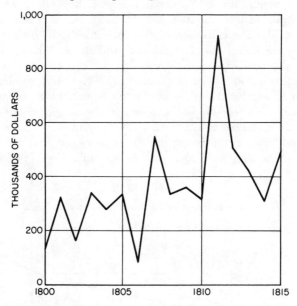

Source: Appendix I, Table B-III.

tended the size of the local market, but even so the high cost of internal transport was an insuperable barrier. Tench Coxe, in his *View of the United States* published in 1792, makes clear the magnitude of the problem.[13]

> To a nation inhabiting a great continent not yet traversed by artificial roads and canals, the rivers of which above their natural

---

[13] Tench Coxe, *A View of the United States, in a Series of Papers* . . . (Philadelphia: William Hall, Wrigley & Berryman, 1794).

navigation have been hitherto very little improved, many of whose
people are at this moment closely settled upon lands which actually
sink from one-fifth to one-half of the value of their crops in the
mere charges of transporting them to the seaport towns, and
others of whose inhabitants cannot at present send their produce
to a seaport for its whole value, a thorough sense of the truth
of the position is a matter of unequalled magnitude and importance.[14]

With the exception of the movement of livestock eastward across
the mountains, the interregional trade of the period, when the
only available transportation was by land, was a trickle of high
value goods. The expansion of the coastwise trade, both regional
and interregional, was of significant proportions. Like the foreign
trade, the coastwise traffic grew very little between 1790–1792,
but beginning in 1793 it expanded rapidly. Unfortunately, there
are no figures for the value of this trade, but there are statistics
for the volume of shipping enrolled in the coastwise trade, and
these are presented in Chart IX-III.[15] They show rapid expansion
after 1792 and again during the Embargo period.

Foreshadowing its larger role in the subsequent period, the

CHART IX-III

Tonnage Engaged in Coastwise and Internal Trade

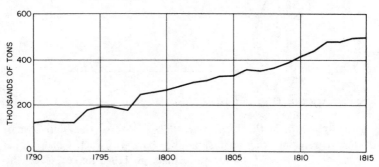

Source: Appendix II, Table C-III.

---

[14] Quoted in Johnson, *et al., History,* p. 205.

[15] These figures contain cumulative errors as a result of the failure annually
to take off the rolls ships which had been lost, broken up, and so on. There
were important clearances of figures in 1801-1802 and 1811. However, in general, they indicate the volume of expansion for the overall period.

other interregional trade which showed the beginnings of expansion was that between the West and the South, particularly New Orleans, on the Mississippi River system. In 1795 Spain granted to the United States the right of navigation in this area, and by 1799 $1 million worth of goods was received at New Orleans from up river. In 1802 the amount was $2,634,564, but in October of that year the Spanish suddenly closed the port. Navigation was reopened before the purchase of Louisiana had been concluded, and the downriver trade continued to grow, reaching $5,370,555 in 1807. This trade was primarily one-way, since it was before the use of steamboats, and movement upriver was slow and freight charges high.

Movement of people was the most important interregional flow of productive factors. This movement was general throughout the period, although far more pronounced in the decade 1800–1810 than in the previous ten years. Table 1 gives the population of the

TABLE 1

POPULATION OF THE WESTERN STATES AND TERRITORIES

State	1790	1800	1810
Kentucky	73,677	220,955	406,511
Tennessee	35,691	105,602	261,727
Ohio		45,365	230,760
Indiana		5,641	24,520
Illinois			12,282
Mississippi		8,850	40,352
Louisiana (Missouri)			20,845
Territory of Orleans (Louisiana)			76,556
Michigan			4,762

Source: E. R. Johnson and collaborators, History of Domestic and Foreign Commerce of the United States, Table 12.

western area for the three census years. There are no figures for interregional capital movements, although it is clear that settlers did take some capital with them.

This brief statistical summary of international and interregional flows will serve as the basis for exploring the way in which expansion took place in this country, but the initiating influences were not within the United States. They resulted rather from events abroad, and the explanation must proceed from there.

IV

THE INTERNATIONAL SETTING—1793-1814

One need look no further than to events in Europe to account for almost every twist and turn in the fortunes of the American economy during these years. From the outbreak of war between England and France in 1793 to the final peace settlement in 1814, the commercial and military policies of England and France and the response of the American government to them were the source for every expansion and contraction. The succession of events and their influence upon our external economic relations will be summarized briefly.[1]

I

Between the outbreak of the war and the brief interlude of peace following the Treaty of Amiens in 1801, the United States benefited greatly from the expansion of the re-export and carrying trades, while at the same time in continual conflict with the chief belligerents. The expansion of the carrying and re-export trades was a result of the disappearance from international trade of the ships of every belligerent save England. Holland, France, Spain, and others ultimately drawn into the conflict were all important carriers, leaving the vast colonial trade of Europe in the hands of neutrals, specifically the United States. While the products of the trade were sometimes exported directly, it was only as exports of a neutral that they could reach European ports without being intercepted en route. Tropical products were imported into the United States

---

[1] Cf. Anna C. Clauder, *American Commerce as Affected by the Wars of the French Revolution and Napoleon, 1793-1812* (Philadelphia: University of Pennsylvania Ph.D. Thesis, 1932). Hereafter cited as *American Commerce.*

and duties paid on them. They were then re-exported, entitling the importer to a drawback of all but a small percentage of the duties. Similarly, manufactures from Europe found their way to colonial ports via the United States. Even Britain, despite her naval superiority, found it advantageous to open her West Indies trade to our ships on a temporary basis.

Continual harassment by the chief belligerents characterized the first eight years of the war. British condemnation of American-owned goods threatened to pull the United States into the war until the Jay Treaty, in which Britain promised compensation of $10,000,000. Seizures by the French in 1796 led to several engagements and, in effect, undeclared sea war until the conclusion of a treaty in 1800.

In 1797, French seizures on the one hand and talk of peace on the other led to drops in shipping activity, and in prices and freight rates which were reflected in the brief dip in American earnings; and then followed unparalleled prosperity in 1799 and 1800. It was not until 1801 that a treaty between France and England was concluded. For the next one and a half years the United States was back in its position of 1790, as the precipitous drop in earnings from both re-exports and the carrying trade indicate. The years 1803-1807 were a duplication of the earlier war period, with United States shipping taking advantage of the renewal of conflict. 1806-1807 were peak years, but the reaction of the belligerents to this unrestrained trade already foreshadowed its end. With the *Essex* decision in 1805, the British reverted to a 1756 rule that neutrals in time of war could carry on only that trade which had been carried on in peace time. This meant the end of the re-export trade, if the ruling were effectively enforced. The Monroe-Pinckney Treaty, which would have legalized this trade, was vetoed by Jefferson. Napoleon's Berlin decree, establishing a blockade of Britain and creating the Continental System, was followed by Britain's Orders in Council of November, 1807. The former made every American ship entering Britain subject to capture; the latter equally prohibited trade between the United States and Europe. The American Secretary of State estimated that between 1803-1807 the British had seized 528 American ships, the French 389.[2] The reaction

---

[2] Quoted in Johnson, *et al.*, *History*, II, 29.

in the United States Congress was to pass the Embargo Act [3] in December, 1807, closing down the foreign trade. The resulting economic distress ultimately forced the government to repeal the act and substitute the Non-Intercourse Act of March 1, 1809, by which commercial intercourse was permitted with all countries except England and France. Harassment and seizure characterized the next three years, and as a result recovery was partial and incomplete. With the declaration of war in 1812 the British effectively ended our external trade and concluded an era of growth based on American neutrality in a world at war.

II

The colonial trade, which had been a source of European jealousies and wars for several centuries, rested on a number of tropical and semitropical goods in growing demand in the Western World. The sugar trade in particular had been a lucrative source of income, which made the West Indies possessions important bases for the economic growth of England and France in the eighteenth century. Coffee, tea, pepper, and cocoa were also a valuable part of the colonial trade, in addition to a number of less valuable commodities. The extent to which the European wars threw this trade into the hands of American merchants for re-export to Europe in the guise of neutral trade can be seen in Chart I-IV, which shows the volume of the four principal tropical goods exported from the the United States during the years 1792–1815. Holland, France, the German ports (Hamburg, Bremen, and so on), Italy, and Great Britain were the major destinations of these goods. Of lesser importance was the trade in European manufactures re-exported to the colonies. While textiles were the most important single commodity of this trade, it included a wide variety of other finished goods.[4]

---

[3] The act was passed before official news of the Orders in Council had reached the United States.

[4] While England dominated this trade, continental European goods and particularly textiles and metal goods from Germany also played an important part.

Though certainly of less spectacular dimensions, the growth of domestic exports during this period was significant for the Amer-

CHART I-IV

Volume of Exports in Pounds: 1792–1814
Cocoa, Coffee, Pepper, and Sugar

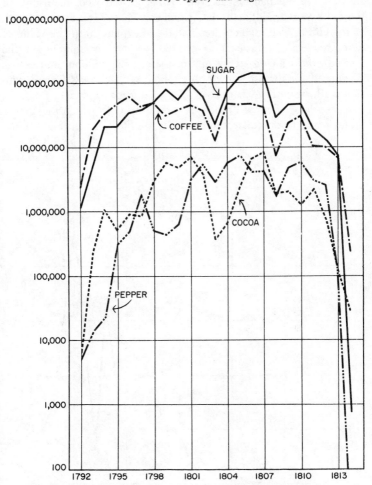

Source: Appendix I, Table A-IV.

ican economy. Foodstuffs, particularly wheat and flour, increased with the cutting off of part of the Baltic and Mediterranean trades. In 1801, as a result of crop failure, the West Indies, Spain, Portugal, and Great Britain were the major buyers. Marine and forest products, particularly lumber, naval stores, pot and pearl ashes, showed some expansion as well. Tobacco and rice, mainstays of the old export trade, made less significant gains. It was the growth of the cotton trade which dominated the expansion in the value of domestic exports. From 1791 to 1807 exports originating in the United States increased by approximately $30 million, and cotton accounted for almost half of this total ($14,232,000). This expansion is illustrated in Chart II-IV. The major markets were England, and, to a lesser degree France. The rapidity with which the United States came to dominate the cotton trade of Great Britain is strik-

CHART II-IV

Volume of Cotton Exports: 1791–1815
(in Millions of Pounds)

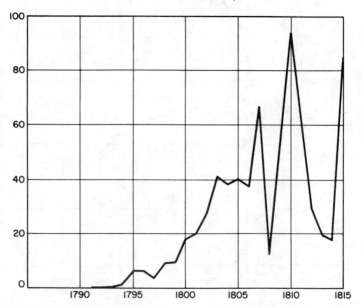

Source: Appendix I, Table B-IV.

ing. In 1787 over half of Britain's raw cotton imports came from British, Spanish, French, Dutch, and Portuguese possessions, primarily in the West Indies. Smyrna and Turkey provided approximately another quarter of the total. The origins of imports into London, Liverpool, and Glasgow in 1807 were as follows: [5]

From the United States	171,267	bales
British West Indies	28,969	
Dutch colonies	43,651	
Portuguese colonies	18,981	
East Indies	11,409	
All other	8,390	
	282,667	

United States shipping, which had carried but 59 per cent of its foreign trade in 1790, increased this proportion to 90 per cent in 1795 and 92 per cent in 1807. It was not only that American ships came to dominate the country's external trade completely, but that the degree of utilization of ships was increased as well. An index of this activity is contained in Chart III-IV, which divides the gross registered tonnage in foreign trade into ships from foreign countries entered into United States ports (1796–1800 = 100). This increased efficiency resulted from the greater demand for shipping and the restricted supply, and from the relaxation of navigation laws and commercial policies that limited utilization of a country's ships, causing a substantial portion of shipping time to be spent in ballast rather than carrying cargo.

The principal trade routes of the period were the North Atlantic, the West Indies and South American trades. These routes were familiar during colonial times, although they were severely circumscribed during the ten years of peace, and several new routes, on which the profits were very high, developed during the war years. These were the trade in the Dutch East Indies, which first assumed significant proportions in 1797, and the China trade, frequently in conjunction with fur trade of the American Northwest. The latter route was initiated in 1784, but expanded in the 1790's, when the United States became the major shipper of tea to Europe

---

[5] From Sir Alexander Baring's inquiry relative to the British Orders in Council, 1808, as quoted in Pitkin, *A Statistical View*, p. 112.

during the war. While these new trades employed only a small fraction of the American tonnage registered for foreign trade, their earnings were probably a higher proportion of total income in the carrying trade.

CHART III-IV

United States Shipping Activity Index

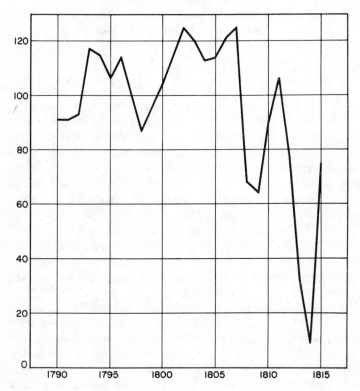

Source: Appendix I, Table C-IV.

III

Both the carrying trade and the re-export trade were concentrated in northeastern ports. New York, Boston, Philadelphia, and

Baltimore were the principal shipping centers, both with respect to registry and as centers of the re-export trade. They were followed by many smaller ports which were the shipbuilding centers of the period. The registration of ships was more widely scattered than the entrepôts of the commodity trade, which were concentrated in the four major sea ports. The concentration of the shipping trade in the Northeast is shown in Table 2. This was true of the coast-

TABLE 2

REGISTERED TONNAGE OF THE UNITED STATES BY STATES,
EMPLOYED IN FOREIGN TRADE 1799

States	Tons	95ths
New Hampshire	19,875	14
Massachusetts	191,067	31
Vermont	--	--
Rhode Island	18,562	39
Connecticut	31,632	63
New York	120,253	06
New Jersey	1,271	34
Pennsylvania	90,944	30
Delaware	2,217	16
Maryland	81,446	81
Virginia	46,858	68
North Carolina	19,214	52
South Carolina	38,567	42
Georgia	286	18

Source: Seybert, Statistical Annals, p. 321.

wise fishing and whaling trade as well as the ships registered for foreign trade. The earnings of the carrying trade flowed initially into ports north of the Potomac.

As indicated above, the re-export trade was even more highly concentrated than the shipping industry. In 1806, $52.9 million out of $60.3 million of re-exports came from the four states of Massachusetts, New York, Pennsylvania and Maryland, and the four ports discussed above accounted for most of the total. Table 3 shows the value of re-exports from each state for the years 1803–1807. The lucrative earnings of the re-export trade, like those of the carrying trade, went initially to merchants in the major seaboard cities of the Northeast.

Domestic export trade was more widely scattered. As Table 4

TABLE 3

THE VALUE OF RE-EXPORTS FROM EACH STATE, 1803-1807

States	1803	1804	1805	1806	1807
New Hampshire	51,093	262,697	218,813	383,884	314,072
Vermont	27,940	55,795	67,405	102,043	55,816
Massachusetts	3,369,546	10,591,256	13,738,606	14,577,547	13,926,377
Rhode Island	611,366	817,935	1,506,470	1,142,499	915,576
Connecticut	10,183	29,228	90,190	193,078	105,644
New York	3,191,556	8,580,185	15,384,883	13,709,769	16,400,547
New Jersey	--	--	110	7,363	5,123
Pennsylvania	3,504,496	6,851,444	9,397,012	13,809,389	12,055,128
Delaware	240,466	517,315	280,556	374,319	151,580
Maryland	1,371,022	5,213,099	7,450,937	10,919,774	10,282,285
Virginia	151,441	395,098	660,985	428,709	367,713
North Carolina	26,296	9,142	12,469	3,576	4,229
South Carolina	947,765	2,309,516	3,108,979	2,946,718	3,783,199
Georgia	25,488	74,345	43,677	--	34,069

Source: Pitkin, A Statistical View, Chapter III, Table 3, p. 55.

TABLE 4

THE VALUE OF DOMESTIC EXPORTS FROM EACH STATE, 1803-1807

States	1803	1804	1805	1806	1807
New Hampshire	494,620	716,091	608,408	795,263	680,022
Vermont	117,450	191,725	169,402	193,775	204,285
Massachusetts	8,768,566	16,894,378	19,435,657	21,199,243	20,112,125
Rhode Island	1,275,596	1,735,671	2,572,049	2,091,835	1,657,564
Connecticut	1,248,571	1,516,110	1,443,727	1,715,828	1,624,727
New York	10,818,387	16,081,281	23,482,943	21,762,845	26,357,963
New Jersey	21,311	24,829	20,743	33,867	41,186
Pennsylvania	7,525,710	11,030,157	13,762,252	17,574,702	16,864,744
Delaware	428,153	697,396	358,383	500,106	229,275
Maryland	5,078,062	9,151,939	10,859,480	14,580,905	14,298,984
Virginia	6,100,708	5,790,001	5,606,620	5,055,396	4,761,234
North Carolina	952,614	928,687	779,903	789,605	745,162
South Carolina	7,811,108	7,451,616	9,066,625	9,743,782	10,912,564
Georgia	2,370,875	2,077,572	2,394,846	82,764	3,744,845

Source: Pitkin, A Statistical View, Chapter III, Table 1, pp. 52-53.

illustrates, over half came from the same four states, with New York in the lead. But staple crops such as tobacco from Virginia and rice from the Carolinas were the basis of wider origins of export. It was particularly the cotton trade that accounted for the increase from South Carolina, Georgia, and the Mississippi. While more than half the income from the export trade went to the four northern states, a growing percentage was flowing into the southern states in exchange for cotton.

V
THE GROWTH OF THE ECONOMY, 1790-1814

An analysis of the American economy during this
period subdivides into three distinct parts. The first
covers the years from the ratification of the Constitution to the outbreak of the European War in 1793;
the second ends with the imposition of the Embargo at the end
of 1807; the last terminates with the peace treaty of 1814.

The most important developments for subsequent growth in the
economy before 1793 took place in the domestic sector. They were
the policies of Alexander Hamilton, specifically the funding of the
foreign, domestic and state debts, and the creation of the first Bank
of the United States, and they formed the monetary and fiscal
underpinnings of the new nation. The first established a sound
credit basis; the second was an important beginning of an elaborated capital market.

Between 1793 and 1808, the economic development of the United
States was tied to international trade and shipping. In the light of
previous analysis, one would expect that the rapid growth of these
years would reflect the strategic role of the carrying and re-export
trades in inducing expansion. Since direct income from both of
these trades flowed into the Northeast, it might be supposed that
the maritime cities of this section and particularly the four major
seaports would grow most rapidly. In the same manner one might
predict the equally rapid development of Charleston and other
ports of the cotton trade. The disposition of income from the carrying and re-export trade, however, was very different from that of
the cotton trade, and consequently the development which took
place in the Northeast was in sharp contrast to that of the cotton
South.

I

Expansion in the Northeast during the period is striking. One need only read contemporary accounts of the opulence evident everywhere in maritime ports to be struck by the enormous effect of the neutral trade. A loyalist returning to Boston for a visit in 1808 wrote:

> The great number of new and elegant buildings which have been erected in this town within the last ten years, strikes the eye with astonishment, and proves the rapid manner in which the people have been acquiring wealth.[1]

S. E. Morison, in his *Maritime History of Massachusetts, 1783-1860*, points out that Boston was practically rebuilt during the period and that State Street was lined with new banks and insurance companies to accommodate the commercial expansion.[2] Striking as it was, the growth of Boston was less than that of the other three major cities. Adam Seybert, a careful observer, described the period with mixed emotions.

> Independent of our newly acquired political character, circumstances arose in Europe, by which a new and extensive field was presented for our commercial enterprize. The most memorable of revolutions was commenced in France, in 1789; the wars, consequent to that event, created a demand for our exports, and invited our shipping for the carrying trade of a very considerable portion of Europe; we not only carried the colonial productions to the several parent states, but we also became the purchasers of them in the French, Spanish and Dutch colonies. A new era was established in our commercial history; the individuals, who partook of these advantages, were numerous; our catalogue of merchants was swelled much beyond what it was entitled to be from the state of our population. Many persons, who had secured moderate capitals, from mechanical pursuits, soon became the most adventurous. The predominant spirit of that time has had a powerful effect in determining the character of the rising generation in the United States. The brilliant prospects held out by commerce, caused our citizens to neglect the mechanical and manufacturing

---

[1] Quoted in Samuel E. Morison, *Maritime History of Massachusetts, 1783-1860* (Boston: Houghton Mifflin Co., 1921), p. 125. Hereafter cited as *Maritime History.*

[2] *Ibid.,* p. 125.

branches of industry; fallacious views, founded on temporary circumstances, carried us from these pursuits, which must ultimately constitute the resources, wealth and power of this nation. Temporary benefits were mistaken for permanent advantages; so certain were the profits on the foreign voyages, that commerce was only pursued as an art; all the knowledge, which former experience had considered as essentially necessary, was now unattended to; the philosophy of commerce, if I am allowed the expression, was totally nelected; the nature of foreign productions was but little investigated by the shippers in the United States; the demand in Europe for foreign merchandise, especially for that of the West Indies and South America, secured to all these cargoes a ready sale, with a great profit. The most adventurous became the most wealthy, and that without the knowledge of any of the principles which govern commerce under ordinary circumstances. No one was limited to any one branch of trade; the same individual was concerned in voyages to Asia, South America, the West Indies and Europe. Our tonnage increased in a ratio, with the extended catalogue of the exports; we seemed to have arrived at the maximum of human prosperity; in proportion to our population we ranked as the most commercial nation; in point of value, our trade was only second to that of Great Britain.

By our extended intercourse with other nations we not only augmented our pecuniary resources, but we thereby became acquainted with their habits, manners, science, arts, resources, wealth and power. At home we imitated them in much that was useful and adapted to our condition; fixed and permanent improvements were established throughout the United States; the accumulated capital of our merchants, enabled them to explore new sources of wealth; our cities were augmented and embellished, our agriculture was improved, our population was increased, and our debt was diminished. The merchants who had been long engaged in trade, were confounded by the changes which were so suddenly effected; the less experienced considered the newly acquired advantages as matters of right, and that they would remain to us; they did not contemplate a period of general peace, when each nation will carry its own productions, when discriminations will be made in favour of domestic tonnage, when foreign commerce will be limited to enumerated articles, and when much circumspection will be necessary in all our commercial transactions.[3]

One need not depend solely on literary description. Urbanization in America increased from 5.1 per cent of the population in 1790 to 7.3 per cent in 1810, and most of this increase was ac-

---

[3] Seybert, *Statistical Annals,* pp. 59-60.

counted for by the four major ports. Their growth for the census years of 1790, 1800 and 1810 is given in Table 5. Other New

TABLE 5

POPULATION OF CITIES AT EACH CENSUS, 1790 TO 1810

City	Census Year		
	1790	1800	1810
Baltimore	13,503	26,114	35,583
Boston	18,038	24,937	33,250
New York	33,131	60,489	96,373
Philadelphia	42,520	69,403	91,874

Source: U. S. Census Bureau, Compendium of the Seventh Census, J. D. B. De Bow, Supt. of U. S. Census (Washington: Senate Printer, 1854), p. 192. It will be noted that there are discrepancies in the figures here reported and those found in U. S. Census Bureau, Sixteenth Census of the United States, Population, Vol. I (Washington: Government Printing Office, 1942), 32-33, as well as those cited in U. S. Census Bureau, A Century of Population Growth in the United States, 1790-1900 (Washington: Government Printing Office, 1909), p. 78. As noted in the latter volume, these differences appear to arise because the later estimates covered only the original city areas in each case.

England shipping and shipbuilding ports accounted for much of the remaining increase. The consequences of this expansion in income from the export sector may conveniently be broken down into the growth of subsidiary, complementary, and residentiary types of economic activity induced by export industries.

Shipbuilding was the major subsidiary industry.[4] Its expansion followed closely the movements in ocean freight rates, as comparison of Chart I-III and Chart IV-III in Chapter III indicates. New tonnage sold at approximately $60 a ton,[5] and accordingly a rough estimate of the value of shipbuilding may be derived. Shipfitting industries, particularly ropeworks and sail-making, developed and flourished around the shipbuilding areas.

More significant, particularly for later development, was the

---

[4] This was not strictly a subsidiary industry, since it was also an export industry (See Table A-III, Appendix I). However, its growth during the period was primarily related to our shipping trade.

[5] Cf. North, "Balance of Payments," *loc. cit.*

variety of complementary industries that arose to serve the re-export and carrying trades. Not only did commission merchants, brokers and other business organizations evolve to implement these trades,[6] but marine insurance companies [7] and banks, and facilities for warehousing and docking also grew up as the carrying trade expanded. Of these complementary facilities, only banking was not

TABLE 6

INSURANCE COMPANIES

Year	Number	Capital
1791		
1792	1	600,000
1793	2	900,000
1794	4	1,200,000
1795	7	2,500,000
1796	8	3,000,000
1797	9	3,300,000
1798	9	3,000,000
1799	12	4,000,000
1800	15	5,000,000
1801	22	6,000,000
1802	29	7,500,000
1803	36	9,000,000
1804	40	10,000,000

Source: Blodget, *Economica*, p. 64.

completely dependent on the shipping and re-export trade for its development. While it is clear that banking provided credit for a wide variety of urban undertakings in addition to internal and external trade, the international economic influences discussed above were the initial force promoting expansion.

Shipping and the re-export trade are the kinds of industries which, directly and indirectly, encourage increased urbanization. The income effect of these industries is to produce a multiplier effect through the growth of a variety of locally oriented manufactures and services to meet the needs of a growing urban population. The rapid growth of New York and the other major ports

---

[6] Norman S. Buck, *The Development of the Organization of Anglo-American Trade, 1800-1850* (New Haven: Yale University Press, 1925). Hereafter cited as *Anglo-American Trade*.

[7] Blodget, *Economica*, p. 64. Also, see Table 6 herein.

reflected the development of a local consuming market. There was an increased demand for foodstuffs for this urban population, with a consequent widening of the market area around these urban centers and concerted efforts to reduce internal transport costs. It is in this connection that the increasing pressure for turnpikes can be understood.

This expansion of local trade was evident to contemporaries everywhere. Writing of the period, McMaster stated:

> But the movement of the people westward not only went on with increasing rapidity. The high price of wheat, of corn, of flour, due to the demand for exportation sent thousands into the Genesee country and the borders of Lake Champlain to farm and from them came back the cry for better means of transportation. The people of the shipping towns were quite as eager to get the produce as the farmers were to send it, and with the opening of the century the old rage for roadmaking, river improvements and canals revived . . . once aroused the rage for turnpiking spread rapidly over the whole country. In a few years, a sum almost equal to the domestic debt at the close of the Revolution was voluntarily invested by the people in the stock of turnpike corporations. By 1810, twenty-six had been chartered in Vermont and more than twenty in New Hampshire, while in all New England the number was upward of one hundred and eighty. New York, by 1811, had chartered one hundred and thirty-seven. This combined capital was over seven millions and a half of dollars. Their total length was four thousand five hundred miles of which fully one-third was constructed.[8]

Expansion in urban and agricultural economic activity and the significant increase in the size of the market should not obscure the fact that the region still had a high propensity to import. The revenue tariffs of the period were no obstacle to the inflow of manufactured goods, and what manufacturing did develop in the Northeast during this period was limited to goods in which we had a comparative advantage (lumbering, shipbuilding, and so on), or those which were locally oriented because of transport costs. Europe, and England in particular, provided the finished goods, especially the luxury goods sought with increased incomes.

---

[8] John B. McMaster, *History of the People of the United States from the Revolution to the Civil War*, 8 Vols. (New York: Appleton-Century-Crofts, Inc., 1892-1919), III, 462-63. Hereafter cited as McMaster, *History*.

II

Expansion in the Northeast and in the South stand in marked contrast to each other. Since the nature of the southern cotton economy is a central part of the study after 1815, it will be dealt with only briefly here. The cotton gin was unquestionably the most significant invention during the years between 1790 and 1860, and the story of its development needs no extended description. The growing dilemma of the South was that the demand for its traditional export staples was no longer increasing and its heavy capital investment was in slaves. The concerted search for new export staples and the experiments with cotton all reflect the problems of the region; invention of the cotton gin can be viewed as a response to the dilemma rather than as an independent accidental development.

The rapid spread of cotton culture throughout Georgia and South Carolina is reflected in Chart II-IV. As the South shifted out of a diversified agriculture into cotton and its income increased, the effect was quite different from that generated in the Northeast by rising incomes from the re-export and carrying trade. Urbanization did not increase. The growth of Charleston, major cotton port of the period, was less than the rate of population growth for the country as a whole. Charleston's population grew from 16,000 in 1790 to 24,000 in 1810, well behind the other urban centers. Only New Orleans had a significant expansion of population, and this is attributable to its role as entrepôt of the western river trade rather than to the cotton trade. The technical characteristics of cotton growing at the time, as well as the income and social structure of a slave economy, simply did not induce urbanization—nor even the growth of an extensive food growing independent yeomanry. The notable fact about cotton is that the income of the South flowed directly out in the form of: (1) services and transport to implement that trade; (2) import of foodstuffs to feed slaves and planters; (3) import of manufactured goods—cheap textiles and iron goods for the slaves, luxury articles for the planting class. It was this demand for goods from outside a region of developing specialization which was responsible for the rapid development of the coasting trade and for the expanding shipments of foodstuffs down the Mississippi.[9] A new South was growing up which specialized in the lucrative export trade of a single staple, with rice, sugar, and tobacco as subsidiary exports, and relied on the rest of the country and foreign imports to provide the rest of its needs.

III

The years 1793–1808 were years of unparalleled prosperity. True, this was a hectic era, and the prosperity was interrupted on two occasions—1797–1798 and the Twenty Month Peace of Amiens 1801–1803—by the external forces which had created it. Yet the evidence suggests that this period was a high water mark in individual well-being which was to stand for many years, and laid important foundations for the growth of the economy after 1815.

Contemporary accounts amply attest to the prosperity of the period. It is logically ascribable to:

(1) The importance of the export sector in the total economy;
(2) The five-fold (or more) expansion of this sector during the period;
(3) The equally large increase in imports for consumption at favorable import prices;
(4) The expansion in the domestic economy induced by the increase in income from the export sector.

While there are no reliable national income figures for the period,[10]

---

[9] However, during this period, there was a major export market for these foodstuffs as well.

[10] Robert F. Martin's figures in *National Income of the United States, 1799-1938* (New York: National Industrial Conference Board, 1939) show a higher per capita real income in 1799 than at any subsequent decade date until the mid-nineteenth century. I believe that this relative figure is correct (if not for 1799 then at least for 1806-1807). This is not to say that I agree with Martin's methods or the relative movement of the figures on subsequent census years. Simon Kuznets, in "Current National Income Estimates for the Period Prior to 1870," International Association for Research in Income and Wealth, *Income and Wealth Series II: Trends and Structure in the United States* (Cambridge: Bowes and Bowes, 1952), provides ample criticism of his methods, which are further elaborated by William Parker and Franklee Whartenby in "The Growth of Output Before 1840," *Trends in the American Economy in the Nineteenth*

the incomplete statistical data in Chapter III and the literary testimony are sufficient proof. One would have to posit a tremendous decline in agricultural productivity to counteract the very substantial expansion in the international sector of the economy, and there is no evidence of such a decline. The increased productivity of shipping, the rise in freight rates, and the favorable terms of trade combined to produce an era of unequaled affluence. The market was being steadily widened by the movement of people out of self-sufficiency into the money economy, in response either to the demand for labor in the burgeoning urban areas or to the high price of agricultural goods and lower internal transport costs. There is a noteworthy point in connection with the current account terms of trade. Where earnings of the carrying trade were concerned there were simultaneously a substantial increase in efficiency—the result of more efficient utilization of ships with suspension of the navigation laws—and improvement in the terms of trade with the rise in freight rates. The growing concentration of the South on cotton and the emergence of a pattern of regional specialization also reflected a more efficient utilization of resources.

This groundwork for later development was vital to the economy's long run future. Shipping and the re-export trade favorably affected the disposition of income from this sector, since the augmented income reacted to widen the domestic market through rapid urban development, the growth of residentiary industry, and the construction of turnpikes linking urban areas and the agricultural hinterland. In addition, the expanded export sector promoted the rapid growth of banking and insurance, improving the capital market.

Though the times immediately ahead were to be difficult ones, these developments provided an important base for the subsequent period of expansion. But the interim years, years of disengagement and then of gradual involvement in the European war, were trying.

Century. Studies in Income and Wealth, Vol. 24 (Princeton University Press for the National Bureau of Economic Research, 1960). Neither Kuznets nor Parker and Whartenby devote sufficient attention to the very large earnings from shipping nor the favorable terms of trade. The answer to this lengthy controversy which Martin initiated is not that individual well-being was declining from 1799 to 1829 but that the brief period 1793-1807 was an extraordinary and unique era which raised per capita real incomes far above the previous or subsequent years.

IV

The effect of the Embargo is graphically described by McMaster:

> The newspapers were full of insolvent-debtor notices. All over the country, the court-house doors, the tavern doors, the post-offices, the cross-road posts, were covered with advertisements of sheriffs sales. In the cities, the jails were not large enough to hold the debtors. At New York during 1809, thirteen hundred men were imprisoned for no other crime than being ruined by the embargo. A traveler who saw the city in this day of distress assures us that it looked like a town ravaged by pestilence. The counting-houses were shut or advertised to let. The coffee-houses were almost empty. The streets along the water-side were almost deserted. The ships were dismantled; their decks were cleared, their hatches were battened down.[11]

If there were any doubts of the strategic importance of the carrying and re-export trade to the American economy, the Embargo swiftly removed them. Collapse in domestic prices, widespread unemployment, and the passage of stay laws against seizure of property in the southern states testify to the severity of the collapse. Even such advocates of Embargo as Justice Story saw ruin, evasion, and open rebellion in the wake of the act, which "had prostrated the whole commerce of America. . . ." [12] He earned the epithet "pseudo-republican" from Jefferson, who credited him with the repeal of the Embargo. The Non-Intercourse Act of March 1809 reopened trade with all except French and British territories.[13] It was followed in May, 1810, by the Macon Bill under which, in return for the lifting of restrictions by one belligerent, we agreed to end commercial intercourse with the other. Throughout the whole of the period before the second war with England, trade with that country was permitted for only fifteen months. Recovery of the re-export and carrying trades was only partial, even under the Non-Intercourse and Macon Acts. The ingenuity of Yankee mariners in

---

[11] McMaster, *History*, p. 415.

[12] William W. Story, Ed., *Life and Letters of Joseph Story, Associate Justice of the Supreme Court*, 2 Vols. (Boston: C. C. Little and J. Brown, 1851), I, 183.

[13] It also excluded British and French goods.

evading the combination of American prohibitions and British and French restrictions led to greater recovery in the carrying trade than in the re-export trade.[14]

At the outbreak of war in 1812, the British Navy, with its long European experience, established an effective blockade of American ports. One of the remarkable aspects of this war was the American trade with the Iberian Peninsula to provision Wellington's army, primarily with flour. The British licensed this extraordinary trade, and permitted some trade with their West Indies. There was also substantial smuggling through Passamaquoddy Bay and Amelia Island.[15] As a result, the carrying and export trades did not disappear altogether in 1813. When the British obtained grain from the Baltic in 1814, however, the trade was closed down, and the blockade was complete except for the trickle of ships which could elude British frigates.

Although resources thus idled in 1808 were never completely reabsorbed in external trade during this period, the consequences were not altogether disastrous. The closing off of the import trade was effective in promoting the rise of domestic manufactures, and capital which had been devoted to shipping and foreign commerce was partially absorbed in a rapid growth of industry. Before 1808 only fifteen cotton mills had been built in the United States: one in 1791, one in 1795, two more in 1803 and 1804, and ten between 1804 and 1808. By the end of 1809 eighty-seven additional mills had been constructed, and capacity had been increased from eight thousand spindles in 1808 to thirty-one thousand at the end of 1809 and an estimated eighty thousand by 1811. Other branches of manufacturing also made substantial gains through 1814.[16]

---

[14] Cf. Clauder, *American Commerce*, Chapters V and VI; and R. G. Albion and Jennie B. Pope, *Sea Lanes in Wartime: The American Experience, 1775-1942* (New York: W. W. Norton & Co., 1942), Chapter IV. Hereafter cited as *Sea Lanes.*

[15] Albion and Pope, *Sea Lanes,* pp. 116-17.

[16] Tench Coxe, *A Statement of the Arts and Manufactures of the United States for the Year 1810* (Philadelphia: A Cornman, 1814); and *Supplementary Observations* (September 1814), carry Coxe's description on up to that date. The prosperity of Philadelphia during this era was in contrast to other major seaport towns. It reflected the rapid development of manufacturing there. See "Philadelphia and the Embargo of 1808," by Louis M. Sears, in *Quarterly Journal of Economics* XXXV (February 1921), 355-59.

Albert Gallatin cautiously observed in 1810 that some of the causes impeding the progress of manufactures had been removed.

> The most prominent of those causes are the abundance of land compared with the population, the high price of labor, and the want of sufficient capital. The superior attractions of agricultural pursuits, the great extension of American commerce during the late European Wars, and the continuance of habits after the causes which produced them have ceased to exist, may also be enumerated. Several of those obstacles have, however, been removed or lessened. The cheapness of provisions had always, to a certain extent, counterbalanced the high price of manual labor; and this is now, in many important branches, nearly superseded by the introduction of machinery; a great American capital has been acquired during the last twenty years; and the injurious violations of the Neutral commerce of the United States, by forcing industry and capital into other channels, have broken inveterate habits, and given a general impulse, to which must be ascribed the great increase of manufactures during the last two years.[17]

Gallatin was correct about the diversion of capital and labor into manufacturing as a result of the end of the neutral trade, but his statement that the other stumbling blocks to the progress of manufacturing had been removed was wrong. Events after 1815 demonstrated that the changes had been only temporary. The rapid rise in the price of manufactures due to the absence of competing foreign goods was responsible for the boom. Prices of manufactures rose as imports decreased, and it was this price rise which induced the surge of manufacturing of the period.

The advent of war graphically illustrated the growing regional specialization in the previous interval. With its increasing concentration on a few export staples, the South was particularly hard hit. New England, which had shifted at least part of its capital to manufactures and had continued a smuggling trade of imports through Canada,[18] sold its goods to the rest of the country on very favorable terms. As these goods were paid for primarily in specie, the specie reserves in Massachusetts banks between 1812 and 1814

---

[17] Albert Gallatin, in *American State Papers, Finance* (Washington: Gales and Seaton, 1832-61), II, 426.

[18] This trade must have been substantial, and an important reason for the relative well being of New England during the war. Newspaper accounts describe this trade, but there is no account of the amount involved so far as I know.

nearly doubled.[19] The heavy drain on banks in the rest of the country left them eager to avail themselves of the chance to suspend specie payments when the British invaded Maryland in 1814.

The shift of resources out of foreign and carrying trade into manufacturing represented an inefficient utilization of labor and capital. Moreover, the idled resources were never completely reabsorbed into the market economy except for rather brief periods. These points, together with the unfavorable movement of the terms of trade, give clear evidence that the years between 1808 and 1814 never reached the prosperous level attained during the era of neutral trade. The prosperity and growth of the economy was interrupted as this country became drawn into the European wars.

---

[19] Smith and Cole, *Fluctuations,* p. 28.

PART TWO

1815-1860

VI

THE ECONOMY IN 1815

1815 ushered in more than an era of peace for the United States; it marked a transitional period in the American economy. Some features of the new era were not apparent until 1819 and the depression that followed three years after the end of the war, but even in 1815 it was clear that the Atlantic economy and its components were very different from the western world of 1790. Only war-induced distortion in the economies of the countries of the Atlantic community delayed some of the consequences.

The re-export and carrying trades, main sources of expansion in the economy during the boom years prior to the Embargo, never again played so important a role. The re-export trade revived partially after the war and into the 1820's, but declined absolutely thereafter until almost 1850, and was unimportant in our foreign trade relative to domestic exports. The carrying trade remained significant in our international economic accounts, but the radical decline in freight rates after 1818, revival of navigation laws, and vigorous competition of other ocean carriers prevented earnings from equalling the years of the neutral trade. While it remained an important credit in our balance of payments, it was no longer an expansive force in the economy.

The rapid development of manufacturing after 1807, which partially substituted for re-exports and shipping, likewise suffered a serious setback. English manufactured goods, denied the lucrative American market during the war, made up for lost time in the years 1815–1818. Industrialization had proceeded apace in Britain even during the war years, and English supremacy in manufacturing was immediately felt by higher cost competitors throughout the world after 1815. A combination of technological leadership, the ability of English manufacturers to dump upon the American market during the years 1815–1818, and the auction system of distribution proved disastrous to a good deal of American manufacturing. The textile industry in particular found that it could not compete in quality goods.

As a result of these circumstances, the decade 1810–1820 was the only one in our history in which urbanization did not increase. Indeed, there was a slight decline: from 7.3 per cent of the population to 7.2 per cent. The major seaports of New York, Philadelphia and Boston barely held their own in population growth. Secondary ports such as Salem and Providence, which had grown rapidly as shipbuilding and re-export centers, showed little increase. Only Baltimore [1] among the seaports and inland Cincinnati exhibited rapid growth. In the South, New Orleans alone grew rapidly, particularly after the beginning of upriver steamboat traffic in 1816. Charleston grew scarcely at all, despite the cotton boom after the war.

While neither the re-export nor the carrying trade were ever again as important relatively, or absolutely, for the economy, the cotton trade in 1815 showed every sign of vigorous if not wildly speculative prosperity. Cotton prices began to rise in 1812; by 1815 they were in excess of twenty cents a pound in New York. The growing demand of the English cotton textile industry was not matched by an equal expansion in supply, and the downward trend in cotton prices which had commenced in 1801 was reversed. Prices reached a peak of twenty-nine cents a pound in 1816 and remained high until 1818. The boom in land sales and cotton expansion was under way well before the end of the war. By 1815 the South was committed to cotton, and an era had begun which was to continue until the Civil War.

Whatever the problems of readjustment to a world at peace,[2] the American economy in 1815 exhibited a marked contrast to the conditions of 1790 described in Chapter I. The population was

---

[1] The rapid growth of Baltimore reflected the boom in wheat and flour exports both immediately before and after the War of 1812. See Chart VIII-III for the growth of internal trade to Baltimore in response to this external demand.

[2] See Chapter XIII for a detailed discussion of the period 1815 to 1823.

approximately 8,400,000,[3] more than twice the figure for 1790. Since immigration had been negligible, this reflected a high rate of domestic increase. A striking feature was the regional differentiation which characterized the Northeast, the South, and the West. Climate, topography, and resources, together with the level of technology (particularly in transport), had conspired to produce three sharply different areas. Border states like Maryland, Delaware, and Kentucky did not fit as neatly into the separate regional patterns, but they were minor exceptions to the increasingly distinct patterns of economic life that developed.

Almost one-half of the total population resided in the Northeast, and it was in this region—the New England and Middle Atlantic States—that urbanization and the resulting commercial market were most highly developed. Both New York and Philadelphia had populations in excess of 100,000.[4] Boston and Baltimore were in excess of 35,000; Salem, Albany and Providence were all in excess of 10,000. The heritage of rapid growth in international commerce and shipping prior to 1807 was evidenced by the Northeast's preeminence in the development of a capital market, marketing and transport facilities, insurance companies, and other social overhead facilities connected with shipping and external trade. With the decline of the re-export trade, merchants in the Northeast had become closely tied to cotton. New York in particular became both the center of the import trade and the financial center for the cotton trade.[5]

Slightly more than one-third of the people in the United States lived in the South. Virginia, once the most populous state in the Union, increased only slightly. South Carolina, Georgia, Alabama, and Louisiana all showed rapid population growth, although they

---

[3] George R. Taylor, *The Transportation Revolution, 1815-1860*, Vol. IV of *Economic History of the United States* (New York: Rinehart, 1951), p. 3, cites this figure. Since it was not a census year it is an estimate. Hereafter cited as *Transportation Revolution*.

[4] In 1810, the populations of New York and Philadelphia were, respectively, 96.4 and 91.9 thousand. In 1820 they were 125.7 and 112.8 thousand.

[5] Margaret Myers, *The New York Money Market*, 2 Vols. (New York: Columbia University Press, 1921), I, *Origins and Development*, 49, 70. The growth in the use of trade acceptances stemmed largely from their widespread use in financing the cotton trade.

did not show a corresponding increase in urbanization. Cotton
plantations extended up navigable waterways, and as the land
closest to water transport was taken up, plantations developed
farther from these transport arteries. The extensive waterways of
the South permitted a vast expansion of improved acreage not far
removed from the only cheap method of shipping cotton. The
towns that did develop were collection points for cotton and for
the reshipment of imports to the upriver plantations. New Orleans,
an important entrepôt since the days of French and Spanish pos-
session, was the one city in the South exhibiting all the signs of
commercial expansion which characterized Northeastern ports. As
the shipping port for the vast hinterland of the Mississippi, Ohio,
and Missouri river systems, its expansion had just begun with the
application of steam to water transport and its successful initiation
on the Mississippi in 1816.

By 1815, population growth west of the mountains had become
substantial. In 1810 the census listed 1,337,946 people living in the
Mississippi Valley; by 1820 there were 2,419,369. As of 1815, however, the West still had little influence upon the American economy. The bulk of the populace was still either outside the market
or peripheral to it, as described in Chapter I. Approximately two
million people were scattered over a vast area effectively separated
from eastern markets by the intervening mountains. The one-way
trade down the Mississippi, the driving of livestock over the mountains, or wagon shipment of high value goods which could take the
overland freight rates were supplements to a self-sufficient way of
life geared to local exchange in the small trading centers which
sprang up throughout the area. The most characteristic feature of
the emerging pattern of urbanization was the small town providing
a wide variety of local trade and manufactures. Ties with the national economy were still tenuous, and such a pattern supported
few large urban areas. Cincinnati was the outstanding center,[6] and
Pittsburgh also developed rapidly. As Callender has pointed out,
nothing better illustrates the frontier, self-sufficient character of the
area than the fact that a population of two million people supported

---

[6] Cf. Thomas S. Berry, *Western Prices Before 1861; a Study of the Cincinnati Market.* Harvard Economic Studies LXXIV (Cambridge: Harvard University Press, 1943), for a discussion of the early growth of Cincinnati. Hereafter cited as *Western Prices.*

almost no urbanization.[7] In 1815 the integration of the West into the American economy awaited the development of cheap means of transportation and markets.

---

[7] Callender, "The Early Transportation and Banking Enterprises of the States in Relation to the Growth of the Corporation," *loc. cit.*

VII

THE ECONOMY 1815-1860—AN OVERVIEW

Between the end of the second war with England and the firing on Fort Sumter were nearly fifty years of peace, interrupted only briefly by the Mexican War on this continent and the Crimean War abroad. Neither was a major disturbing force, although the latter had repercussions upon economic stability in the 1850's. It was an era of tremendous expansion for the Atlantic economy as a whole and for the United States in particular.

The contrast between the sources of expansion in periods just before and after the War of 1812 is striking. In the former period the Western World was at war, and the rapid development of the American economy for fourteen years reflected our ability to take advantage of this war. The exigencies of war relaxed the mercantilist restrictions of European powers, and war created the demand for shipping and re-exports and the very favorable terms of trade that produced unequalled American prosperity up to 1808.

The period following 1815 was not only one of peace, but one in which artificial national barriers to the free movement of goods, services, productive factors, and ideas were being relaxed. An international economy was emerging in which the parts were interrelated by the forces of comparative prices of goods, services, and productive factors. An analysis of the United States economic development must necessarily be put into the context of the expansion of the Atlantic economy. Institutions and national policies which both impeded and fostered the international exchange of goods, services, productive factors and ideas must be continually brought into view. It was the "anonymous," impersonal forces of the evolving international economy which were the basic influence on the developing Atlantic economy and its constituent parts. National policies and institutional influences modified rather than generated the economic growth that ensued. The very forces of the Atlantic economy which were inducing expansion in the United States were thereby making this country increasingly independent of the international economic context, so that during these years there was a fundamental shift away from dependence upon the Atlantic economy toward dependence on our own internal economy as the mainspring of expansion.

In 1815 the international context was still critical. The expanding industrialization of England and Europe in the years after the Napoleonic wars was accompanied not only by the gradual relaxation of restrictions on trade and factor mobility, but the resultant structural changes accelerated the movement of productive factors in response to differential rates of return. While the immigration of people and particularly capital into the United States played an important part in our growth in the thirty years after 1815, it was the growth of the cotton textile industry and the demand for cotton which was decisive. In 1815 the previous sources of expansion, the re-export and carrying trade and manufactures, were declining as a result of peacetime competition. The West was still largely unintegrated into the national economy. The United States was left with only cotton as the major expansive force. The vicissitudes of the cotton trade—the speculative expansion of 1818, the radical decline in prices in the 1820's and the boom in the 1830's—were the most important influence upon the varying rates of growth of the economy during the period. Cotton was strategic because it was the major independent variable in the interdependent structure of internal and international trade. The demands for western foodstuffs and northeastern services and manufactures were basically dependent upon the income received from the cotton trade. This dependence resulted not only from the developing regional specialization, but from the characteristics of the South itself.

A marked characteristic of the South was that income received from the export of cotton (and sugar, rice and tobacco) flowed directly out of the regional economy again in the purchase of goods and services. The South provided neither the services to market its own exports nor the consumer goods and services to supply its own needs, and had a very high propensity to import. It was the West which provided food for the South and, since the South was the West's major market until the problems of cross-mountain transport had been solved, the growth of the market for western foodstuffs was geared to the expansion of the southern cotton economy.

The Northeast provided not only the services to finance, transport, insure, and market the South's cotton, but also supplied the South with manufactured goods, either from its own industry or imported and reshipped to the South. Major markets for the Northeast were the South and the West. Both depended, directly in the first case and indirectly in the second, on the income from the cotton trade.

It was cotton which was the most important influence in the growth in the market size and the consequent expansion of the economy: the slow development of the 1820's, the accelerated growth in the 1830's. In this period of rapid growth, it was cotton that initiated the concomitant expansion in income, in the size of domestic markets, and creation of the social overhead investment (in the course of its role in the marketing of cotton) in the Northeast which were to facilitate the subsequent rapid growth of manufactures. Cotton also accounted for the accelerated pace of westward migration as well as for the movement of people out of self-sufficiency into the market economy.

Cotton was not the only expansive influence in the economy during this period. Clearly there were others, and they will be considered. Had there been no cotton gin, it is certain that the resources directly and indirectly devoted to the cotton trade would have been at least partially absorbed in other types of economic activity. Given the social structure, attitudes and motivation of American society, and the rich quantity and quality of resources which made even the self-sufficient farmer well off as compared with his European counterpart, the United States economy would not have stagnated. But cotton was the commodity for which foreign demand was significantly increasing, it accounted for over half the value of exports, and the income directly or indirectly from cotton was the major independent influence on the evolving pattern of interregional trade. Without cotton the development in the size of the market would have been a much more lengthy process, since there was no alternative way to expand the domestic market rapidly without recourse to external demand. In short, cotton was the most important proximate cause of expansion, and by tracing out the resulting interrelationships light may be shed on the pace and character of the economy's development, particularly in the years up to 1843.

The argument advanced in the first chapter with respect to the strategic role of certain industries is pertinent here. A great deal of economic activity is a passive rather than an active source of economic expansion. It grows up either dependent upon an "active" industry or in response to the growth of income initially generated by the carriers [1] of economic change. In the examination of economic change it is important to distinguish between an independent variable initiating the change and the expansion of dependent economic activity which is induced by the "carrier" industry. This distinction is undoubtedly more difficult to make today than it was before 1860, when transport barriers and distinct patterns of regional specialization and internal trade all pointed to the strategic role of cotton. Direct income from the cotton trade was probably no more than 6 per cent of any plausible estimate of national income which we might employ,[2] but when income from cotton exports, including shipments to textile mills in our own Northeast, grew from $25 million in 1831 to $70 million in 1836, it set in motion the whole process of accelerated expansion which culminated in 1839.[3] Certainly the views of contemporaries, northern observers as well as southerners, support the position that in this period cotton was indeed king.

The cotton trade remained an important influence upon the economy until 1860, but its role declined in relative importance after the boom and depression that followed 1839. It is not that income from cotton did not grow. On the contrary, the 1850's represented another prosperous era, though not as wildly speculative as former ones, in which the value of the cotton trade exceeded any former period. However, a major consequence of the expansive period of the 1830's was the creation of conditions that made possible in-

---

[1] The term is Rutledge Vining's. See his article, "Location of Industry and Regional Patterns of Business Cycle Behavior," *Econometrica* XIV (January 1946), 37-68.

[2] However, if we took into account the income generated in the course of transport, financing, and marketing cotton (that is, the directly dependent industries) it would be significantly greater.

[3] And the era of depressed prices in the 1820's had an equally depressing effect on economic activity in that decade.

dustrialization in the Northeast. Transport facilities developed to
connect the East and West more efficiently; a new market for
western staples developed in the rapidly urbanizing East and,
sporadically, in Europe. The dependence of both the Northeast and
the West on the South waned.[4] The discovery of gold in California
in 1848 created a third source of expansion outside the South. The
Far West was not only a major market for the goods and services
of the Northeast, but its one export, gold, played a vital role in
the whole expansion of the 1850's.

It should not be forgotten that the United States expansion was
taking place within the larger context of the Atlantic economy.
While the demand for cotton in England and to a lesser extent in
France played perhaps the most prominent part, the terms of trade,
relative price levels here and abroad, the movement of productive
factors, and the flow of ideas, particularly technological information, were all a part of the interrelated pattern of development.

Throughout the whole period the secular movement of the terms
of trade became increasingly favorable. In the expansive surges of
1815–1818 and 1832–1839 they became very favorable, reflecting
a rapid rise in the price of American exports. In these two periods,
it was cotton that accounted for the rise and appeared to initiate
the subsequent flow of capital in response to the increased profitability of opening up and developing new sources of supply of the
export staple and western foodstuffs.[5] The consequent divergence
of domestic and foreign price levels, and the increase in imports
and specie movements, determined the timing of cyclical movements. Attractive employment opportunities during these surges of
expansion were the pull which brought immigrants to American
shores in increasing numbers.

Expansion in the 1850's, unlike that of the two previous booms,
was not preceded by favorable movements of the terms of trade—

---

[4] The most striking evidence of the changing role of cotton is provided by
its role in cyclical turning points. While cotton set the pace in the booms and
depressions of 1815-1823 and 1823-1843, it lagged a full two years behind the
recovery that began in 1843 and was clearly not a major influence in the
cyclical downturn of 1857. In fact, the South was relatively unaffected by that
depression.

[5] This argument is elaborated in my article, "International Capital Flows and
the Development of the American West," *Journal of Economic History* XVI,
No. 4 (December 1956), 493-505.

instead it was the domestic price level which began to rise before the export price index. Cotton played a part in the boom, but it was industrialization in the Northeast and the opening up of the West and Far West which were primarily responsible for the growth of the 1840's and 1850's. The influence of the international economy was felt less in the flow of capital than in the flow of people, with the first big wave of immigration coming in this period.

The foregoing summary has emphasized surges in growth followed by periods of depression, then gradual expansion preceding still another boom. The explanation of these long swings is that these movements are initiated by the movement of prices in the key "carrier" industries. Shifts in supply and demand result in a shift of resources into these areas in periods of rising prices. There is concomitant expansion in the wide variety of subsidiary, complementary, and residentiary activities whose fortunes are tied to the growth of the "carrier" industries and to the rise in income that is initiated by these surges of expansion. The process is a lengthy and cumulative one, ultimately overlayed with speculative excesses; the tremendous expansion in supply results in a painful period of declining prices and readjustment. In the first two expansive periods analyzed here, 1815 to 1818 and 1832 to 1839, cotton was the key industry in both the boom and the subsequent collapse and readjustment. In the last period the sources of expansion are more diffuse, but grain in the West played the most important role.

Underlying the uneven pattern of development were the shape of the supply curve of cotton (or grain) and the way in which the supply curve shifted. During each period of expansion, millions of acres of new land were purchased from the government for cotton production. Once this land had been cleared and a crop or two of corn planted to prepare the soil, the amount of cotton available could be substantially increased, and the supply curve of cotton shifted very sharply to the right. With the depressed cotton prices that followed such expansion, a good deal of this land was devoted to alternative uses. For the most part, it was put to crop and livestock use to feed slaves and reduce the costs of purchasing foodstuffs. In effect, it represented unused capacity with respect to cotton, and any slight increase in cotton prices could and did lead to shifting some of this land into cotton. In the old South, where slaves as such were an important intermediate good, this was clearly a rational redirection of resources during periods of depressed prices. The result is that the supply curve of cotton approximated the shape indicated in Chart I-VII.[6] It was highly elas-

CHART I-VII

Shape of Supply Curve of Cotton

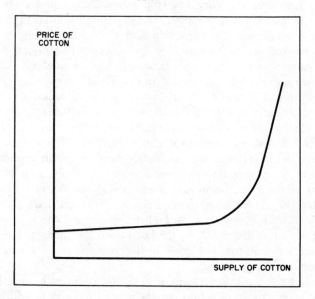

tic over a range of output which included all the available land that had been cleared and readied for crop production and was suitable for cotton. Even with the rapid growth in demand that characterized the cotton textile industry in the first half of the nineteenth century, it took a decade for demand to shift to the right sufficiently to absorb this potential supply. During this decade very little new land was sold in the cotton states, and the expansion of potential capacity was at a much slower rate than during the

[6] For a pioneering elaboration of the general argument with respect to a different industry, see Tjallman Koopmans, *Tanker Freight Rates and Tankship Building* (Haarlem: De erven F. Bohn, n.v., 1939), Chapter V.

previous boom. When the growth of demand for cotton finally brought all this potential capacity into production, a further increase in demand resulted in substantial price increases as the supply curve became increasingly inelastic. With the readily available cotton land already in production, higher prices brought forth little additional production in the short run.

While there had been little incentive to buy and clear new land for cotton during the period of low prices, rising prices triggered a land boom in the new South. Millions of acres of virgin land were sold; planters and their slaves migrated in large numbers to open up and exploit the rich land in the Southwest—Alabama, Louisiana, Mississippi, and Arkansas were the major states. A lengthy period intervened between the initial impetus from rising prices and substantial output increases for putting this land into production. While imperfections in the capital market and land speculation partially explain this delay, the more important reasons were the time it took to obtain slaves from the old South, clear the land, and plant a crop or two of corn to prepare the soil. The results of this delay are clearly evident in Chart II-VII. Note the output of cotton in the five cotton states. There was a lag of approximately four years between the peak in land sales and a large increase in cotton production. The consequence was a vast shift to the right in the supply curve of cotton and the beginning of a new period of depressed prices. Cotton output actually fell as some of this land was diverted into corn with the low cotton prices that prevailed after 1839.

In the West, the same general pattern prevailed with respect to wheat and corn. Land sales in the western states paralleled the prices of those staples, with one important difference. Little transportation or other social overhead investment was necessary to increase the supply of cotton in the South. In the West, transportation was the major limiting factor in increasing supply. The accessible lands close to water transportation were taken up first. Initially, the rise in prices brought into cultivation land further and further from cheap transportation. As a result, the supply curve of wheat and corn land was probably less inelastic than cotton as it began to slope upward. However, it also encouraged a boom in land sales and at the same time a growing agitation for large-scale investment in new transportation facilities. Canal and railroad building was a lengthy process, but a completed canal or railroad opened up large amounts of new land. The canal construction era of the 1830's and the railroad construction period of the 1850's each served to make possible, along with the land sales and influx of settlers that accompanied them, a large shift to the right in wheat and corn supplies, with much the same results as cotton.

CHART II-VII

Land Sales, Cotton Production and Prices: 1833–1843
(Ala., Ark., Miss., Fla., La.)

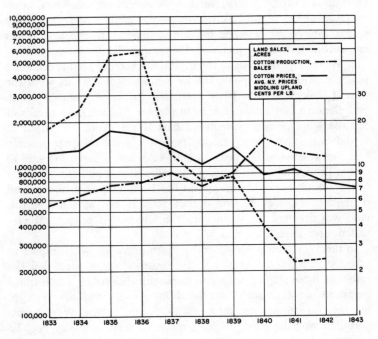

Source: Appendix I, Table A-VII.

VIII

INTERNATIONAL ECONOMIC FLOWS—1815-1860

The Statistical Evidence

The quantitative data to analyze America's international economic relations during these years may be conveniently organized and analyzed under four separate headings: the balance of payments, the terms of trade, the flows of immigrants, and the acquisition of land.

I

While the quality of the data in the balance of payments from 1815 through 1819 is similar to that for the earlier period, after 1820 there are important improvements and the data are far more reliable.[1] During this period our international economic relations were the subject of extensive discussion, and there are many direct estimates of the various components, as well as qualitative evaluations, against which to check the figures and their significance.

As a percentage of the value of exports, tobacco, rice and lumber products declined during this period. Wheat and flour were erratic, being 16 per cent of exports from 1816 to 1820 but declining thereafter until the last fifteen years, when they increased slightly. Manufactures were a slightly declining percentage of exports in the 1830's and thereafter showed a modest gain. Cotton, of course, dominated the export trade. It constituted 39 per cent of the value of exports from 1816 to 1820, and increased to 63 per cent of total export values from 1836 to 1840. Thereafter it dropped somewhat,

---

[1] See the introduction to my study, "Balance of Payments," *loc. cit.*, for an evaluation of the quality of the data.

but the level continued high—over half of the value of exports for the remaining years to the Civil War. Chart I-VIII shows the

CHART I-VIII

Value of Total Exports and Cotton Exports: 1815–1860
(in Millions of Dollars)

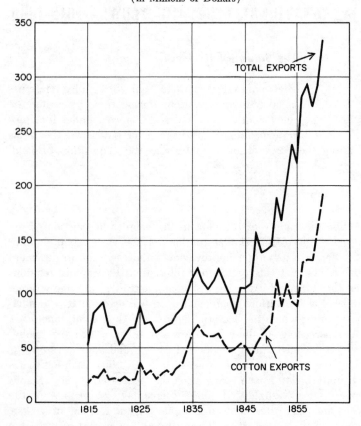

Source: Appendix I, Table A-VIII.

value of total exports and the value of cotton exports from 1815 to 1860.

The value of exports showed little increase in the 1820's but expanded rapidly from 1831 through the ensuing boom. After a decline during the depression of the early 1840's, the value of exports increased during most of the period up to 1860. Several years of extraordinarily high export values (in comparison to the secular trend) reflected special circumstances, such as the cotton speculation in 1825 and the Irish famine in 1847.

The United Kingdom alone took almost half of our exports, with France taking an additional 12 to 17 per cent (based on five year averages). The West Indies, which had been a major market for American exports and took 19 per cent in the years 1821 to 1825, were a continually declining percentage thereafter, being only 7 per cent in the five years preceding the Civil War.

After exports, the next most important credit in the balance of payments was shipping earnings. Unlike the earlier period when they accounted for perhaps a third or more of total international credits, in this period they were never more than about 10 per cent of credits and were actually a decreasing percentage throughout. The revival of navigation laws and foreign competition, as well as the expansion of the cotton trade, resulted in American shipping being confined primarily to our export and import trade and engaged less in trade between foreign countries. Foreign shipping was increasingly important from 1845 to 1860, presaging our transition from creditor to debtor status in this sphere during the war years. United States and foreign shipping earnings in our international accounts are shown in Chart II-VIII.

The funds that immigrants brought with them were an important credit in the last fifteen years of the period under study, when the first great wave of immigration occurred. Over 90 per cent of the immigrants were from Britain, Ireland or Germany. There was a striking difference in their well-being; the Germans were relatively prosperous while the Irish were desperately poor, with little left after their passage money. Approximately two-thirds of them came in American ships, providing an additional credit in the United States account.[2]

The three items discussed above—exports, shipping earnings, and

---

[2] See Section III of this chapter for a discussion of the significance of immigrant fares. My study on the United States balance of payments provides further discussion of this subject, and Appendix III in this study summarizes the quantitative data on immigrant funds.

CHART II-VIII

Net U.S. Shipping Earnings and Earnings of Foreign Ships Carrying U.S.
Imports: 1815–1860
(in Millions of Dollars)

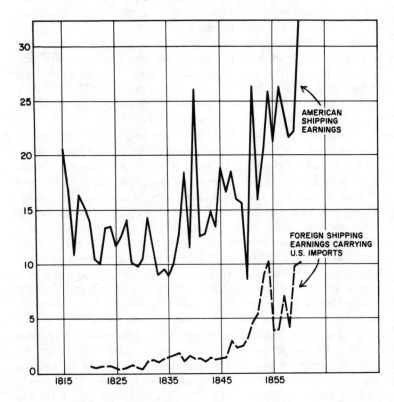

Source: Appendix T, Table B-VIII.

immigrant funds—comprise the net credits on current account of
the United States balance of payments during this period.

Imports were the major debit item. There were two major classes
of imports, manufactured goods and tropical (or semitropical)
goods such as coffee, tea, sugar, and cocoa. Manufactures were the
most important, with textile imports (cotton, wool, silk, and linen)
comprising a third or more of the value of this sector. Iron and

steel imports assumed increased importance during the first big railroad boom in the early 1850's.

Import values were more volatile than exports, rising more rapidly in periods of expansion and dropping more precipitously in times of slower growth. Their value is shown in Chart III-VIII.[3] Britain was the major source of imports, accounting for somewhat more than a third. France supplied another 9-18 per cent (again based on five year averages). Cuba and the West Indies accounted

CHART III-VIII

Value of Imports: 1815–1860
(in Millions of Dollars)

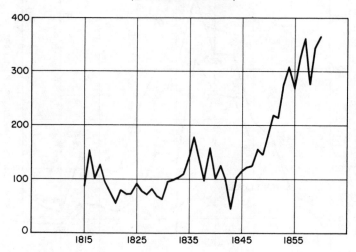

Source: Appendix I, Table C-VIII.

---

[3] It should be noted that the value of imports shown here differs from the official figures in that it makes an allowance for undervaluation from 1832-1860. See "Balance of Payments," *loc. cit.*, Appendix B, for a discussion of the basis for the allowance.

for most of the tropical goods, which reached a high of 28 per cent of imports from 1821–1825 and a low of 17 per cent from 1851–1855. Among invisible items, immigrants' remittances and tourist expenditures were the major net debits. The former grew

CHART IV-VIII

Immigrants from the United Kingdom: 1844–1860. Graphed with a Three-Year Lag Against Remittances to the United Kingdom: 1847–1863

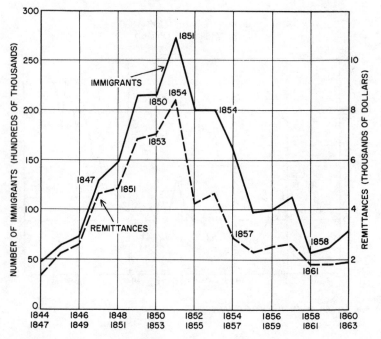

Source: Appendix I, Table D-VIII.

rapidly during the wave of immigration after 1845. These remittances were primarily for passage money to bring over relatives and friends, and most of them went to Ireland. They bear an interesting relationship to immigration, which is illustrated in Chart IV-VIII. Remittances to the United Kingdom moved directly with the volume of immigration from there three years earlier. The most plausible explanation for this close relationship is that it took Irish immigrants approximately three years to save passage fares for friends and family in Ireland.

The flow of specie during this period served both as a mechanism of adjustment between the price levels of the United States and foreign countries (particularly the United Kingdom), and in the 1850's as another export industry which financed a large import surplus and helped sustain the expansion of that decade. Specie flows were particularly important in relating the monetary systems of the United States and the United Kingdom. When domestic price levels diverged significantly, the resulting flow of specie tended to lead to international price readjustment in a fashion to be expected by monetary theorists. Chart V-VIII shows specie flows against an index in which United States wholesale prices (Warren-Pearson) are divided by British wholesale prices (Sauerbach index) to illustrate this relationship. It is clear that after the discoveries of 1848 gold plays an additional role, and is in effect another export commodity as well as an inflationary influence upon United States and foreign prices.

Interest and dividends were a continuous debit item in our balance of payments. Not only did the amount vary with the level of foreign debt and of the interest rate, but it was strongly affected on two occasions during this period by repudiation of debts—1816–1818, and 1841–1845. Chart VI-VIII presents the interest upon foreign indebtedness.[4]

The balance of trade of the United States was generally unfavorable. Chart VII-VIII not only illustrates the fact that imports exceeded exports for all but a few years (primarily the 1840's), but also shows the greater volatility of import values. Long swings are also evident in both exports and imports.

The balance of payments (see Appendix I for complete balance)

---

[4] Cf. "Balance of Payments," *loc. cit.*, for a discussion of the method of estimating the interest change.

reveals three periods of capital inflow, one of outflow, and a period
in which there is little net movement. The years 1815–1818, 1832–
1839, and 1850–1857 were periods of significant foreign borrowing.
The 1840's were a decade of debt repudiation and return of securities to America, while the 1820's show relatively little net capital

CHART V-VIII

Quotient of United States Wholesale Price Index (Base 1830) Divided by
English Wholesale Price Index (Base 1830). Graphed against
Specie Flows: 1815–1860

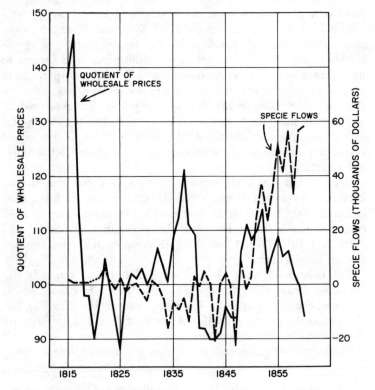

Source: Appendix I, Table E-VIII.

movement. Chart VIII-VIII shows the residual of the balance of payments [5] and illustrates the long swings that characterize its movement.

The resulting aggregate foreign indebtedness of the United States shows a substantial increase in the three periods of capital inflow, with the most significant rate of increase occurring during the pe-

CHART VI-VIII

Interest and Dividends on Foreign Indebtedness: 1815–1860
(in Millions of Dollars)

Source: Appendix I, Table F-VIII.

---

[5] It should be pointed out that the residual of the balance of payments and net capital movements are the same thing only under certain assumptions about the figures and inclusiveness of the component parts. For a discussion of this, see the text of my study on the United States balance of payments.

1815-1860

CHART VII-VIII

Value of Imports and Exports of the United States: 1815–1860
(Figures from "U.S. Balance of Payments, 1790–1860.")

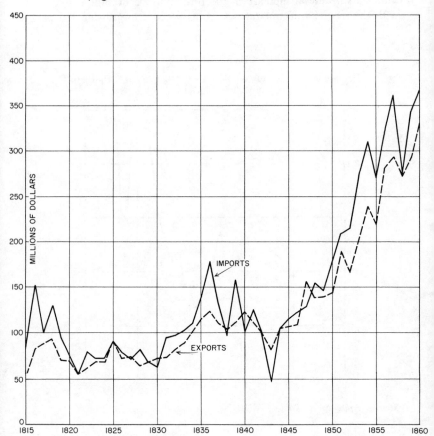

Source: Appendix I, Tables A-VIII and C-VIII.

CHART VIII-VIII

Residual Balance of Payments: 1790–1860
(in Millions of Dollars)

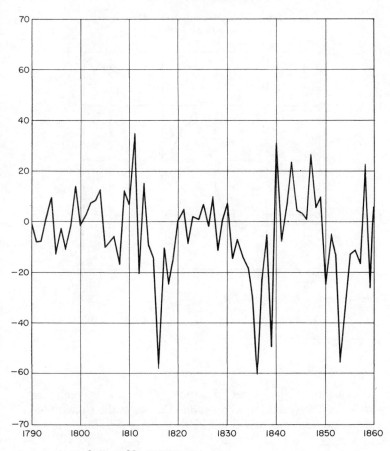

Source: Appendix I, Table G-VIII.

riod 1832–1839.[6] Our aggregate foreign indebtedness is presented in Chart IX-VIII.[7]

CHART IX-VIII

Aggregate Foreign Indebtedness: 1815–1860
(in Millions of Dollars)

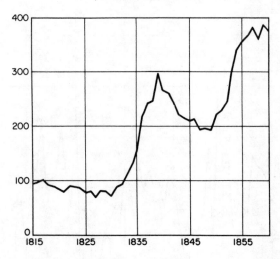

Source: Appendix I, Table H-VIII.

II

Movements of the prices of exports and imports, both commodities and services, played an important role in the United States expansion during this period just as they did earlier. Since no such

---

[6] We were repudiating debt while incurring it from 1816-1819. See Appendix A, "Balance of Payments," *loc. cit.*

[7] See Appendix C, "Balance of Payments," *loc. cit.*, for independent direct estimates of aggregate indebtedness as corroboration of the figures in Chart IX-IX.

indices exist, the manner in which they were developed for this study is treated in detail in Appendix III; the results of the study are summarized here.

CHART X-VIII

Export Price Index and the Price of Cotton: 1815–1860
(Base 1830)

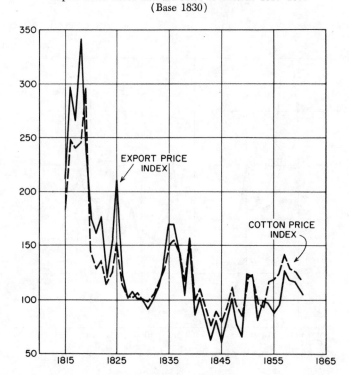

Source: Appendix I, Table I-VIII.

The export price index is dominated by the price of cotton, as Chart X-VIII indicates. In general, export prices declined substantially from the 1818 peak throughout the 1820's, with the exception of 1825, when a short-lived speculation in cotton occurred. The

1830's witnessed a surge in export prices which began in 1831–
1832 and extended, with a break in 1837–1838, to 1839. The price
decline in the 1840's was not so severe as that which followed the
boom of 1818. The sharp rise in 1847 resulted from the demand

CHART XI-VIII

Export Price Index and Warren-Pearson Wholesale Price Index: 1815–1860
(Base 1830)

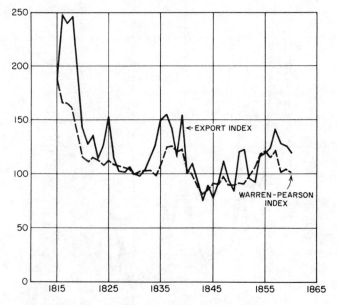

Source: Appendix I, Table J-VIII.

for wheat due to the Irish famine. The irregular rise in the 1850's
reflected another period of expansion in the American economy.
Prices of exports were more volatile than domestic goods, as a
comparison of the export index with the Warren-Pearson wholesale
price index in Chart XI-VIII indicates. Export prices fell more

rapidly from 1818–1830 and rose more in periods of expansion, particularly that of the 1830's. The volume of exports was far steadier, as Chart XII-VIII indicates. It does show that there was considerable price elasticity in the demand for exports, since years

CHART XII-VIII

Volume Index, U.S. Exports: 1815–1860
(Base 1830)

Source: Appendix I, Table K-VIII.

with a sharp price break (1819, 1838, 1840, 1853) were periods of significant increases in export volume.

The import price index and its separate components are shown in Chart XIII-VIII. The overall index shows a fairly persistent downward trend until the end of the 1840's. Manufactures fell significantly in the years after 1815, but manufactured goods fell even more sharply between 1815 and 1830. The fall of raw material and food prices was not large in the early period, but after 1820 they fell almost as much as manufactures. All of our import prices

CHART XIII-VIII

Import Price Index and the Indices of its Component Parts: 1815–1860

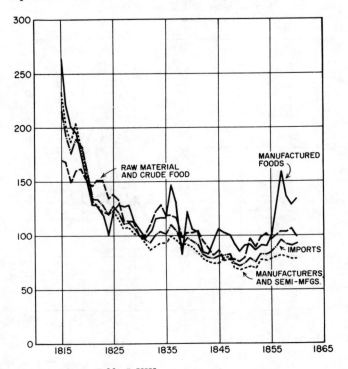

Source: Appendix I, Table L-VIII.

fell during the period. The overall index shows no such spectacular rises during the surges in the United States expansion as occur in the export price index. Increased import values meant an increased volume of imports, and little of the increased demand was absorbed by price increase. Chart XIV-VIII shows the deflated value index for the period.

CHART XIV-VIII

Real Value of Imports (Deflated Value Series)
(in Thousands of Dollars)

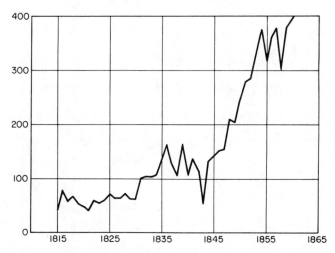

Source: Appendix I, Table M-VIII.

A comparison of the export and import price indices illustrates the marked difference in their behavior, Chart XV-VIII. The resultant net barter terms of trade, Chart XVI-VIII, not only show that the secular trend was towards improvement in the terms of trade, but also demonstrate that, in expansive periods of the economy, the terms of trade became extremely favorable. This is particularly true from 1815–1818 and 1831–1839. The correspondence between changes in the terms of trade and in the international flow of capital (as indicated by the residual of the balance of payments) is striking. Until 1845 (and less so thereafter), almost every movement of the terms of trade was paralleled by a reverse move-

1815-1860

CHART XV-VIII

Export and Import Price Indices: 1815–1860
(Base 1830)

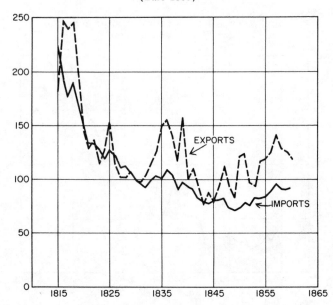

Source: Appendix I, Table N-VIII.

CHART XVI-VIII

Terms of Trade: 1815–1860
(Base 1830)

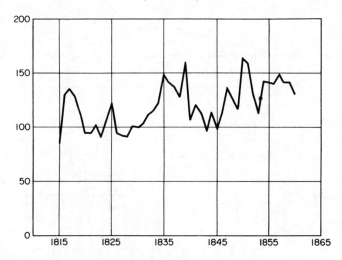

Source: Appendix I, Table O-VIII.

ment in the residual in the balance of payments, as Chart XVII-
VIII shows. There was increased capital inflow when the terms of
trade became more favorable and decreased inflow or actual outflow when they became relatively less favorable.

CHART XVII-VIII

Terms of Trade Graphed with the Residual Balance of Payments: 1815–1860
(Base 1830)

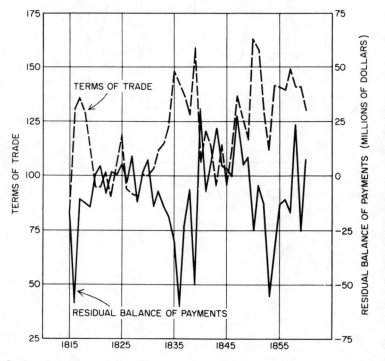

Source: *Appendix I, Table P-VIII.*

Are movements of the terms of trade significantly affected by the
price behavior of non-commodity items? The price behavior of the

non-commodity items is at times divergent from commodity trade, but the magnitudes are relatively small, and the overall effect is not great. Freight rates fell dramatically during these years, particularly during the early period, and the price of shipping fell more

CHART XVIII-VIII

Freight Rate Index, U.S. Exports: 1815–1860
(Base 1830)

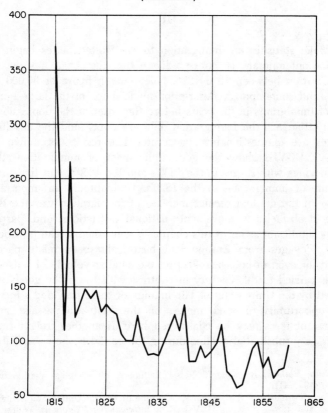

Source: Appendix I, Table Q-VIII.

than that of exports, as Chart XVIII-VIII shows. On the other hand, the price of capital showed no significant drop and actually rose in the 1850's (see Appendix I). However, neither of these two dampening effects on the terms of trade would be very large.

III

Official statistics on immigration to the United States begin in 1820. Contemporary accounts indicate that there was a surge of immigration between 1816–1818. Niles cites a figure of 30,000 in 1817, and contemporary description made much of the large number of immigrants in the years before the onset of the depression.[8] Even after 1820 the immigration data are poor,[9] and the absolute figures are unquestionably inaccurate. The results as shown in Chart XIX-VIII show the general behavior of immigration, the long swings with surges in the 1830's and the 1850's, and the small volume of immigration in the 1820's. Undoubtedly an important factor in the gradual secular increase of immigration was the decline in obstacles to movement: national restrictions, and, particularly significant as far as this chapter is concerned, ocean transport costs. Voyages from Europe had historically been made partly empty or even in ballast, reflecting the smaller volume of finished goods carried to this country in contrast with the bulky goods exported by the United States. The immigrant trade provided a lucrative opportunity to make money on the westward passage, and immigrant fares may be considered here as another freight rate. Their very substantial decline during the period is shown in Table

---

[8] *Niles' National Register,* 75 Vols. (Baltimore, Philadelphia, Washington: 1811-1849), XIII, 35-36.

[9] For a critique see Marian Davis, "Critique of Official United States Immigration Statistics," Appendix II, Vol. II of *International Migrations,* Walter F. Willcox, Ed. (New York: National Bureau of Economic Research, 1929-1931).

7. Although the pull of differential real income and employment was the fundamental cause, the decline in the cost of steerage passage did implement the movement.

As pointed out above, the origin of immigrants during this period was primarily from Ireland, England, and Germany, with all other countries together accounting for only 10 per cent of their number. Equally interesting is the changing composition of immigrants by occupation. While the figures here are rough (since they include

CHART XIX-VIII

Immigration to the United States: 1815–1860

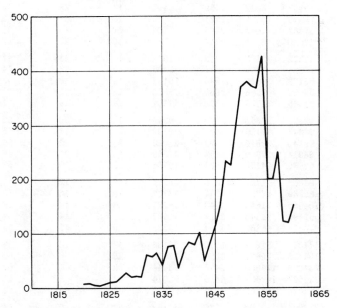

Source: Appendix I, Table R-VIII.

returning Americans), they do show a declining portion of merchants and skilled people, and a rising proportion of unskilled labor (Table 7).

TABLE 7

IMMIGRANT ORIGINS AND OCCUPATIONAL DISTRIBUTION

Year	Total	Irish	English	German	Labor	Merchants	Mechanics & Farmers
		Alien Arrivals			Occupation as Percentage of Total Arrivals		
1820	8385	3974	1782	948	9%	25%	31%
1	9127	3388	1036	365	8	27	31
2	6911	2421	856	139	9	31	24
3	6354	1908	851	179	8	33	27
4	7912	2606	713	224	8	38	24
5	10199	5857	1002	448	10	29	32
6	10837	6032	1459	495	11	29	29
7	18875	10971	2521	425	18	21	31
8	27382	14047	2735	1806	21	19	31
9	22520	8331	2149	582	20	28	22
1830	23322	3105	733	1972	12	25	41*
1	22633	7639	251	2395	10	27	44
2	53179	16665	944	10168	13	18	46**
3	58640	8648	2966	6823	13	15	33
4	65365	33724	1129	17654	14	14	51***
5	45374	29350	468	8245	15	20	55
6	76242	43156	420	20139	29	11	55
7	79340	39810	896	23036	28	12	55
8	38914	17860	157	11369	18	20	55
9	68069	34172	62	19794	22	16	58
1840	84066	41704	318	28581	22	12	63
1	80289	53723	147	13727	28	13	55
2	104565	71542	1743	18287	33	10	53
3	52496	24542	3517	11432	23	14	57
4	78615	46460	1357	19226	29	12	54
5	114371	61942	1710	33138	32	10	56
6	154416	70626	2854	57010	28	6	62
7	234968	124880	3476	73444	32	4	62
8	226527	142631	4455	58014	43	3	52
9	297024	207162	6036	60062	45	3	50
1850	310004	169533	5276	63168	38	5	54
1	379466	266257	5306	71322	48	7	42
2	371603	161351	30007	143575	44	7	48
3	368645	165130	28867	140653	48	7	42
4	427833	105931	48901	206054	37	7	53
5	200877	51877	38871	66219	39	13	45

*Large per cent not stated this year
**Missing quarter
***Large per cent not stated this year

Source: Bromwell, William J., History of Immigration to the United States, (New York: Redfield 1856).

IV

Chart XX-VIII illustrates graphically the territorial expansion of the economy during this period. The most striking aspect of this chart is not the addition of Louisiana, which has always been accorded the role of almost doubling the size of the country, but

CHART XX-VIII

United States Territorial Expansion: 1790–1860
(in Millions of Square Miles)

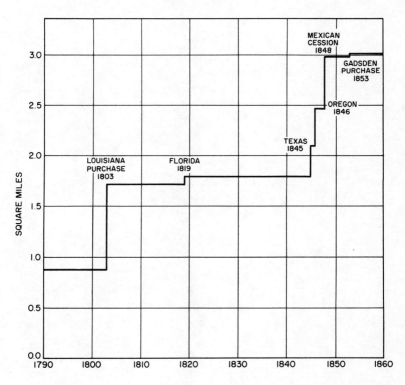

the even greater increase in territorial expansion which occurred in three short years between 1845 and 1848. More than 1.2 million square miles were added to the country's territorial boundaries, including California, which was quickly exploited for its discoveries of gold.

IX

INTERREGIONAL FLOWS—1815-1860

The Statistical Evidence

It is possible to present fairly complete statistics upon our international economic relationships throughout this period, but no complete quantitative picture is available for internal movements of goods, services, and productive factors. Although the statistics are fragmentary, and no attempt has so far been made even to piece them together, there is a wealth of descriptive material in government reports and contemporary books and magazines to provide a general outline and fill in many of the gaps. It will be necessary to supplement the available statistical fragments with literary description and, while the result is perhaps a less precise picture, the general movements are clear and the evidence sufficiently conclusive to support the analysis. The interregional movements of goods, of people and of capital will be treated in turn.

While the data on interregional trade are incomplete, the general pattern of this trade has been carefully examined in a number of government studies of United States internal commerce.[1] Yet G. S. Callender's comment of a half-century ago that the significance of this pattern of trade has been slighted by the economic historian is still appropriate.[2] In describing the trade between western farmers and southern planters he said:

> This commerce between different agricultural communities in America has played a more important role in our economic history

---

[1] Cf. Louis B. Schmidt, "Internal Commerce and the Development of a National Economy Before 1860," *Journal of Political Economy* XLVII (December 1939), 799, sources cited in footnote 2 therein.

[2] The best account of the internal commerce of the period is contained in the excellent article by Louis B. Schmidt cited in footnote 1.

than seems to have been appreciated. It began in colonial times and shows itself in the trade between the Northern Colonies and the West Indies which was reckoned by the colonists themselves to be of vital importance to their prosperity. It appears again in the first part of the nineteenth century when a trade grew up on our western rivers between the lower South and the new states of the West of exactly the same character as that which went up and down the Atlantic coast between the West Indies and the Northern Colonies during the eighteenth century. It was in both cases a trade between a community of planters using slave labor to produce a few valuable staples which found a ready sale in the markets of the world on one hand, and a community of small farmers (who in many cases were partly fishermen) producing food and crude supplies on the other. The basis of the trade in both cases was the fact that the planter found it more profitable to devote his slave labor to the production of valuable staples to be sold in the markets of the world than to use it in producing the food and other agricultural supplies which he needed. So long as there were other agricultural communities ready and willing to furnish these supplies it was cheaper to procure them by trade than by direct production.[3]

Certainly the pattern of this trade between the West, the South, and the East has long been familiar. While its beginnings antedate the second war with England, it was of negligible importance until the close of the war. With the innovation of the steamboat on the Mississippi in 1816, the West used that artery to ship foodstuffs to the South. The South, in addition to the foreign export of cotton, sugar, tobacco, and rice, shipped these staples to the Northeast and to a lesser extent upriver to the West. The Northeast provided banking, insurance, brokerage, and transport services to the South, and shipped finished goods, both its own and imports, to the South and the West. The trade between the Northeast and South was a coastwise trade, while that with the West was overland when it involved valuable manufactured goods which could stand the high cost of wagon transportation, or by coastwise trade to New Orleans and thence upriver if they were bulky items. Beginning in the 1830's, this pattern of trade gradually changed. Before 1835 almost all of the produce going eastward over the Erie Canal came

---

[3] Callender, *Economic History,* pp. 300-301.

only from western New York,[4] but with the completion of the Ohio canals there was a gradual redirection of western produce to the eastern seaboard. It was not until the last two decades of our period that the pattern of internal trade was significantly altered. When, in addition to the Erie and Pennsylvania Canals, East-West railroads were completed in the early 1850's, the nature of internal trade had been fundamentally changed. It is not that the West's trade with the South declined absolutely; on the contrary, it increased and the 1850's were a golden era in Mississippi trade, but percentagewise the growing volume of western foodstuffs and a few mining products, such as lead from Missouri, were going increasingly to eastern markets. At the same time, the West became an important market for eastern finished goods, although the South continued to be a major market for eastern services and manufactures. Schmidt's succinct summary of this mutual interdependence is worth quoting.

> The rise of internal commerce after 1815 made possible a territorial division of labor between the three great sections of the Union—the West, the South, and the East. The markets which were developed for various products opened the way for the division of labor in regions where it had been practically unknown before. Each section tended to devote itself more exclusively to the production of those commodities for which it was best able to provide. There was fostered a mutual economic dependence between sections and the establishment of predominant types of industry in each which were in turn dependent on foreign commerce. The South was thereby enabled to devote itself in particular to the production of a few plantation staples contributing a large and growing surplus for the foreign markets and depending on the West for a large part of its food supply and on the East for the bulk of its manufactured goods and very largely for the conduct of its commerce and banking. The East was devoted chiefly to manufacturing and commerce, supplying the products of its industries as well as the imports and much of the capital for the West and the South while it became to an increasing extent dependent on the food and the fibers of these two sections. The West became a surplus grain- and livestock-producing kingdom, supplying the growing deficits of the South and the East.[5]

---

[4] Schmidt, "Internal Commerce," *loc. cit.*, p. 811.
[5] *Ibid.*, p. 820.

The quantitative measures of this trade are certainly incomplete, but parts of it can be presented. The trade between the West and the South is recorded in receipts at New Orleans (Chart I-IX). However, these gross receipts include downriver shipments of cot-

CHART I-IX

Value of Receipts of Produce from the Interior at New Orleans: 1815–1860
(in Millions of Dollars)

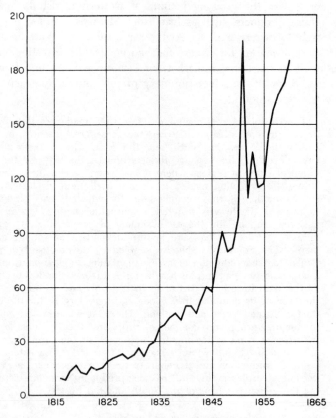

Source: *Appendix II, Table A-IX.*

ton, sugar, hemp, and tobacco as well as western foodstuffs. After 1845 the proportion of total receipts made up of southern staples for export (either abroad or to the Northeast) increased as western foodstuffs were increasingly diverted East or found their way to the southern states by railroad. While New Orleans was the great entrepôt of the South, a great deal of western produce either found markets in the South above New Orleans,[6] or in the case of live-stock, was driven directly to the Southeast.[7] An 1845 estimate states that in 20 years the southern planter had purchased $900,000,000 worth of products from the western and border states.[8]

In 1836, over four-fifths of the tonnage coming to tidewater over the Erie Canal came from western New York State and less than one-fifth came from western states. By 1847, tonnage from western states exceeded that from western New York. Chart II-IX presents tonnage from western New York State and from the western states that came over the Erie Canal from 1836 to 1860 and dramatically illustrates the rise of West-East trade. The growth of this trade was, of course, greatly implemented by the Great Lakes and the canals connecting them with the Mississippi River system. Chart III-IX shows the growth of traffic on both of these waterways. Chart IV-IX shows the rapid growth of receipts on the Ohio canals as they opened up interior Ohio (it also gives evidence of the effect of railroads on those canals in the 1850's). An important part

---

[6] U.S. Congress, House, *Report on the Internal Commerce of the United States*, 50th Congress, 1st Session, 1888, House Executive Document No. 6, Part 2 (hereafter cited as *Report on Internal Commerce*) estimates that in 1816 as much as 20 per cent of produce was lost on the way downriver; the report goes on to say that "many boats, moreover, stopped along the river on their way down to sell supplies to the planters" (p. 191). Moreover, many Louisiana planters took their produce directly to ships to be exported. The *Report* estimates the value of shipments to Louisiana originating in the West at $13,875,000 instead of the official $8,062,540 in 1816. There was also a great deal of produce shipped to New Orleans and thence back upriver. See Schmidt, "Internal Commerce," *loc. cit.*, pp. 804-5.

[7] A contemporary estimate is that 10,000 head of livestock annually were driven to the South Atlantic states. James S. Buckingham, *The Slave States of America*, 2 Vols. (London, Paris: Fisher, Son & Co., 1842), II, 203-4.

[8] Edward Ingle, *Southern Sidelights, a Picture of Social and Economic Life in the South a Generation Before the War* (New York: Thomas Y. Crowell & Co., 1896), p. 55. Hereafter cited as *Southern Sidelights*.

of the trade was in cereals. The redirection of this trade from the Mississippi to the Atlantic was striking during the 1850's.[9] The

CHART II-IX

Tonnage Over Erie Canal to Tidewater from Western States and from New York: 1836–1860

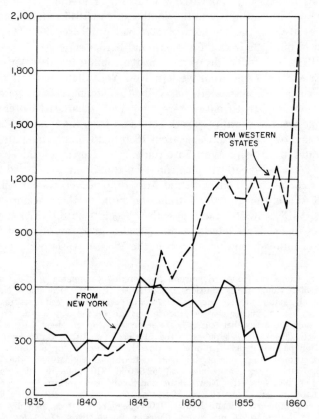

Source: *Appendix II, Table B-IX.*

[9] Cf. Louis B. Schmidt, "The Internal Grain Trade of the United States," *Iowa Journal of History and Politics* XVIII, No. 1 (January 1920), 94-124.

growth in receipts of flour and grains at Buffalo from the West between 1836–1860 is presented in Chart V-IX. Expanded receipts of provisions such as pork, beef, bacon, and lard as well as whiskey were also features of this redirected trade.[10] The change of trade

CHART III-IX

Tonnage of Vessels on the Western Rivers: 1816–1860; and Tonnage Employed in the Lake Trade: 1830–1860
(in Thousands of Tons)

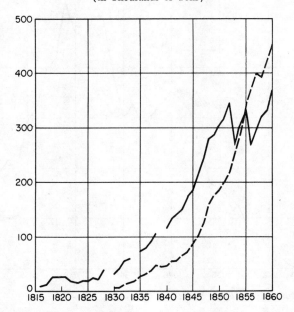

Source: Appendix II, Table C-IX.

---

[10] Cf. U.S. Congress, Senate, *Statistics of Foreign and Domestic Commerce*, Senate Executive Document No. 55, 38th Congress, 1st Session, 1864, p. 162, for statistics. Hereafter cited as *Statistics of Foreign and Domestic Commerce*.

of the West from the South to the East is summarized in the House *Report on Internal Commerce of 1887*.

CHART IV-IX

Receipts on All Ohio Canals: 1827–1860
(in Thousands of Dollars)

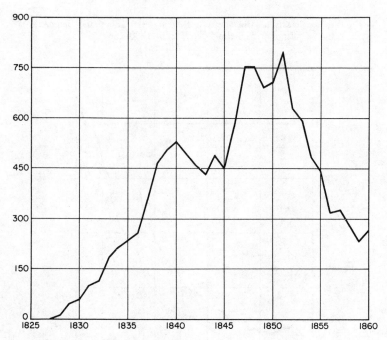

Source: Appendix II, Table D-IX.

In the twenty years between 1840 and 1860 during which the competition of river and rail had been inaugurated, the production of the Mississippi Valley had increased far more rapidly than the receipts at New Orleans. The river traffic had increased in the aggregate, but lost relatively. The Mississippi carried a much larger tonnage, but a far smaller percentage of the total traffic of the Valley. The loss was most marked in western products. Forty

CHART V-IX

Receipts of Flour and Grain at Buffalo from the West: 1836–1860

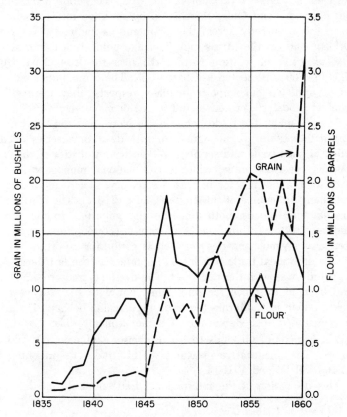

Source: Appendix II, Table E-IX.

years before these had constituted 58 per cent of the total receipts at New Orleans. In 1859-60 they had fallen to 23 per cent although in that period the West had made the greatest increase in population and production.[11]

The trade of the East with the West was of longer standing than the reverse movements, since the East sent relatively high value manufactured goods to the West through costly overland transportation even before the development of more efficient transport media. Until the advent of the Erie Canal and the four railroad systems, the New York Central, the Erie, the Pennsylvania, and the Baltimore and Ohio, there is no quantitative measure of this trade either directly across the mountains or indirectly via New Orleans and up the Mississippi. Tonnage going to western states (i.e. exclusive of western New York) over the Erie Canal from 1836 to 1860 is presented in Chart VI-IX. The commodities moving west paralleled our imports in many respects; they were either tropical goods (sugar, coffee, and so on) or manufactures.[12]

There remains the trade between the North and the South. Unfortunately there are no figures to provide a time series of the value of such trade and services. We do have statistics of the tonnage in coastwise trade, which was a national monopoly. These, with some allowance for increased efficiency, give a good idea of the changing volume of this trade (Chart VII-IX). The North sent manufactured goods, both domestic and imported, to the South, and received in return southern staples (cotton, tobacco, naval stores, sugar, molasses, rice) as well as cotton for export.

One additional trade which was important in the last decade of this study was with the Far West. The overland trade to Santa Fe had been in existence for some time, but with the discovery of gold in 1848 in California the trade via Panama or Cape Horn by ship assumed real significance for the economy. The East sent finished goods of all kinds to San Francisco and received gold in return. The quantitative measures of this trade are presented in Charts VII-IX and VIII-IX.

This discussion of the interregional trade of the United States

---

[11] *Report on Internal Commerce*, p. 215.
[12] *Statistics of Foreign and Domestic Commerce*, p. 132.

is really a means of getting at the income flows between these specialized, interdependent parts. The trade was paralleled by reverse flows of income or at least by claims which were frequently settled by a more circuitous route. We now have some idea of interregional trade, but not of an interregional balance of payments. Unfortu-

CHART VI-IX

Tonnage Going to Western States by Erie Canal: 1836–1860
(in Thousands of Tons)

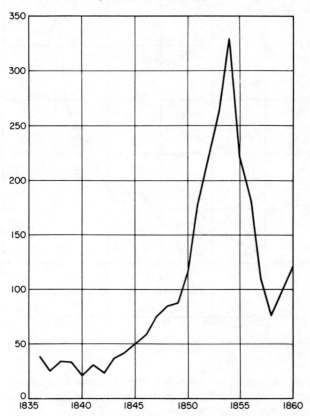

Source: Appendix II, Table F-IX.

nately, no comprehensive figures are available on this score. Contemporaries were aware of the importance of the invisible items in the settlement of claims between the North and the South, not to

CHART VII-IX

Tonnage in the Coasting Trade: 1816–1860
(in Thousands of Tons)

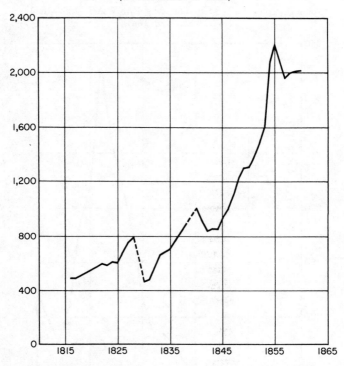

Source: Appendix II, Table G-IX.

mention the flow of capital into the West. From their accounts, we can get at least a qualitative picture of this subject supplemented by some contemporary estimates.

It was evident at the time, and indeed the subject of bitter reproach on the part of southern partisans,[13] that the income of the South flowed out to the North and the West. The fact that it had very little regional multiplier effect will be considered in the following chapter, but the reason it flowed out to the North rested not just on the interregional trade, but upon the other items in the

CHART VIII-IX

California Gold Production and Gold Exports: 1848–1860

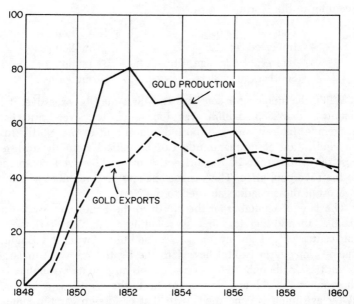

Source: Appendix II, Table H-IX.

balance of payments. The North provided the South with transportation, insurance, and marketing services, as well as a good deal

---

[13] Cf. Herbert Wender, *Southern Commercial Conventions, 1837-1859*. Johns Hopkins University Studies in Historical and Political Science, Series XLVIII, No. 4 (Baltimore: The Johns Hopkins Press, 1930).

of the capital for southern plantation expansion. In addition, it provided the summer residence of the wealthy planter class who migrated northward to escape the hot and pestilent summers in the South, so the South paid the North for these services. Their magnitude must remain conjectural to a degree, but they were clearly important. Kettell's estimate for 1859 was little more than a guess, but it does give some indication of the likely magnitudes. He estimates southern produce, raw materials, and so on sent north at $462 million, which is balanced by the following credits accruing to the North: [14]

Domestic goods	$240 million
Imported goods	106 million
Interest, brokerage, etc.	63 million
Southern travellers	53 million

While the amount for southern travellers may be excessive, it is doubtful that $63 million was too much to cover insurance, brokerage, interest and transportation accruing to the North. Just one indication of its magnitude can be gained from the *transfer* cost of cotton, that is, the price the planter received compared to the Liverpool price. The various changes are presented in Table 8. Most of these changes accrued to the North.

The flow of capital from the North to the South and West was sizable. In addition to the flow resulting from New York being the center of the money market [15] and linked with the English market, long term capital flowed to the South and West in large quantities. Although there is no quantitative data available on these flows, the ebb and flow of capital to the West was consistent, as far as timing is concerned, with that of foreign capital coming into or leaving the country. Moreover, the terms of trade between the agricultural West and eastern finished goods also showed

---

[14] Thomas P. Kettell, *Southern Wealth and Northern Profits, as Exhibited in Statistical Facts and Official Figures* . . . (New York: G. W. and J. A. Wood, 1860), p. 75.

[15] Cf. Margaret Myers, *The New York Money Market*, I, Chapter VI for a discussion of seasonal money flows which reflected the trade patterns discussed above.

TABLE 8

TRANSFER COSTS OF COTTON:
CHARGES ON A BALE OF COTTON AT MOBILE

A statement of the Charges incurred at the Port of Mobile, exclusive of Insurance, calculated on a Bale of 420 Pounds, with Freight at 3/4 d., and Prices at the present Rates.

Wharfage, per bale	$ .10	
Weighing	.125	
Draying to press	.125	
Storage, average, day	.20	
Factor's commissions, average this season	.80	
Add for freight to city	1.50	
Chargeable to planter		$ 2.85
Brokerage	.25	
Storage until compressed	.125	
Drayage to vessel or lighter	.08	
Wharfage	.10	
Commission on purchase, average, say	.80	
Freight and primage, say	6.645	
Chargeable to purchaser		$ 8.00
Compressing	.80	
Lighterage to lower bay	.25	
Stowing, (done by the day) say	.25	
Chargeable to vessel		$ 1.30
Total charges on a bale		$12.15
Add port charges at Liverpool		6.00
Total, on both sides, per bale		$18.15

Source: Hunt's Merchants' Magazine, and Commercial Review, March 1840, pp. 267-78.

a pattern similar to that of the international context. In this connection it is worth quoting T. S. Berry's study of *Western Prices before 1861* at some length:

Nevertheless, the admission of an important dynamic factor into the analysis—the ebb and flow of capital investment (and immigration) to and from the West—may serve to clear up the apparent disharmony between eastern exchange rates and commodity prices between 1838 and 1843. Various evidence points to the fact that net new British investment in the United States, which was admittedly large in the years prior to 1837, continued in sizable volume through 1839; it was not until the collapse of the latter year that the tide turned and capital commenced to flow back. A good deal of these funds were lent to the West directly, and much of the capital lent in New York and other eastern centers from abroad was reinvested in western lands and public works. It has been found that (1) New York commodity prices exceeded London figures in the middle thirties but fell below them in the early forties, and (2) a similar turnover occurred between 1839 and 1840 in the values of domestic and foreign commodities in the New York market. In other words, the inflowing capital itself, which must be associated with lower rates on foreign exchange, tended to raise prices in the receiving region as compared with those in the paying region; conversely, the withdrawal of capital (1840 and later) tended to raise exchange rates but to depress prices in the United States, especially those of domestic goods.

The same general reasoning may profitably be applied to the western state of affairs, particularly between 1838 and 1843. Western prices remained above eastern, taken as a whole, and Index A stayed higher than Index B so long as the net flow of capital was from East to West (1838 and 1839). This flow of capital *per se* prevented eastern exchange rates from rising above par to any extent. However the period of severe liquidation witnessed not only a large decline of general prices in the interior as compared with New York and England but also a tendency of western export values (Index A) to fall in relation to import values (Index B). At the same time, exchange rates on the points whither capital was heading were sent higher and higher according to the demand for the transfer of funds. As the demand for funds became more acute in the West, efforts were made to offset the effects of withdrawing capital from the region by issuing various kinds of more or less convertible currency; the pressure upon commodity prices does not appear to have been greatly relieved, according to the behavior of Cincinnati index numbers, whereas the ceiling on the eastern exchange market was removed.

Indeed, the thesis elaborated above may be applied to the whole period before 1861. In times of expansion the high values of western crops and the shipment of funds from the East for investment and speculation operated temporarily to reduce the rate of exchange. Western bankers felt free to issue a larger volume of currency, so that western prices advanced relative to eastern—this appears to have happened in 1816–1817, in 1834–1835, and again in the mid-fifties. In each case, a delayed crisis finally brought liquidation and a call of funds back to the East, and the exchange situation was rendered more acute by a drastic shrinkage in the mass value of agricultural exports. As eastern exchange rose to a higher premium and western paper currency depreciated bit by bit, the strain grew heavier upon the note-issuing banks. The latter proved least able to withstand it in 1820–1822, when a final solution was found only in wholesale deflation and reestablishment of a specie currency. In the great crises of 1819 and 1839, deflation occurred first in the East, and the shrinkage in export profits was only partly compensated by a temporarily high exchange premium—western prices were eventually forced to realign themselves with the East. As the depression wore on, old stocks of commodities and old currencies were cleared away, and debts were either paid or written off. This continual pressure, which seemed especially severe to the West, was not relieved until eastern exchange subsided and western products began to improve in price. The terms of trade were about as unfavorable to the interior as they had been favorable in time of prosperity. Here again, matters were probably worse in 1821 than in 1842; the western price structure of the former year was stretched beyond recognition.[16]

Berry's terms of trade between western agricultural goods and eastern finished goods are presented in Chart IX-IX.

It is reasonable to assume that the flow of capital into the South approximated the periods of expansion in cotton: 1816–1819, 1832–1839, and to a lesser extent the 1850's. There is abundant contemporary description to support this view. Both British and northeastern capital were particularly attracted to the South in the 1830's.

There is better evidence on the internal flows of people. Perhaps the best indication of internal migration is land sales in the southern and western states. These are presented in Charts X-IX and XI-IX. They show surges of migration to the South in 1816–1818, 1832–1839, and only modest inflow into the Southwest in the 1850's. Internal migration was accelerated to the West in each period of expansion, but was greatest in the 1850's. While speculation certainly played a part in the timing of land sales, the evidence of population movements suggests that they bore a close relation-

---

[16] Berry, *Western Prices,* pp. 466-68.

1815-1860

CHART IX-IX

Western States Terms of Trade: 1816–1860
(Base 1824–1846)

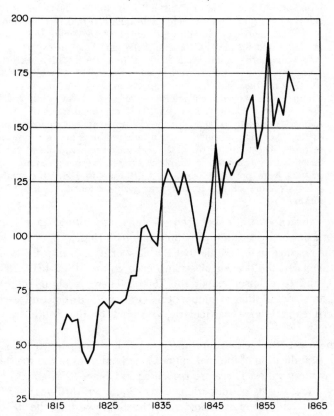

Source: Appendix II, Table I-IX.

CHART X-IX

Receipts from Public Land Sales in Five Southern States: 1815–1860
(in Millions of Dollars)

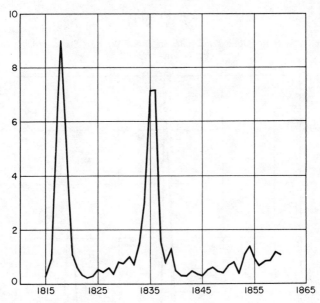

Source: Appendix II, Table J-IX.

ship to the westward movement.[17] The movement in the southern states was primarily an intraregional movement from the old South to the new South (see Chapter X). The flows into the West came partly from already settled western areas, but particularly from

CHART XI-IX

Receipts from Public Land Sales in Seven Western States: 1850–1860
(in Millions of Dollars)

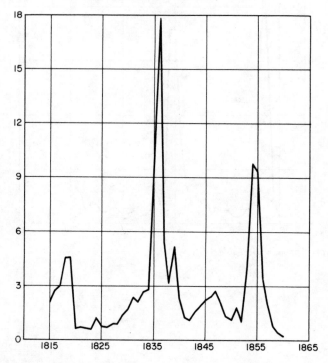

Source: Appendix II, Table K-IX.

[17] Cf. Arthur H. Cole, "Cyclical and Sectional Variations in the Sale of Public Lands, 1816-60," *Review of Economics and Statistics* IX, No. 1 (January 1927), 50.

the East. Chart XII-IX presents the decennial census figures for population changes by region. It indicates the remarkable rapidity with which Americans moved west and the rapid relative change in regional population distribution.

CHART XII-IX

Population Distribution by Regions: 1810–1860

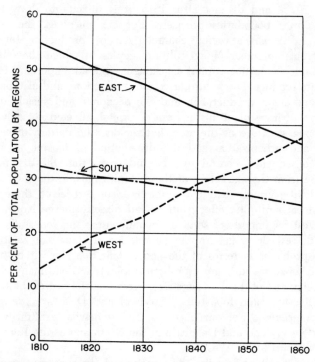

Source: Appendix II, Table L-IX.

X

THE ECONOMIC STRUCTURE OF THE SOUTH

While the three regions became increasingly separate
and distinct after 1815, it is difficult to draw their
boundaries precisely. For our purposes, the South
was a region characterized by production for the
market of a number of agricultural staples in which slave labor
was both the major capital investment and an important intermediate product. The nature of cotton production (and of tobacco,
rice, and sugar production), and the economic and social consequences of investment in this form of capital, affected not only the
economic structure of the area, but molded the pattern of settlement and urbanization and the distribution of income as well.
The consequence, central to this study, was that the expanding
income from the marketing of these staples outside the region induced little growth within the South. Income received there had
little local multiplier effect, but flowed directly to the North and
the West for imports of services, manufactures and foodstuffs.

With respect to geographic boundaries, a state like Kentucky
poses problems in terms of the above definition since it both exported tobacco and hemp (southern staples), and had many of the
characteristics of the western states, providing the rest of the South
with livestock and foodstuffs. Maryland and Delaware present a
similar problem. For our purposes, and somewhat arbitrarily, we
include Maryland and Delaware in the North and assign Kentucky
and Missouri to the West.

It is difficult to describe the structure of the southern economy
in the space of a single chapter. The description must oversimplify
the structure at any specific point of time, and can scarcely do
justice to the changes wrought over several generations. Yet the
general outlines are clear enough, and are attested to by contemporary descriptions of both residents and travellers, drawing a picture consistent with the meager statistical data available.

Apart from slavery, the most noteworthy feature of the South, which influenced both its structure and the pattern of internal migration of productive factors from East to West, was the enormous comparative advantage of cotton. This comparative advantage varied with changes in the price of cotton, the costs of cotton production, and the prices of goods which represented an alternative use of resources. It was only for a brief period in the 1840's that the price of cotton was so low as to suggest that the southerner might profitably shift his capital and labor to other employment. Even in the dark days of 1843–1845, with six or seven cent cotton, the planter viewed the price depression as temporary. It was not simply that cotton production was the most efficient use of resources; throughout the period investment in new cotton lands in the West yielded a return upon capital[1] high enough to attract funds from the old South,[2] the Northeast, and Europe.

Alternative uses of resources in the South, even in the old South, were limited. Rice was always a profitable crop in the limited coastal areas of South Carolina and Georgia, but even there it was in competition with long staple cotton.[3] Sugar, like rice, could only be planted in a very limited area. Virginia and North Carolina, marginal to or outside the cotton belt, found no satisfactory alternative use of resources when the tobacco trade ceased expanding, and the rapid relative decline of Virginia from its early preeminence in the Union attests to the persistent difficulties faced by that state. An old southern state like South Carolina, which had continuously lost slaves and capital to the Southwest, and for which the secular decline in cotton prices was a continuing source of dismay and agitation, found no profitable substitute for cotton production.[4]

The secular decline in the price of cotton between 1818 and

[1] Cf. A. H. Conrad and John R. Meyers, "The Economics of Slavery in the Ante-Bellum South," *Journal of Political Economy* LXVI, No. 2 (April 1958), 95-130. Hereafter cited as "Economics of Slavery."

[2] A universal cause of complaint in the old South was the drain of capital to the Southwest. See Alfred G. Smith, Jr., *Economic Readjustment of an Old Cotton State, South Carolina, 1820-1860* (Columbia: University of South Carolina Press, 1958), pp. 33, 38, 123. Hereafter cited as *Economic Readjustment*.

[3] Actually, rice production did shift from internal swamp areas to coastal areas where the tides could flood the lands when needed.

[4] Cf. Smith, *Economic Readjustment*, for a thoughtful discussion of the readjustment problems of South Carolina throughout the period.

1845 (Chart I-X) reflected the fact that, despite the enormous growth in demand of the English cotton textile industry and to a lesser degree that of France, the rest of Europe and the north-

CHART I-X

Public Land Sales and Cotton Prices: 1814–1860

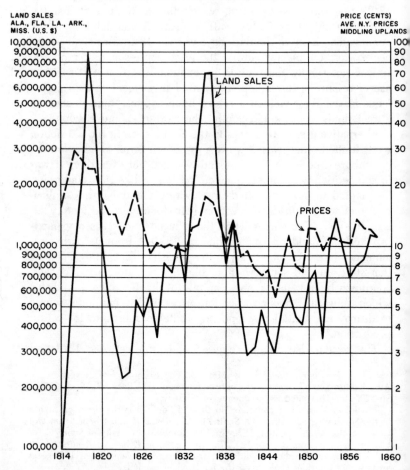

Source: Appendix II, Table A-X.

eastern United States, the supply of cotton grew even more rapidly. This was primarily a result of the expanded acreage (although yields were much higher in the Southwest) that came about with the great migration into western lands between 1815 and 1839.

Any discussion of the costs of cotton production must be qualified with respect to its generality and implications. Costs varied widely, even among planters in the same district. While there can be no doubt of the profitability of ten cent cotton, eight cent cotton (on the plantation) was considered marginal in some areas and five cent cotton was profitable only in the Southwest.[5] Two generalizations may be made about production costs of cotton: yields in the Southwest were greater and production costs substantially lower than in the old South, and the optimum unit cost combination entailed substantial amounts of labor and land, so that there were important economies of scale.[6] It is not surprising to find that the scale of operations was increasing, particularly in the Southwest. Not only were the size of plantations and number of slaves per plantation much greater than in either the Southeast or the border states, but between 1850 and 1860 there was a marked increase in concentration of slaveholdings in the area.[7]

Efficient development of the cotton trade was accomplished with relatively minor amounts of capital for social overhead investment or dependent industries. Internal transport problems were mitigated by the abundance of rivers in the South. Planters not located on rivers usually had only short hauls by wagon to a navigable waterway, from which the cotton went to an inland or coastal port. Here it was baled, or rebaled if packed in "square bales" on the plantation, by a steam press, and readied for shipment.

---

[5] Governor Hammond is quoted as saying that on land that would average 2,000 pounds of ginned cotton for each full hand, it was possible to realize 7 per cent at a net price of 5 cents a pound. Lewis C. Gray, *History of Agriculture in the Southern United States to 1860* (Washington: The Carnegie Institution, 1933), p. 709. Hereafter cited as Gray, *History*. For estimates, see Matthew B. Hammond, *The Cotton Industry; an Essay in American Economic History*. Part I, The Cotton Culture and the Cotton Trade (New York: Macmillan, for the American Economic Association, 1897), p. 118.

[6] Cf. Gray, *History*, pp. 478-80. In sugar and rice production the heavy fixed costs incurred provided even greater advantages to large scale organizations.

[7] Gray, *History*, Chapter XXIII.

The factor played an important role as intermediary between the planter and the "outside world." He acted as selling agent for the cotton, purchaser of the plantation's consumption and capital goods, and as a source of credit.[8]

The only requirements for efficient marketing of cotton were a few strategically located ports acting as export centers for the crop and import centers for the planter's consumption and capital goods, and a factorage system which linked him with outside sources of capital, ocean transportation, and insurance for the cotton in transit. The earlier development (1793–1808) in the Northeast of merchant houses, banking and insurance ventures to service the shipping trade formed a convenient link with the cotton trade through the factor. An alternative source was the English counterpart of these services. It is important that the institutional structure of the cotton trade through the factorage system could market the crop efficiently, and import the planter's requirements, with a minimal expansion of social overhead investment in the South.[9]

Certain characteristics of water transportation affected the economic structure of the South. The first of these was the rapid fall in ocean freight rates on cotton to Liverpool (see Chart II-X), which improved the comparative advantage of cotton. Second, the transportation of cotton occupied far more shipping space than the return flow of manufactured goods, so the freight rate on the latter was extremely low,[10] and transportation costs gave little protection for the development of local manufacturing. Third, a combination of the existing pre-eminence of New York in trade, commerce and finance, and the law which restricted coastwise shipping to American bottoms, led to that city's being the entrepôt for the South, as, to a lesser degree, were other northern cities. Imports came into New York rather than directly to the South because they

---

[8] For a more detailed description of the organization of the cotton trade see Buck, *Anglo-American Trade*, Chapter IV. When credit was extended under the factorage contract, the planter not only agreed to consign his entire crop to the factor, but paid a penalty if the number of bales fell below a certain level. Gray, *History*, pp. 713-14.

[9] The readjustment problem connected with the westward spread of cotton culture led South Carolina into fairly extensive investment in railroads. The effect was to strengthen cotton culture by opening up inaccessible areas. Smith, *Economic Readjustment*, Chapter V.

[10] Cf. North, "Ocean Freight Rates and Economic Development, 1750-1913," *loc. cit.*

would be assured of more cargo on the westward voyage than by going to a southern port. United States coastwise ships carried the cargo, both imports and northeastern manufactures, to southern ports, and returned with cotton for shipment to Liverpool, Havre,

CHART II-X

Freight Rates, Cotton New York–Liverpool, New Orleans–Liverpool: 1820–1860

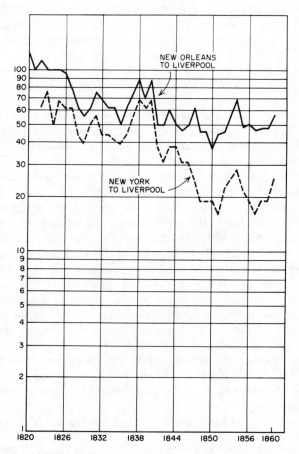

Source: Appendix II, Table B-X.

or perhaps to the New England textile industry. This trade pattern tied the South still more to the services provided by the Northeast.

The salient features of the South's economic structure were these:

1. There was concentrated production for the market (outside the region) of a few staple commodities, with cotton by far the most important.

2. Large scale organization typified production of these staples, reflecting important economies of scale. The plantation system in cotton, sugar, and rice involved the complementary combination of relatively (for agriculture) large amounts of labor and land for lowest unit cost.

3. The supply of labor for the plantation system was, of course, in slaves. They were the major capital investment in the plantation system and, as noted by Conrad and Meyer, the production of slaves was an essential intermediate good.[11] The rise in the price of slaves over the period from 1802 to 1860 from $600 to $1800 (for a prime field hand) represented a rational increased capitalization of slaves. The crop value per slave rose from $14.68 in 1802 to $101.09 in 1860,[12] and when the price of a slave is divided into crop value per slave it shows no tendency to decline, but is on the average higher in the last decade than in the earlier years of the nineteenth century.

4. The availability of land to the West for extensive expansion of cotton culture and the rich quality of this land were salient features of the pattern of internal migration which characterized the region between 1815 and 1860. The pace of this western movement can be illustrated by the growth of population in the states of the Southwest. (See Table 9). It was not a continuous process, but took place in surges that clearly reflected the pull of increased profitability of cotton production on western lands. The price of cotton was the most decisive factor in this regard, and if this is plotted against public land sales in the five new cotton states the relationship is quickly evident. (Chart I-X)

5. Long swings in the price of cotton were the result of periods

---

[11] Conrad and Meyer, "Economics of Slavery," *loc. cit.*, p. 97.
[12] *Ibid.*, Table 17, for annual estimates.

TABLE 9

POPULATION OF FREE (NEGRO AND WHITE) AND SLAVES OF THE
STATES OF ALABAMA, ARKANSAS, FLORIDA, LOUISIANA,
AND MISSISSIPPI 1820-1860

Year	Alabama F	S	Arkansas F	S	Florida F	S	Louisiana F	S	Mississippi F	S	Total All
1820	86,622	41,879	12,638	1,617	------	-----	83,857	69,064	42,634	32,814	371,125
1830	191,978	117,549	25,812	4,576	19,229	15,501	106,251	109,588	70,962	65,659	727,105
1840	337,224	253,532	77,639	19,935	28,760	25,717	183,959	168,452	180,440	195,211	1,470,869
1850	428,779	342,892	162,797	47,100	48,135	39,309	272,953	244,809	296,698	309,878	2,193,300
1860	529,121	435,080	324,335	111,115	78,680	61,745	376,276	331,726	354,674	436,631	3,093,383

Source: U. S. Congress, House. Preliminary Report on the Eighth Census, 1860 (Washington: Government Printing Office, 1862), pp. 126-133.

of excess capacity with a consequent elastic supply curve of cotton over a substantial range of output. Once demand had shifted to the right sufficiently to use all the available cotton land, the supply curve became rather inelastic. A rise in cotton prices precipitated another move into new lands of the Southwest by planters and their slaves. Funds from the Northeast and England financed the transfer of slaves, purchase of land, and working capital during the period of clearing the land, preparing the soil and raising a cotton crop. There was a lag of approximately four or five years between the initial surge and the resulting large increase in output which caused a tremendous shift to the right in the supply curve and the beginning of another lengthy period of digesting the increased capacity.

6. There were several important differences between plantations in the new South and those in the old South. Not only were production costs lower in the Southwest, but plantations tended to be more specialized than in the old South. Part of the answer was that the availability of cheap foodstuffs from the West enabled the planter to keep all his best land in cotton.[13] Western foodstuffs were more costly in the old South because of transportation costs. In addition, the differential return between cotton and corn on most lands was much narrower than in the Southwest. The move in the direction of greater diversi-

---

[13] Gray, *History*, pp. 707-8.

fication of agriculture in the old South was particularly strong during the period of low prices in the 1840's. South Carolina began to raise a greater proportion of its livestock and depend less upon Kentucky and Tennessee.[14] Northern Virginia became an important general farming area. Outside the cotton growing tidewater area of North Carolina there was extensive development of wheat and corn production, although tobacco continued as the major cash crop in many areas.

7. Those members of the southern white population who possessed slaves and engaged in the production of southern staples were in the minority. Aside from the large plantation owner, there were a substantial number of smaller farmers who owned a few slaves and produced small quantities of cotton for the market. The majority, however, owned no slaves at all. A large percentage of the population made very little cash income and cannot be thought of as a regular part of a market economy. Even more striking is the fact that there was little tendency for them to be pulled into the market economy. There was some migration of these self-sufficient farmers into the West with the expansion of economic opportunity there, but there was very little tendency to develop agricultural production for a local market.

8. A notable lack of urbanization characterized the area. Aside from the growth of a few ports to implement the cotton trade (Mobile, Savannah, Charleston, and New Orleans), there was scant increase in urbanization. (See Chart III-X) New Orleans alone gave all the indications of a thriving city and grew rapidly. In 1860 it was the only southern city among the first fifteen (by population) in the United States. Russell describes the conditions in Alabama:

In travelling through a fertile district in any of the Southern States, the appearance of things forms a great contrast to that in similar districts in the Free States. During two days' sail on the Alabama River from Mobile to Montgomery, I did not see so many houses standing together in any one spot as could be dignified with the appellation of village, but I may possibly have passed some during the night. There were many places where cotton was shipped and provisions were landed; still there were no signs of

---

[14] *Ibid.*, p. 917.

enterprise to indicate that we were in the heart of a rich cotton region. Nor is this to be wondered at, for American slavery, in its most productive state, has all the worst features of absenteeism, more particularly where the plantations are managed by overseers. In fact, the more fertile the land the more destitute is the country of villages and towns. And how can it be otherwise? The system of management which is recommended as the most economical and profitable, is to raise and to manufacture on the plantations every thing which the slaves require. Though this is seldom accomplished, yet a great part of the clothing is homemade; and the chief articles imported are bacon and mules from the Northern States. The only article sold is cotton, which is conveyed to the nearest point on a navigable river, and consigned to a commission agent in the exporting town; while the bacon all comes in through the same channel. Of such articles as are in daily use among the rural inhabitants in the poorest districts of the Free States, the slaves are a non-consuming class. An element so essential to rural prosperity is in great measure wanting in the Slave States, and thus few villages are seen. The planters supply themselves with their

CHART III-X

Urban Population as Per Cent of Total Population: 1790–1860

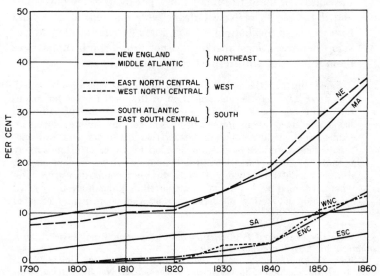

Source: Appendix II, Table C-X.

own necessaries and luxuries of life directly through agents in the large towns, and comparatively little of the money drawn for the cotton crop is spent in the Southern States. Many of the planters spend their incomes by travelling with their families in the Northern States or in Europe during the summer, and a large sum is required to pay the hog-raiser in Ohio, the mule breeder in Kentucky and, above all, the northern capitalists, who have vast sums of money on mortgage over the estates. Dr. Cloud, the editor of the "Cotton Plant," assured me, that after these items are paid out of the money received for the whole cotton and sugar crops of the South, there did not remain one-fourth part of it to be spent in the Southern States. Hence the Slave States soon attain a comparatively stationary condition, and further, the progress they make is in proportion to the increase of freemen, whose labour is rendered comparatively unproductive, seeing that the most fertile land is pre-occupied by slave-owners.[15]

9. It is not surprising that locally oriented industries and services were conspicuously fewer in the South, on a per capita basis, than elsewhere. Even in retail trade, the most rudimentary of residentiary industries, the area was conspicuously deficient. The 1840 census included an enumeration of retail stores by states. Only Louisiana among the southern states was not at the bottom of the list of retail stores per thousand population,[16] and if the parish of New Orleans were omitted, it too would have been at the bottom. Residentiary industry failed to develop because a local market did not grow. Smith summarizes these difficulties with respect to South Carolina:

Since much of the industry of the State was consumer oriented, it is necessary to make an evaluation of the local market for manufactured goods, particularly in view of the fact that lack of patronage has been given as an important reason for the failure of several plants. Such an evaluation indicates that consumer and raw material oriented industries did not develop to a greater extent largely because of lack of markets. Inadequate local purchasing power, competition of already established consumer goods industries elsewhere, coupled with internal transportation difficulties, the job of establishing marketing mechanisms, and the poor quality of local

---

[15] Callender, *Economic History,* pp. 283-84, quoting from Russell, *North America: Its Agriculture and Climate.*

[16] Fred M. Jones, *Middlemen in the Domestic Trade of the United States, 1800-1860,* Illinois Studies in the Social Sciences XXI, No. 3 (Urbana: University of Illinois Press, 1937), p. 56.

goods compared with that of imported goods are all factors that must be considered.

Both plantation and farm had a high degree of self-subsistence, not only with regard to the production of food and feed for home consumption but in respect to manufactured goods as well. Although self-sufficiency rose as agricultural income fell, there does not seem to have been a significant increase in the purchase of locally manufactured goods when farm prices were better.[17]

10. Investment in human capital in the South was conspicuously lower than in the other two regions. The ratio of pupils to white population in 1840 was 5.72 per cent in slaveholding states compared to 18.41 per cent in the non-slaveholding states. Illiteracy as a percentage of the white population was 7.46 in the slaveholding states and 2.13 per cent in the non-slaveholding states.[18] While the slaveholding states in 1850 had slightly less than half of the white population of the northern states (6.1 million compared to 13.2 million), they had less than one-third as many public schools, one-fourth as many pupils, one-twentieth as many public libraries, and one-sixth as many volumes in those libraries. It should be noted, moreover, that Maryland, Delaware, Kentucky, and Missouri are all included in the slaveholding states and all were far higher than the southern average. Had they been excluded, and the population ratio adjusted accordingly, the poorer educational investment in the South would have been even more striking.[19]

Clearly, the structure of the southern economy played a critical role in the South's policy toward education. The concentration on cotton production, the lack of urbanization, and very unequal distribution of income were important factors. Even more significant were the attitudes of the dominant planter class, who could see little return to them in investment in human capital. Expenditures to educate the large percentage of white southerners who were outside the plantation system was something they vigorously op-

---

[17] Smith, *Economic Readjustment*, pp. 133-34.

[18] U.S. Census Bureau, *Compendium of the Seventh Census*, J. D. B. DeBow, Superintendent of U.S. Census (Washington: Senate Printer, 1854), p. 152.

[19] Statistics from Hinton R. Helper, *Compendium of the Impending Crisis of the South* (New York: A. B. Burdick, 1860), pp. 144, 288-89. Hereafter cited as *Impending Crisis*.

posed. This opposition carried over to Reconstruction days, when the effort to expand public education met formidable political and financial obstacles.[20]

---

[20] Cf. W. H. Nicholls, "Some Foundations of Economic Development in the Upper East Tennessee Valley, 1850-1900. II," *Journal of Political Economy* LXIV, No. 5 (October 1956), 410-11. Nicholls also points up the correlation between financial support of schools and subsequent per capita value added and capital per farm worker.

XI

THE ECONOMIC STRUCTURE OF THE WEST

The West was a less homogeneous region than the South, and changes in the regional economy were far more pronounced over the forty-five-year period 1815–1860. The growth in income of the area and its integration into the national economy came basically from the export outside the region of wheat, corn and products derived from these two cereals: flour, meal, livestock products, and whiskey. In terms of the focus of this study, the most important changes in the western regional economy were: (1) the surges of westward expansion, (2) the redirection of its trade from the South to the East and to Europe, (3) the accelerated shift of its population out of self-sufficiency into the market economy during periods of expansion, (4) the development of a far more diversified economic structure than existed in the South, and the creation of the conditions essential to rapid development of manufacturing in the post-Civil War period.

I

The physiographic characteristics of the West were an important part of the explanation of the region's economic organization. The mountains stretching from Maine to Georgia were for many decades an effective barrier to East-West trade. High value goods such as manufactures going west or furs coming east could bear the costs of transport, but the bulky items that constituted the basis of western production had to find other markets until new develop-

135

ments lowered transportation costs.[1] The Mississippi, Ohio, Illinois river systems provided an avenue for transportation to the South. With the successful innovation of the steamboat for upriver transportation in 1816, trade with the South was limited only by the latter's demand for western foodstuffs and the rate of investment necessary to increase the supply in the West. The physiographic features of the West also played an important part in the early pattern of intraregional trade. Advancing settlement into the prairie areas of Indiana and Illinois led to an early demand for lumber, and the lumber trade became the major trade internal to the West. River shipment of other building materials was also important.

The major determinant of the pace of westward expansion before 1860 continued to be the profitability of the traditional staples: wheat, corn, and their derivatives. Waves of western expansion in 1816–1818, 1832–1836, 1846–1847, and 1850–1856 reflected the increased profitability of these products. While cost reduction played a part in increased returns, it was the change in wheat and corn prices which most directly affected western development. Wheat and corn prices and the pace of the westward movement, as reflected in land sales in seven western states, are illustrated in Chart I-XI. The prices of other western foodstuffs derived from wheat and corn show similar long swings in their behavior. Chart II-XI presents a number of these series on a nine year moving average.

While the general timing of these long swings was similar in the South and the West, the pace of movement into the West was different in some respects from that into the new South. All through the 1820's the price of cotton provided little incentive for opening up new lands. In contrast, as early as 1827 the price of wheat improved, and sales of public lands in Ohio, Indiana, Illinois, and Michigan increased markedly. Wheat and corn prices increased in the mid-forties as did land sales in the West, in contrast to the price of cotton. The boom in land sales in the 1850's was a western phenomenon triggered by the rising prices of cereals

---

[1] Cf. Taylor, *Transportation Revolution*, Chapter VII, and Berry, *Western Prices*, Chapters III and IV for transport costs.

during the first half of that decade, while southern cotton prices and land sales rose only moderately. Long swings were a pervasive

CHART I-XI

Land Sales in Seven Western States: 1815–1860
(Ohio, Ill., Ind., Mich., Iowa, Wis., Mo.)

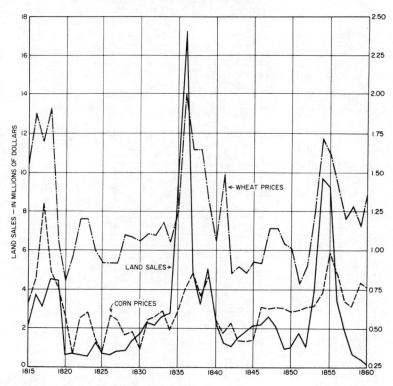

Source: Appendix II, Table A-XI.

influence upon the whole character of the West during this period. Chart III-XI, which shows annual incorporations in Ohio, illustrates the correspondence of formation of new business with long swings. Berry's study provides additional statistical evidence of long swings in the organization and dissolution of banks and other financial series.[2] He concludes that "the settlement of the West did

CHART II-XI

Prices of Pork, Lard, Whiskey, and Corn, Philadelphia: 1815–1857
(9 Year Moving Averages)

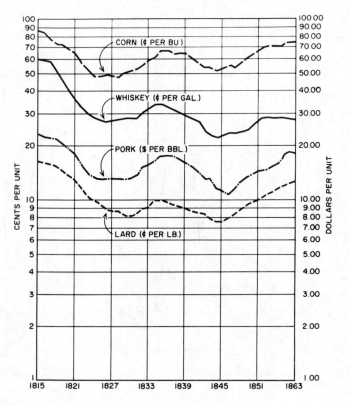

Source: Appendix II, Table B-XI.

---

[2] Berry, *Western Prices,* Appendix B, Table 50.

not, however, proceed at a rate that was even approximately constant. On the contrary, it tended to surge and recede in tides of fairly equal length (eighteen to twenty-two years)."[3] He goes on

CHART III-XI

Annual Incorporations, Ohio: 1800–1851, 1856–1860

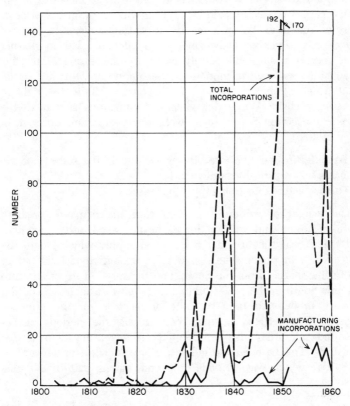

Source: *Appendix II, Table C-XI.*

---

[3] *Ibid.*, p. 530.

to point out that while these tides were most sharply delineated in agricultural prices, they pervaded all aspects of the settlement of the West. High water marks occurred in 1816–1839, 1835–1839, and 1854–1857. The "flood" phase averaged sixteen years while the "ebb" averaged less than four years.[4]

The long swings in prices of western agricultural commodities stemmed from the same market characteristics that obtained in cotton. Surges into new western lands led to large increases in potential capacity which would be utilized with a rise in the price of these commodities. When demand had shifted sufficiently to make use of this capacity, further increase in demand led to sharper price increases, since the supply curve was increasingly inelastic. The result was to set in motion another period of westward settlement which ultimately led to a further large shift to the right in the supply curve. While this general argument is similar to the case of the cotton South, there were some important differences. They related:

1. To shifts in both the rate of increase and in the sources of demand for western foodstuffs, and
2. To the factors affecting supply increases.

The weight of evidence suggests that the demand for both southern cotton and western foodstuffs increased rather steadily,[5] and that it was the irregular response of supply which led to the long swings in prices. The demand for western foodstuffs before 1843 came largely from the South, and the surge of expansion into the new South in the 1830's undoubtedly led to a more substantial increase in demand than the rate of increase for the previous decade. New settlers moving West during the periods of accelerated migration also represented an increasing demand for foodstuffs. The Irish famine led to a sharp increase in demand in 1846–1847 which was "outside" the endogenous pattern of price behavior.

---

[4] *Loc. cit.*

[5] Robert C. O. Matthews maintains that there is no evidence of an acceleration in the rate of growth of demand for cotton in the 1830's over the 1820's. *A Study in Trade Cycle History; Economic Fluctuations in Great Britain 1833-1842* (Cambridge: The University Press, 1954), p. 53. Berry also maintains that the demand for foodstuffs was less susceptible to variation than supply; see *Western Prices*, p. 535.

The sources of demand also changed during these forty-five years. From 1815 to the mid-forties, the primary market for western foodstuffs was the South, supplemented by reshipments out of New Orleans to the East, West Indies, and South America; the rapid extension of cotton culture in the Southwest was the major determinant of expanding demand for corn, hogs, bacon, pork, wheat, flour, and so on. The South remained a market for the West throughout the period, but was displaced by the East in relative terms during the last surge of expansion from 1843–1861. While developments in transportation, to be discussed below, made possible this reorientation of internal trade, the growing demand *per se* stemmed from the rapid industrialization and urbanization of the Northeast, and sporadic demand from abroad as a result of the Irish famine and the Crimean War. The Northeast was rapidly becoming a large food deficit area. The per capita production of wheat in the Middle Atlantic states dropped from 5.75 bushels to 3.75 bushels between 1850 and 1860. New England in 1850 was already a deficit area, with a per capita production of 0.40 bushels. By 1860 this figure had dropped to 0.34 bushels.[6] The Northeast's deficit in corn production also increased. During this period the major wheat growing states "moved West." In 1839 Ohio, Pennsylvania, New York, and Virginia, in that order, were the leading states. By 1859 Illinois was first, followed by Indiana, Wisconsin, and Ohio.[7] Transportation developments accounted for both the shift in the direction of trade and the uneven pattern of supply response to the growing demand for foodstuffs. Early settlers took up land along navigable waterways, and as people poured into Ohio, Indiana, and Illinois they had to take up land farther from water transportation. Navigation improvements on the rivers and the building of canals represented the first major effort to open up new western lands to markets. Approximately 2000 miles of canals were constructed in the 1830's.[8]

---

[6] Schmidt, "The Internal Grain Trade of the United States," *loc. cit.*, 103.

[7] Louis B. Schmidt, "The Westward Movement of the Wheat Growing Industry in the United States," *Iowa Journal of History and Politics* XVIII, No. 3 (July 1920), 399-401.

[8] Taylor, *Transportation Revolution*, p. 79.

II

The redirection of trade had as its initial impetus the opening of the Erie Canal in 1825, but it was almost two decades before this canal began to have a significant effect in moving western bulk goods to the eastern market. Initially, both the Erie and Pennsylvania Canals shipped eastward goods originating largely in western New York and Pennsylvania, rather than effectively reorienting the trade of the West. Transportation developments along the Great Lakes gradually widened the area tributary to eastern markets, and after the middle of the 1840's the re-direction in trade accelerated rapidly. Almost 10,000 miles of railroad were constructed in the West in the 1850's. The westward extension of the New York Central, Pennsylvania, Erie, and Baltimore and Ohio railroads effectively completed the ties between Northeast and West, and the 1850's witnessed a shift in trade which had far-reaching effects on the structure of the western economy. Table 10 shows the rapid growth of railroad mileage in the West between 1845–1861.

TABLE 10

GROWTH OF MIDDLEWESTERN RAILROADS 1845-1861

State	1845	1850	1852	1854	1856	1858	1860	1861
Ohio	84	575	756*	1317*	1807*	2651	2946	2946
Michigan	238	342	431	444	501	642	779	810
Indiana	30	228	756*	1317*	1807*	2014	2163	2175
Illinois	22	111	412	788	2235	2781	2790	2917
Wisconsin		20	71	97	276	826	905	933
Iowa					254	533	655	701
Missouri				38	144	547	817	838

* Identical mileage for Ohio and Indiana for the years 1852, 1854, and 1856 have been reported by Poor in previous and subsequent editions of The Manual of the Railroads of the United States. Other sources have not been located to confirm or correct these figures.

Source: Henry V. Poor, Manual of the Railroads of the United States, for 1869-70 (New York: H. V. and H. W. Poor, 1869), pp. xxvi-xxvii.

Areas advantageously located to the new East-West transport facilities grew very rapidly. The pattern of urbanization reflected this new trade pattern with Chicago, connected by rail and water with the rest of the West, and the eastern seaboard showing the most striking growth. Other cities along the Great Lakes and the East-West rails also grew rapidly, and breaks in the transport system, such as Buffalo, became early flour milling centers. Cincinnati, the dominant city of the early West, was effectively connected with the East by rail, but did not occupy the commanding position in the East-West trade which it had held in the trade with the South. It was large-scale investment in transportation which resulted in the opening up of new areas of market production. The river improvements and canal building in the 1830's made possible large increases in supply of western foodstuffs in Ohio, Indiana, Illinois, and Michigan. In the 1850's the railroad accomplished the same result in conjunction with the expansion of Great Lakes traffic.

The large-scale capital investments necessary for canal and railroad construction brought the individual state governments into the transportation business, either to float the loans or provide subsidies for railroad construction. During both periods of expansion, the initial domestic capital was largely supplemented by foreign borrowing.[9] While such transportation developments took a number of years between their initial conception and completion, the ultimate result in each case was to open up new areas of western land and substantially increase the supply of foodstuffs.

III

The shift from pioneer self-sufficiency to a market oriented agriculture took place throughout most of the western states during this period. The most pervasive influence affecting this shift was the decline in transport costs. The change in the price differential

---

[9] Cf. Douglass C. North's "International Capital Flows and the Development of the American West," *loc. cit.*

between Cincinnati and New Orleans (Chart IV-XI), and between
Cincinnati and New York (Chart V-XI) on staple commodities
from the West illustrates the great decline in transportation costs
which occurred during these years. Taylor estimates that on the

CHART IV-XI

Cincinnati, New Orleans Wholesale Commodity Prices. Average Absolute
Differences by Five-Year Periods. Lard, Mess Pork, Flour, and Corn:
1816–1860.

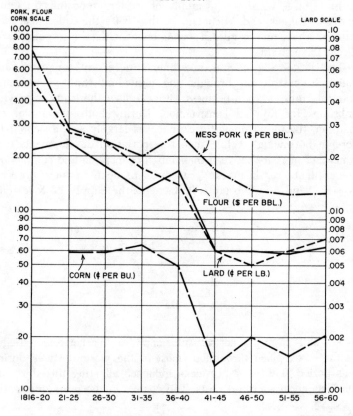

Source: Appendix II, Table D-XI.

Ohio-Mississippi system, downstream rates in 1860 were 25-30 per cent of the 1815–1819 period, and that upstream rates were 5-10 per cent of the earlier period.[10] The cost per ton-mile of moving

CHART V-XI

Cincinnati, New York Wholesale Commodity Prices. Average Absolute Differences by Five-Year Periods. Lard, Mess Pork, Flour, and Corn: 1816–1860

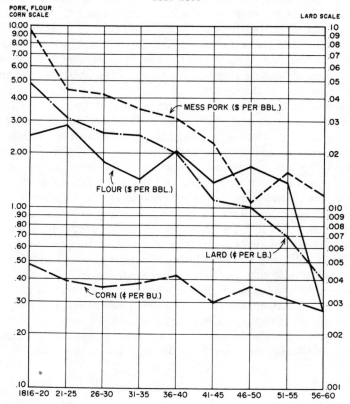

Source: Appendix II, Table E-XI.

---

[10] Taylor, *Transportation Revolution*, p. 136.

freight from Buffalo to New York in 1817, before the Erie Canal was opened, was 19.12 cents. The average over the Erie Canal for the 1857–1860 period was 0.81 cents.[11] Railroad rates on the four major railroads to the West also showed substantial freight rate declines in the 1850's.[12]

An additional influence affecting the growing market orientation of western agriculture was the substantial improvement in the terms of trade of western staples vis-à-vis other commodities, particularly eastern manufactured goods. Berry's terms of trade index, on a base of 1824–1846 equal to 100, rises from 57 in 1816 to 176 in 1859.[13] The major reason for this improvement was transport cost declines, but another was the rapid productivity increases in eastern manufactures resulting from technological changes and the increased size of the market.

Rising prices and accelerated investment in western transport occurred simultaneously in the years 1832–1839 and 1849–1856.[14] In the short run this investment in transport resulted in still higher agricultural prices, since it diverted some real resources out of agriculture into transportation construction. During these surges of westward expansion, the supply of labor was more elastic than it is in the contemporary economy, because of the shift integrating the western farmer into the national economy. The primary importance of this shift for American economic growth was not that the farmer's output was directly measured in the income flows. This in itself may represent little in the way of a real addition to output. It was that he became more specialized, with all that is implied by increased division of labor, and that there were market-induced pressures for greater productivity through increased use of capital and advancing technical knowledge.

It is worthwhile devoting some attention to an individual case study of the changes wrought in Illinois between 1850 and 1860.[15]

---

11 *Ibid.*, p. 137.

12 *Ibid.*, Appendix 2, Table 2.

13 Berry, *Western Prices*, Appendix B, Table 19.

14 In 1846-47 there was a substantial rise in cereal prices as a result of the Irish famine.

15 The material presented below, including the two maps, is from a paper presented in my seminar in American Economic History by Mr. Charles J. Jorgensen. I am indebted to him for permitting me to summarize it here.

MAP 1

Population Density by County, and Transportation Facilities, Illinois: 1850

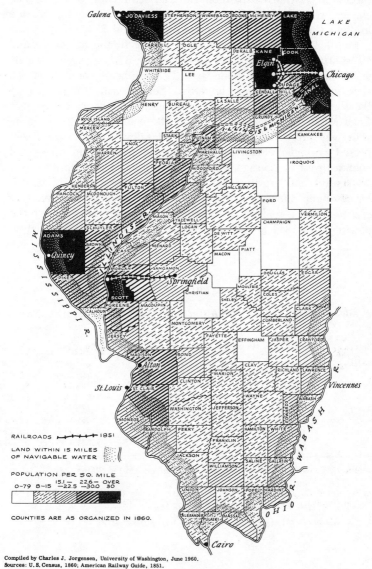

RAILROADS ━┿━┿━┿━ 1851

LAND WITHIN 15 MILES
OF NAVIGABLE WATER

POPULATION PER SQ. MILE

| 0-79 | 8-15 | 15.1–22.5 | 22.6–30.0 | OVER 30 |

COUNTIES ARE AS ORGANIZED IN 1860.

Compiled by Charles J. Jorgensen, University of Washington, June 1960.
Sources: U. S. Census, 1860; American Railway Guide, 1851.

They not only point up the growth of a market oriented economy, but also illustrate the first two points made in this chapter: the surges of westward expansion and the redirection of trade. The changes described for Illinois were paralleled during this decade in other states, such as Wisconsin, Indiana, and Iowa.

Map 1 illustrates the population density of Illinois by county, and transportation facilities available in 1850. With navigable waterways on almost every boundary, the peripheral counties of the state were the most densely settled. Settlers had also pushed up the Illinois river, and after the connection of that waterway with Lake Michigan at Chicago in 1848, the counties along the entire waterway prospered. The 111 miles of railways in the state connected Springfield with the Illinois river and opened up several counties west of Chicago. While the counties adjacent to navigable waterways had grown rapidly, the interior counties had experienced much slower expansion. Table 11 presents data on four counties in the middle of the state, selected at random, for the census years 1840 and 1850. Only one county had a population

TABLE 11

GROWTH OF POPULATION AND SELECTED PRODUCTS, ILLINOIS
1840-1850

County		Population	Wheat, bu.	Corn, bu.	Swine
Dewitt	1840	3,237	25,400	285,600	15,000
	1850	5,002–56%	22,000	705,000	10,000
Logan	1840	2,333	12,400	234,500	16,600
	1850	5,128–82%	27,000	840,000	16,000
Macon	1840	3,039	21,300	173,000	13,300
	1850	3,988–30%	22,000	698,000	17,000
McLean	1840	6,565	44,500	350,800	25,700
	1850	10,163–55%	64,000	1,227,000	30,000

Source: U. S. Census Bureau, Sixth Census of the United States, 1840
(Washington: Blair and Rives, 1841).
U. S. Census Bureau, Seventh Census of the United States, 1850
(Washington: Government Printing Office, 1852).

All production figures rounded to nearest hundred.

MAP 2

Population Density, by County, and Transportation Facilities, Illinois:
1861 (April 1)

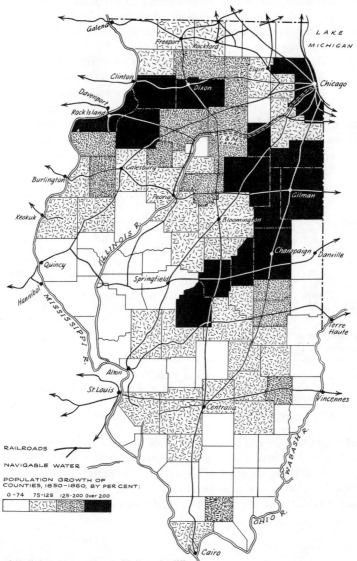

RAILROADS

NAVIGABLE WATER

POPULATION GROWTH OF
COUNTIES, 1850-1860, BY PER CENT:

0 - 74   75-125   125-200   Over 200

Compiled by Charles J. Jorgensen, University of Washington, June 1960.
Sources: U. S. Census, 1860; G. R. Taylor and I. D. Neu, "The American
Railroad Network, 1861-1890," Harvard University Press, 1956.

growth above the state average for the decade (79 per cent); the
others were substantially below the average. Wheat expanded very
little. The big increase was in corn, as feed for livestock. At this
time the major market of Illinois was still to the South, and Illinois
farmers who lived close to navigable waterways sent their produce
to New Orleans. Chicago and the lake trade to the East were just
becoming important.

The rapid changes of the 1850's can be seen from Map 2. The
population of the state increased by 101 per cent; the railroad network of about 2700 miles opened up the whole interior of the
state and connected it effectively with the East. The largest increase was in the interior counties which the railroad made accessible. Table 12 shows the striking growth of the same four

TABLE 12

GROWTH OF POPULATION AND SELECTED PRODUCTS, ILLINOIS
1850-1860

County		Population	Wheat, bu.	Corn, bu.	Swine
Dewitt	1850	5,002	22,000	705,000	10,000
	1860	10,820-112%	151,000-585%	1,409,000-100%	18,000-80%
Logan	1850	5,128	27,000	840,000	16,000
	1860	14,272-178%	254,000-840%	2,656,000-216%	45,000-180%
Macon	1850	3,988	22,000	698,000	17,000
	1860	13,738-242%	151,000-585%	1,637,000-134%	24,000-41%
McLean	1850	10,163	64,000	1,227,000	30,000
	1860	28,772-184%	464,000-625%	3,229,000-163%	52,000-73%
State Average % increase		101%	114%	101%	19%

Source: U. S. Census Bureau, Census of 1850.
U. S. Census Bureau, Eighth Census of the United States, Agriculture
(Washington: Government Printing Office, 1865).

All production figures rounded to nearest hundred.

counties in Table 11. The importance of the growth of wheat output was that it was a cash crop for export to the East—striking
evidence of the growing market orientation of the farmer. The
growth of the export trade to the East was impressive indeed.
Chart VI-XI shows the growth of grain exports out of Chicago.

CHART VI-XI

Shipments of Flour and Grain from Chicago: 1839–1861

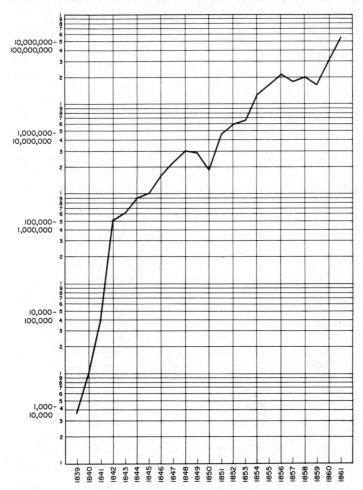

From approximately two million bushels in 1850, they grew to fifty million bushels in 1861. If we add the exports from other Lake Michigan ports, of which Milwaukee was the most important, the figure was sixty-nine million bushels.[16] Shipments of livestock and other products to the East also gained markedly during the decade.

Table 13 shows the consequences of the expansion in Illinois. Though the number of farmers increased by only 39 per cent,

TABLE 13

SELECTED FARM PRODUCTION IN ILLINOIS
1850-1860

Item	Unit	1850	1860	% Increase
Farmers		141,000	196,600	39
Improved Acres		5,039,545	13,251,473	163
Farm value, gross	$	96,133,000	432,531,000	350
Acre value	$	19.20	31.85	65
* * * * * * * related to production * * * * * * *				
Wheat	bu.	9,414,000	23,837,000	114
Corn	bu.	57,646,000	115,175,000	101
Hay	ton.	601,952	1,834,265	205
Butter	lb.	12,526,000	28,337,000	126
Swine	ea.	1,915,000	2,280,000	19
Milk cows	ea.	295,000	533,000	81
Other cattle	ea.	541,000	882,000	63

Source: U. S. Census Bureau, Census of 1850.
          U. S. Census Bureau, Census of 1860, Agriculture.

improved acreage increased by 163 per cent and gross farm value by 350 per cent. Individual commodity output showed equally impressive gains. The small increase in swine production reflected a relative decline in exports to the South, since it was the major market for cured pork. The relatively greater increase in corn than in beef cattle reflected the fact that, before the advent of the

---

[16] U.S. Census Bureau, *Eighth Census of the United States, 1860, Agriculture* (Washington: Government Printing Office, 1865), p. cl. While railroads were instrumental in bringing the grain to lake ports, water transport was still cheaper than rail to New York. The necessity for several transfers as a result of different gauges was an element in early railroad costs.

railroad, cattle were driven to Ohio, fattened, and then sent East. After the railroad, they were fattened on corn in Illinois and then shipped by rail.[17] All of this added up to a market-oriented agriculture in which productivity was growing rapidly.

IV

The economic structure of the West, even when it was still primarily oriented to river trade, was in marked contrast with that of the South. The pattern of land ownership and the size of individual farms reflected the different production possibilities of the two areas. The vigorous growth of Cincinnati, Louisville, St. Louis, and Pittsburgh had no counterpart in the South outside New Orleans. Even more striking were the many small towns and villages which dotted the West and showed every sign of vigorous expansion. (See Chart III, Chapter X.) Locally oriented manufacturing trade and services developed along with the widespread pattern of towns in order to serve local consuming markets.

In the years between 1843 and 1860, western growth gave evidence of the promise that would be realized in the post-Civil War era. The redirection of its trade and the increased market orientation of western producers hastened the growth of towns and cities, and led to increased specialization in cash crops. A growing diversity of economic activity supplemented the early dependence upon cereal production. In contrast to the South, the growing income from the export sector of the West and the economic structure of the region resulted in expansion and diversification of the area's economy. The salient characteristics which made this development possible were:

1. The broad range of production possibilities made possible a variety of exports.[18] While the region's factor endowments provided an obvious comparative advantage for agricultural products, specifically wheat and corn, the West early produced lead

---

[17] In 1859 livestock was the most important single commodity in through-traffic eastward on the Pennsylvania Railroad. Johnson, *et al., History,* I, 240.

[18] Cf. Arnold Zellner and George G. S. Murphy, "Sequential Growth, the Labor Safety Valve Doctrine, and the Development of American Unionism," *Journal of Economic History* XIX, No. 3 (September 1959), 402-21.

in Missouri, copper in Michigan, and iron—first at Pittsburgh and then in the Lake Superior area. Lumber was still another major extractive industry.

2. The major export industries resulted in a variety of subsidiary industries, some of which became important new exports. There were obvious locational advantages to processing wheat and corn into flour, corn meal, ham, bacon, salt pork, and whiskey within the region. Soap and candles were additional by-products of the processing industry in Cincinnati. In addition to the McCormick reaper plant at Chicago, the agricultural machinery and implement industry developed in Canton and Dayton, Ohio, and in a number of other western urban areas.[19] Pittsburgh manufactured iron in a variety of semi-finished forms.

3. It was necessary to have substantial investment in transportation and other social overhead facilities in order to increase the supply of western staples. Canals, railroads, warehouses and the various urban facilities which developed in the West effectively reduced the cost of producing and exporting goods as well as the production costs of goods produced for the regional market.

4. Distribution of income was influenced by the distribution of property ownership and the factor proportions in the major export commodities. Wheat and corn could be produced most efficiently on the "family-size farm," given early nineteenth century technology. Slavery existed only in the border states. As a consequence, income was more evenly distributed than it was in the South. The growing income from the export sector immediately affected a large portion of the western populace, and led to a pattern of consumer demand which was the most important immediate influence in the widespread growth of small towns and residentiary industry which characterized the West. Retail trade, services, small machine and tool shops, printing and publishing, glass and stone products, leather goods, wood products, metal fabrication, and so on, developed in western urban areas in response to regional consumer demand. Some

---

[19] The value of agricultural implements produced in the West grew from $1.9 million in 1850 to $7.9 million in 1860. U.S. Census Bureau, *Preliminary Report on the Eighth Census* (Washington: Government Printing Office, 1862), p. 169.

were by nature residentiary; some could be efficiently produced on a moderate scale of production and developed in the larger cities of the West, like Cincinnati.[20] Others were initially protected by the high transport cost of imports. As income grew in the West, manufactures and services grew with it, and resulted in an increasingly diversified economy and the development of new exports.

5. The attitude of the West towards investment in skills, training, and education led to an early willingness of westerners to devote tax money for education and training. The statistics on schools per 100 square miles, literacy among the white population, per cent of whites in school, and tax money devoted to public education all show a great difference in favor of the West over the South.[21] The westerner looked upon education as a capital investment with a high rate of return. The pattern of income distribution resulted in a broad tax base and equally broad benefits to the families whose children received a public education. The structure of productive activity demonstrated to the western producer the advantages that would accrue from improvements in skills and knowledge. The westerner invested heavily in spreading the skills, knowledge and technology which were an essential prerequisite to taking advantage of the agricultural and industrial opportunities clearly evident in the decade before the Civil War.

---

[20] Cincinnati was an early center of production for the regional market. Clothing, boots and shoes, furniture, liquor, paper and publishing, iron manufactures, and many other commodities were produced there. For statistics on such production, see Berry, *Western Prices,* pp. 254-55.

[21] Cf. *Compendium of the Seventh Census,* pp. 141-54.

XII

THE ECONOMIC STRUCTURE OF THE NORTHEAST

The New England and Middle Atlantic states may be combined into a single region for purposes of analysis. There were important differences (the Middle Atlantic states had a far more favorable agriculture and accessibility to the West), but the region as a whole shifted from commerce and trade to become a manufacturing region between 1815 and 1860. While the beginnings of its manufacturing go back to the earlier period, particularly to the Embargo era, the period 1815–1819 was marked by significant readjustments in the face of English competition. Sustained and accelerated growth of manufacturing came later. Daniel Webster's celebrated speech against the tariff in 1824 and his equally celebrated remarks of 1828 in favor of protection have frequently been taken to mark the transformation, at least of New England. Webster himself said that with the passage of the Act of 1824, New England did avail herself of the new opportunities and engage in manufacturing. Taussig, however, offers convincing evidence that the Tariff Act of 1824 played very little part in accelerating manufacturing.[1] If we are to explain the structural transformation of the Northeast, we must look further than the tariff.

---

[1] Frank W. Taussig, *The Tariff History of the United States*, 6th Ed. (New York: G. P. Putnam's Sons, 1914), Chapters III, IV, V, and VI. Hereafter cited as *Tariff History*. The act of 1816 did accelerate cotton spinning after 1819 when the drop in price of cotton yarn made the effective rate very high on coarse grade cotton. Taussig concluded that by 1824 cotton spinning could stand on its own feet.

I

It is important to distinguish the manufacturing development which I have in mind from the widespread existence of household manufacture and locally oriented handicraft activities which accounted for so much of the census totals of manufactures in early periods. *Niles' Register* gives a census of the manufacturing interests in and around Mt. Pleasant, Ohio, in 1815, a town described as having a population of about 500.

> . . . 3 saddlers, 3 hatters, 4 blacksmiths, 4 weavers, 6 boot and shoemakers, 8 carpenters, 3 tailors, 3 cabinet makers, 1 baker, 1 apothecary, and 2 wagon makers shops—2 tanneries, 1 shop for making wool carding machines, 1 with a machine for spinning wool, 1 manufactory for spinning thread from flax, 1 nail factory, 2 wool carding machines. . . . Within the distance of six miles from the town were—9 merchant mills, 2 grist mills, 12 saw mills, 1 paper mill with 2 vats, 1 woolen factory with 4 looms and 2 fulling mills.[2]

This wide variety of manufacturing existed because of the isolation of the local market from imported goods as a result of high transfer costs. Reduction in transport costs and the extension of the size of the market resulted in specialization, division of labor and the localization of industry. The diverse activities which characterized the isolated town of 1815 would be reduced, as the market widened, to only those which are typically residentiary in character. The decline of household manufactures between 1820 and 1845, as the Erie Canal opened up western New York, has been illustrated graphically in Arthur Cole's *The American Wool Manufacture.*[3]

Industrialization of a region means the development of manufacturing for a larger market than the particular geographic area, which implies the localization of manufacturing activity. If this localization reflects only the location advantages of processing an exhaustible resource such as lumbering or copper smelting, it hardly qualifies as an industrial area. Such processing, while it may

---

2 *Niles' National Register* X (June 8, 1816), as quoted in Taylor, *Transportation Revolution,* pp. 207-8.

3 Two Vols. (Cambridge: Harvard University Press, 1926), p. 280.

lead to further manufacturing development, has two important disadvantages as a base for sustained manufacturing expansion:

1. It is immediately tied to a resource which is subject to diminishing returns.
2. It is of a character which induces little additional manufacturing activity in the way of subsidiary or complementary industry.

The first of these points is obvious. It is the second which gets at the heart of the much abused notion of industrialization. An industrial revolution consists of a dynamic series of changes in which initial developments in manufacturing provide strong inducements for additional investment in subsidiary or complementary industries.[4] Not only must the initial manufacturing be of a character that has extensive backward and/or forward linkages,[5] but the factor endowments of the region must be such that these new industries will be located within the region rather than outside it. It is difficult to generalize about a particular kind of manufacturing initiating industrialization. The process depends both upon linkages associated with a given industry at a particular state of technology [6] and upon other factor endowments, which dictate to what degree this induced investment will occur within the region or nation rather than elsewhere. While these linkages are important in getting industrialization under way when the region is a marginal producer of manufactures, and facilitate investment decisions in initiating new industries, the sustained development and spread of manufactures ultimately requires that the region's factor endowments improve. While analysis of the early manufacturing development of an economy inevitably focuses on the industries that first succeeded and upon the complementary and subsidiary industry that evolved, a discussion of the spread of manufacturing beyond these immediate industries requires an examination of a region's changing factor endowments.

---

[4] Hirschman's emphasis on unbalanced growth strikes me as a particularly useful way to look at the whole process. Albert O. Hirschman, *The Strategy of Economic Development* (New Haven: Yale University Press, 1958), Chapter IV.

[5] Hirschman, *Strategy of Economic Development*, Chapter VI.

[6] Quite obviously these linkages would change at different states of technology and as a result an industry might well set off industrialization in one era and not in another.

One aspect of the localization of industry is the growth of a large number of specialized firms. Localization of industry has not necessarily implied large plants, but it has meant an increasing specialization of function in large numbers of relatively small plants. As the market grew larger, the firm became increasingly specialized. Auxiliary activities, which initially had to be undertaken by an individual firm in order to produce or market a product, could be more efficiently done by other firms concentrating on producing the equipment, supplying the raw material, marketing the product, or even training the labor force. It was this growth of specialized function with the increasing size of the market that resulted in Adam Smith's classic argument that productivity of labor is fundamentally influenced by specialization of function.[7] It was the development of a large number of complementary and auxiliary manufacturing activities in typically small, but growing, plants which characterized the emergence of the Northeast as a manufacturing center, and which contributed significantly to increased efficiency in the economy.

II

The development of manufacturing in the United States before 1860 was primarily of two kinds: resource-oriented manufacturing consisting, at least initially, of the simple processing of raw materials in which there were location advantages to sites near raw materials (lumber, meat packing) or at breaks in transportation (flour milling); and manufacturing in which capital requirements were relatively modest (cotton goods, boots and shoes, men's clothing, leather, and woolen goods). The former were the major types of manufacturing in the West. They influenced the evolving pattern of western urbanization, Cincinnati and Chicago, for example. The Northeast, which accounted for three-fourths of the country's manufacturing employment in 1850 and for 71 per cent of it in 1860, concentrated on the latter type. Table 14 gives a breakdown of the leading branches of manufacturing in 1860. Tex-

---

[7] Cf. Stigler, "The Division of Labor is Limited by the Extent of the Market," *loc. cit.*

TABLE 14

LEADING BRANCHES OF MANUFACTURE IN THE UNITED STATES, 1860

Item	Employment	Value of Product (000's of $)	Value Added by Manufacture (000's of $)	Rank by Value Added
1. Flour & Meal	27,682	$248,580	$40,083	4
2. Cotton Goods	114,955	107,338	54,671	1
3. Lumber	75,595	104,928	53,570	2
4. Boots & Shoes	123,026	91,889	49,161	3
5. Men's Clothing	114,800	80,831	36,681	5
6. Iron (cast, forged, rolled, wrought)	48,975	73,175	35,689	6
7. Leather	22,679	67,306	22,786	9
8. Woolen Goods	40,597	60,685	25,030	8
9. Liquors	12,706	56,589	21,667	10
10. Machinery	41,223	52,010	32,566	7

Source: U. S. Census Bureau, Eighth Census of the United States, 1860, Manufactures (Washington: Government Printing Office, 1865), pp. 733-742.

tiles played the leading role, and were strategic in terms of backward and forward linkages in the case of four of the ten leading
manufactures (cotton goods, men's clothing, woolen goods, machinery).

After Samuel Slater's initial undertaking at Pawtucket, early developments in the cotton textile industry were modest in size and
scattered throughout the East. Between 1815 and 1831, however,
the number of spindles per establishment tripled, and by 1860 the
number had tripled again.[8] Introduction of the power loom and
the performance of all cloth-making operations with water power
initiated the growing size, specialization, and localization of the
industry.[9] While the Boston Manufacturing Company at Waltham
in 1813 was spectacularly successful,[10] and the industry revived
and expanded in the 1820's, it was not until the decade of the 1830's

[8] V. S. Clark, *History of Manufactures in the United States*, 3 Vols. (New
York: McGraw-Hill, for the Carnegie Institution, 1929), I, 452. Hereafter cited
as *History of Manufactures*.

[9] Clark, *History of Manufactures*, I, 450-53.

[10] So successful that even during the difficult period of British dumping of
manufactures from 1816-19 it earned a very good rate of return.

that the tendency toward specialization and localization was clearly evident.[11] Before 1830, mills in Virginia had about the same number of spindles as those in Massachusetts. By 1860 the average cotton factory in New England had nearly 7000 spindles, compared to 2000 in the South and West.[12] The average number of looms per factory was one hundred and sixty-three in New England, twenty-four in the South, and forty-nine in the West.[13] The localization of the industry was also marked. In 1860 70 per cent of the capital was invested in New England mills, and 75 per cent of the cloth came from there. Another 23 per cent came from the Middle Atlantic states.[14]

The early success of the Waltham mill was a result of producing a coarse cloth in growing demand in America, and which could be woven on the new power loom. This plain white "sheeting" lent itself to mass production, and met a wide variety of needs in a predominantly agricultural society. New England mills following in the footsteps of the Boston Manufacturing Company found they could compete with British textiles in this type of product, and had a market that grew with the developing regional interdependence.

Between 1820 and 1860, the relative efficiency of cotton textile firms improved vis-à-vis competition from abroad,[15] and the product line was broadened somewhat. Forward linkages from the cotton textile industry in the form of final consumer goods were an important part of the spread of manufacturing in the Northeast, particularly after the innovation of the sewing machine. It was the backward linkage into the textile machinery industry which had the more important consequences for the growth of manufacturing. Between the creation of a machine shop as an adjunct of the Boston Manufacturing Company in 1813 and the Civil War, "the manu-

---

[11] Clark, *History of Manufactures,* I, 452.

[12] *Loc. cit.*

[13] *Eighth Census, Manufactures,* pp. x-xiii. Factories in the middle states were smaller on the average than in New England but larger than in the South and West.

[14] *Ibid.,* pp. ix, xi.

[15] The most obvious evidence was the United States ability to enter the export market in cotton textiles in the last three decades before the Civil War. For some indirect evidence of productivity changes, see Caroline Ware, *The Early New England Cotton Manufacture, a Study in Industrial Beginnings* (Boston: Houghton Mifflin Company, 1931), pp. 112-14.

facture of textile machinery evolved from a local trade sporadically practiced by many small shops to an industry characterized by a few large shops and an increasing number of smaller more specialized shops all of which were beginning to compete vigorously for business on a national scale." [16] In the early period, many cotton textile mills made their own machinery, but with the growth of the market the machine shops became separated from the mills, and began to concentrate on machinery construction. Some were highly specialized, building only one or two types of machinery. Others broadened to include a number of different types of textile machinery, plus machine tools, locomotives, stationary engines, and a number of other metal products.[17] This backward linkage into textile machinery had further important linkage effects back into iron casting, machine tools, and metal working, creating in the process skills and training which were effectively applied to other machinery and machine tool undertakings. It is worth quoting Gibb's conclusion with respect to this formative period.

> The manufacture of cloth was America's greatest industry. For a considerable part of the 1813–53 period the manufacture of textile machinery appears to have been America's greatest heavy goods industry, occupying the primary position in point of size and value of product among all industries which fabricated metal. Size, however, is not the most critical measure of importance. From the textile mills and the textile machine shops came the men who supplied most of the tools for the American Industrial Revolution. From these mills and shops sprang directly the machine tool and locomotive industries together with a host of less basic metal fabricating trades. The part played by the textile machinery industry in fostering American metal working skills in the early nineteenth century was a crucial one.[18]

The pattern of development in terms of growing specialization and localization of woolen goods paralleled the cotton textile industry in many respects. The most important difference was the later technical developments in wool, a difference also true in Britain.[19] While the industry experienced rapid technical advance

---

16 George S. Gibb, *The Saco-Lowell Shops, Textile Machinery Building in New England, 1813-1849*. Harvard Studies in Business History 16 (Cambridge: Harvard University Press, 1950), p. 168. Hereafter cited as *Saco-Lowell Shops*.

17 *Ibid.*, p. 168.

18 *Ibid.*, p. 179.

19 Cole, *The American Wool Manufacture*, I, 234.

in the years before 1830, the two succeeding decades were periods of accelerated growth. The woolen industry became highly localized in New England, with Massachusetts assuming the pre-eminent position just as in cotton textiles, and the wool textile machinery industry became effectively separated from the woolen industry. A few large, specialized enterprises dominated loom building, scouring, carding, and spinning machinery.[20] Not only did the wool working mills give up their machine construction and become dependent upon the specialized builder of textile apparatus, but the small local machine shops were also displaced by the specialized machinery producer.[21]

In the final decade before the Civil War the concentration of industry and the growth of large-scale, specialized firms were still further accentuated. Between 1850 and 1860, the value of output in New England mills increased 62 per cent, compared to 7 per cent in the Middle Atlantic States and 10 per cent in the West. In absolute terms, the value of output in New England was $40.6 million compared to $15.9 million in the Middle Atlantic States, $3.1 million in the Western states, and $2 million in the Southern states.[22] The size of firms grew rapidly in the Northeast, geared to a national market, in contrast to the predominantly local market of the West. Writing of the period before 1870, Cole says:

> For the whole area of the Ohio and Upper Mississippi Valleys, the mills averaged less than two sets apiece, although New England factories could boast an average of five to six sets—more productive sets too. Furthermore, the connection of these establishments with the local market remained intimate. . . . Mr. John L. Hays, moving spirit and first secretary of the National Association of Wool Manufactures, summarizes the situation when he reported of Western producers: that they were "confident if they did not attempt to make their mills too large, and continued to seek their principal markets in the counties and local districts where they were established, ... they should be prosperous." [23]

While the boot and shoe industry was more primitive than the textile industry in terms of technology and factory organization, it showed an equal tendency to concentrate in New England, par-

---

[20] *Loc. cit.*

[21] *Loc. cit.*

[22] *Eighth Census, Manufactures,* p. xxxv.

[23] Cole, *The American Wool Manufacture,* I, 276.

ticularly Massachusetts, and for the size of firm there to exceed that of firms elsewhere. Approximately 60 per cent of the industry was located in this area, more than half of these establishments in Massachusetts.[24] Their average capitalization and number of employees were well above the mean for the rest of the country. Between the 1830's and 1860, the industry passed from the domestic stage to the factory system, with the increasing size of the market the most important element in this transformation.[25] By 1860 the sewing machine, which had already revolutionized the clothing industry, was just beginning a similar transformation of the boot and shoe industry.

The products of the iron industry present a varied picture during the period prior to the Civil War. While pig iron production was concentrated in Pennsylvania (580,049 tons out of the United States total of 987,559 tons in 1860),[26] the various products derived from it were more scattered. Bar, sheet and railroad iron were concentrated in Pennsylvania, while Massachusetts was the leading state in iron wire and iron forgings. New York, Pennsylvania, and Massachusetts, in that order, produced the bulk of the iron castings.

An important part of iron output was turned immediately into final consumer goods. Stoves were the major single commodity, with an 1860 value of $10,709,972. Railroads were the most important single demand from industry. The value of bar, sheet, and railroad iron produced in 1860 was almost $32 million. A little less than half that value, equal to 235,107 tons, was railroad iron, yet railroads were not the dominant factor in the iron industry. While the value added of rails was approximately $6.5 million in 1860 and roughly equal to the value added of bar iron, it was dwarfed by the value added of the polyglot classification of iron castings, which was $21 million in 1860. Indeed, the value added in stove making alone was equal to that of iron rails. The iron industry mirrored the state of American manufacturing prior to the era of steel (which was just beginning to develop). Iron was used in a

---

[24] *Eighth Census, Manufactures,* p. lxvii.

[25] Cf. Blanche Hazard, *The Organization of the Boot and Shoe Industry in Massachusetts Before 1875.* Harvard Economic Studies XXIII (Cambridge: Harvard University Press, 1921), Chapters IV and V.

[26] Statistics from this section are from *Eighth Census, Manufactures,* pp. clxxviii-cxvi.

broad range of consumer and producer goods, and casting was the major method by which the metal could be transformed to meet the needs of the time. After 1845, rolling mills especially geared to making heavy rails had developed in eastern Pennsylvania, and they presaged the growing importance of the railroad in inducing large-scale production in the iron and steel industry.[27] But such a development was just beginning before the Civil War.

III

There can be no doubt that American industrialization was well under way before the Civil War. Since Tench Coxe's first rough estimates in 1810, the value of manufacturing output had increased approximately tenfold, while population had increased only four and one-half times.[28] In the final decade before the Civil War, cotton textile output had increased by 77 per cent, wool textiles by 42 per cent, hosiery goods by 608 per cent, carpets by 45 per cent, men's clothing by 55 per cent, boots and shoes by 70 per cent, coal mined by 182 per cent, pig iron by 54 per cent, bar, sheet, and railroad iron by 100 per cent, and steam engines and machinery by 66 per cent.[29]

While the Census data before 1840 are so poor that they are almost worthless,[30] the gross outlines of this manufacturing development are clear. Between 1810 and 1820, manufacturing output showed a drastic decline in every state in the Northeast, a decline much magnified by the incomplete nature of the returns for 1820 and the inclusion of household manufactures in the 1810 figure. By 1830 most northeastern states showed an increase over the 1810 figures, and Massachusetts showed a very substantial increase, indicating that the textile and boot and shoe industries had effectively taken hold during that decade. It is the decade of the 1830's which gives evidence of accelerated growth of manufacturing

---

[27] Clark, *History of Manufactures,* I, 513.

[28] *Eighth Census, Manufactures,* p. v.

[29] Statistics from *Eighth Census, Manufactures,* Introduction.

[30] Cf. Robert C. Morgan and W. A. Shannon, *Treasury Department Technical Paper No. 10,* Executive Documents, 34th Congress, 1st Session, 1855-56, Vol. 4.

throughout the Northeast. Monographic studies of the individual
industries support the very incomplete census returns, which show
a dramatic expansion during that decade in Connecticut, New Jersey, New York, Pennsylvania, and Rhode Island. Manufacturing
incorporations, and/or total incorporations where only the latter
were available, indicate a similar trend.[31] Successive census figures
show a continuing rapid growth of manufacturing and indicate that
by the end of the 1830's the acceleration of manufacturing development was well under way. The ability of the Northeast to weather
the very sharp depression of 1839–1843 and to emerge with expansion in manufacturing during the rest of the 1840's is vivid
evidence of the new position of manufacturing. The *Massachusetts
Manufacturing Census of 1837* shows a value of output of
$86,282,616, while that of 1845, only two years after the bottom
of the depression, was $124,749,457.[32]

IV

The timing, pace, and character of American manufacturing development before the Civil War resulted from the following
factors:

1. By all odds, the most important influence was the growth in the
   size of the domestic market. The two English commissions
   which investigated United States manufacturing in the 1850's,
   whose reports represent the most careful evaluation of American manufacturing progress prior to the Civil War,[33] placed

---

[31] George H. Evans, *Business Incorporations in the United States, 1800-1843*
(New York: National Bureau of Economic Research, 1948), Chart 1, p. 13;
Chart 3, p. 23.

[32] John P. Bigelow, Secretary of the Commonwealth, *Statistical Tables Exhibiting the Condition and Products of Certain Branches of Industry in Massachusetts, for the Year Ending April 1, 1837* (Boston: Dutton and Wentworth,
1838), and Francis DeWitt, Secretary of the Commonwealth, *Statistical Information Relating to Certain Branches of Industry in Massachusetts for the
Year Ending June 1, 1855* (Boston: William White, Printer of the State, 1856).
The figure for 1855 was $295,820,681.

[33] The two investigations were: The official reports presented to the British
Parliament by Sir Joseph Whitworth and George Wallis, later published
separately as *The Industry of the United States in Machinery, Manufactures,
and Useful and Ornamental Arts* (London: George Routledge & Co., 1854),

first emphasis on the size and composition of the market. They noted not only the absolute size and rate of growth of the population, but also the high average wealth of the people. Wallis was particularly impressed by the fact that "all classes of the people may be said to be well dressed and the cast off clothes of one class are never worn by another." [34] They were most impressed by the standardized method of production which lent itself to mechanical techniques and low unit costs geared to large-scale output of a standardized product. The growing localization of industry, specialization of function, and increasing size of firm were all basically related to the growth in the market, which stemmed from the regional specialization and growth of interregional trade beginning after 1815, but was *really* accelerated with the surge of expansion in the 1830's. The markets for textiles, clothing, boots and shoes, and other consumer goods were national in scope, reflecting the decline of self-sufficiency and the growth of specialization and division of labor. Derived demand for machinery and products of iron expanded in response to the consumer goods industries. The cotton trade was the immediate impetus for this regional specialization, and the growth of cotton income in the 1830's was the most important proximate influence upon the spurt of manufacturing growth of that decade. The growth of specialized methods of distribution and the decline of the auction system betokened this new dimension of the market.[35]

This growing interregional specialization was greatly aided by declining transport costs. The fall in ocean freight rates, in western river freight rates, and in rates on the Erie and Pennsylvania Canals were important early influences. Even before the advent of the railroad, interregional trade had effectively

---

and *Report of the Commission on the Machinery of the United States* (Parliamentary Papers, 1854-55, L). They are summarized in D. L. Burn, "The Genesis of American Engineering Competition, 1850-1870," *Economic History,* Supplement to the *Economic Journal* II, No. 6 (January 1931), 292-311. The Whitworth volume is hereafter cited as *Industry of the United States,* the report of the Commission as *Machinery of the United States.*

[34] Whitworth and Wallis, *Industry of the United States,* p. 99.

[35] Cf. Clark, *History of Manufactures,* I, 356-60; Cole, *The American Wool Manufacture,* Chapter VII, p. 286; and the abundant material in *Eighth Census, Manufactures,* Introduction.

widened the market for eastern manufactures. The development of industry in Massachusetts in the 1820's and in the other northeastern states in the early 1830's gives evidence of the rapid development of interregional trade dependent upon declining water transportation rates. The spread of railroads in the Northeast between 1835 and 1850 did play an important role in the further growth and localization of industry. This was true of New England in general and Massachusetts in particular, where the most efficient size firms in textiles and in a variety of other industries tended to develop. The effective connection of East and West by railroad in the 1850's further decreased the transfer cost barrier to localized industry.

2. Concentration of manufacturing in the Northeast stemmed from a number of factors, some of which were specific to a particular industry. The most important underlying reason was the developments in the years before 1815, particularly during the French and Napoleonic Wars, when the groundwork was laid. The growth of large urban centers, the development of a capital market-first around foreign trade and then for the cotton trade, social overhead investment in transportation facilities, and the growing supply of labor-first from agriculture and then from immigrants, will be examined in turn.

By 1815, the major urban centers and the largest market for manufactures existed in the Northeast. Rapid growth during the years 1793–1808 had made New York, Philadelphia, Baltimore, and Boston natural centers for the development of residentiary manufacturing. While Baltimore and Boston remained fundamentally commercial and financial cities, Philadelphia and New York became the two most important manufacturing cities in the country. With manufacturing valued at $136 million and $159 million, respectively, in 1860, they possessed approximately 15 per cent of the country's total manufacturing output. The composition of manufacturing in these cities indicates that much of it was residentiary, or had begun as locally oriented manufacturing and gradually expanded to serve a larger market.[36] The major manufactures in

---

[36] See the breakdown in *Eighth Census, Manufactures,* pp. 379-85, for New York, and pp. 522-27 for Philadelphia.

New York were men's clothing, sugar refining, boots and shoes, bread and crackers, cabinet furniture, machinery and steam engines, and newspaper printing. Philadelphia showed a similar pattern. In contrast to the highly localized manufacturing which developed in New England, the manufactures of these two cities, with a few exceptions such as men's clothing, were primarily geared to serve the expanding local and regional market.

The early development of a capital market in the Northeast around foreign trade and the cotton trade, as compared with its relatively primitive state in the other regions, was another important influence on manufacturing development. The growth of savings institutions and financial intermediaries in the Northeast aided a wide variety of early manufactures. The development of the New England textile industry was implemented by the shift of capital from shipping into textiles.[37] While the location of sites with abundant water power dictated specific locations within New England, the predilection of Boston capitalists for textile manufacturing within the region was a contributing factor.[38] The abundance of financial intermediaries in Boston and the Northeast provided the large amounts of loan capital essential to rapid expansion of the textile firms.[39] It should be noted that while foreign capital went almost exclusively into transportation and financing cotton expansion, the indirect effect was to increase the supply of capital and therefore to facilitate the financing of manufacturing.

Banking, insurance, port facilities, warehousing, the development of a distribution system for imports, and the early growth of roads and turnpikes connecting the hinterland with the major ports were all social overhead investments aiding the development of manufacturing. Manufacturing developed in those industries where imports had been largest, demonstrating that a market existed, and a distribution system to reach that market had been

---

[37] Clark, *History of Manufactures,* I, 368.

[38] It also played a part in the localization of the shoe industry. See Edgar M. Hoover, Jr., *Location Theory and the Shoe and Leather Industries.* Harvard Economic Studies LV (Cambridge: Harvard University Press, 1937), p. 268.

[39] Cf. Lance Davis, "Sources of Industrial Finance: The American Textile Industry, A Case Study," *Explorations in Entrepreneurial History* IX, No. 4 (April 1957), 189-203; and by the same author, "The New England Textile Mills and the Capital Markets: A Study of Industrial Borrowing, 1840-1860," *Journal of Economic History* XX, No. 1 (March 1960), 1-30.

created.[40] While the British recaptured a large share of the market between 1815–1819, the tariff-protected early growth and the solid expansion of the industry in subsequent decades merely followed the path of the well-developed import trade.

While the supply of labor did not reflect the prior development of the region in any immediate sense, in an indirect sense it did in these important respects:

1. The earlier agricultural settlement in New England not only provided the well-known female labor force of the early textile mills, but it was also at an increasing comparative disadvantage in competition with western agriculture, which resulted in ready migration from the farm.[41]

2. The prior development of the major seaports and their dominance of the country's foreign trade resulted in their becoming centers of immigration. English and German immigrants were relatively better off and proved relatively mobile within this country. The Irish were destitute, and formed a reservoir of unskilled labor in the Northeast. In 1850, 55.5 per cent of the immigrants were in the Northeast.[42] Not only did the Irish immigrants shift the supply curve of labor to the right, but their immobility and their lack of skills and social position made them in effect a non-competing wage group at the bottom of the ladder of social structure.[43] They fitted in very well with the needs of an industrializing society.

3. Manufacturing growth in the Northeast reflected a general improvement in its factor endowments vis-à-vis their combination in manufacturing. In the early period, certain industries were leaders in this process and induced further investment, backward into the capital goods industries and forward into final

---

[40] For a discussion of this point in connection with contemporary development problems, see Hirschman, *The Strategy of Economic Development*, Chapter VII.

[41] Cf. Morris D. Morris, "The Recruitment of an Industrial Labor Force in India, with British and American Comparisons," *Comparative Studies in Society and History* II, No. 3 (April 1960), 315-20.

[42] Thomas W. Page, "Distribution of Immigrants in the United States before 1870," *Journal of Political Economy* XX (1912), 676-94.

[43] Brinley Thomas, *Migration and Economic Growth, A Study of Great Britain and the Atlantic Economy* (Cambridge: The University Press, 1954), pp. 166-67.

consumer goods industries.[44] In this regard the textile industry played a leading role. Its backward linkages into textile machinery, machine tools, and iron products in the very early years of manufacturing development have been described above. They were far more important than this quantitative value indicates: witness the numerous other machinery and machine tool products which developed in these shops to provide the needs of other industries. Forward linkages with a vast array of final consumer goods industries to meet the needs of the northeastern urban dweller, the southern slave and planter, and the western farmer made the complex of industries which grew up around cotton and wool the most important in pre-Civil War America.[45] The iron industry too, while a large part of its output served other industries, had important forward linkages in final consumer goods such as stoves and backward linkages in pig iron and coal production.

4. Underlying the backward and forward linkages which induced the chain reaction of manufacturing growth in the Northeast were the conditions that made these subsidiary and complementary industries develop there rather than elsewhere, and which led to sustained technical development of the leading industries themselves. While the growth and structure of the capital market were discussed above, the resource endowments and the quality of labor and entrepreneurial talent deserve further elaboration.

The early growth of the iron industry throughout the Northeast using bog iron and then the Pennsylvania ores led to an early widespread growth of metal work and casting. The large supply of coal in Pennsylvania provided a cheap source of power

---

[44] While the railroad was not itself a manufacturing industry, it did induce manufacturing growth during this period. Its backward linkages into railroad iron, locomotives, and railroad cars were important; yet in the pre-Civil War era it does not compare in importance with the textile industry, as the statistical data in the preceding section indicate. As an impetus to manufacturing development the railroad was more important in its cost reducing effects upon transportation during this period.

[45] The character of consumer demand, therefore, played an important role in forward linkages. The varied demands for clothing in a temperate climate, for example, are in marked contrast to India, where final demand was simply for cloth. I am indebted to my colleague, Morris Davis Morris, for this point.

for steam engines and coke for further iron development. Abundant water power in New England was a critical determinant of textile manufacturing sites. These and other natural resource endowments were clearly vital in the expansion of manufacturing in the Northeast.

Size of the market provided the opportunity, prior development in the Northeast and factor endowments were important in the specific location of manufacturing, but the rapid spread and success of manufacturing, the effective development of backward and forward linkages, owes a basic debt to the quality of labor and entrepreneurial talent. Anyone who reads carefully into the period cannot help but be impressed with:

a. The efficient adaptation of foreign innovations to American manufacturing,
b. The widespread success in innovating a broad range of new manufacturing techniques, particularly labor saving ones, and
c. The widespread mechanical skills and knowledge that made possible the rapid spread of these innovations on the American scene.[46]

Samuel Slater's introduction of spinning machinery was only one spectacular illustration of the introduction of English machinery. Lowell's investigation of the British textile industry, and his subsequent construction of a power loom with the aid of Paul Moody, represented the real beginning of large-scale, efficient cotton textile production. Other illustrations in every branch of manufacturing indicate clearly the willingness and ability of American entrepreneurs and mechanics to take over foreign innovations as their use became practicable.

English investigators of the 1850's were particularly impressed with the American ability to develop new production methods. From Eli Whitney's and Simeon North's development of interchangeable parts and efficient techniques in the small arms industry to the innovations and methods of American arsenals, the armament industries were constantly experimenting in production methods. The lock and clock industries were a source of amazement to the

---

[46] For a more extended discussion of these three points see John E. Sawyer, "The Social Basis of the American System of Manufacturing," *Journal of Economic History* XIV, No. 4 (1954), 361-79.

British commissions,[47] as were the wood-working industries. They noted that individual firms were not necessarily large, but that everything was performed by machinery.[48] Automatic machines for producing wood screws, files, and cut nails all impressed the investigators in comparison with production techniques in Great Britain.[49] The constant concern with laborsaving machinery was considered by the commissioners to be a fundamental explanation of the indigenous development of such innovations, and the relatively high price of labor was considered the driving force.[50] Important innovations developed in every industry, frequently in small shops and firms at the hands of mechanics with little or no formal scientific training.

Equally as impressive as the broad base of mechanical developments was their ready adoption throughout various industries. The commissioners were struck by the different attitude towards machinery in the New World as contrasted with the Old.

> The comparative density of the old and the new countries, differing as they do, will account for the very different feelings with which the increase of machinery has been regarded in many parts of this country [England] and the United States, where the workmen hail with satisfaction all mechanical improvements, the importance and value of which, as releasing them from the drudgery of unskilled labour, they are enabled by education to understand and appreciate.[51]

Contemporaries were in agreement about the underlying causes of the rapid innovation of industrial techniques (whether indigenous or adapted from abroad) and their widespread utilization. Gibb quotes a prevailing view:

> From the habits of early life and the diffusion of knowledge by free schools there exists generally among the mechanics of New England a vivacity in inquiring into the first principles of the

---

[47] Whitworth and Wallis, *Industry of the United States,* p. 12; Parliamentary Commissioners, *Machinery of the United States,* pp. 558, 616, as cited in D. L. Burn, "Genesis of American Engineering Competition," *loc. cit.,* p. 295.

[48] *Ibid.,* p. 294.

[49] *Loc. cit.*

[50] Burn, "Genesis of American Engineering Competition," *loc. cit.,* pp. 306-7. See also Clark, *History of Manufactures,* I, 435, for further testimony from contemporaries on this subject.

[51] Whitworth and Wallis, *Industry of the United States,* Preface, viii.

science to which they are practically devoted. They thus frequently acquire a theoretical knowledge of the processes of the useful arts, which the English laborers may commonly be found to possess after a long apprenticeship and life of patient toil.[52]

Whitworth and Wallis were thoroughly impressed with the importance of broadly based education ". . . so that everybody reads, and intelligence penetrates through the lowest grades of society." [53] It is worth quoting at some length the conclusion of the English investigators with respect to the role of education in American industrialization.

> The compulsory educational clauses adopted in the laws of most of the States, and especially those of New England, by which some three months of every year must be spent at school by the young factory operative under 14 or 15 years of age, secure every child from the cupidity of the parent, or the neglect of the manufacturer; since to profit by the child's labour during three-fourths of the year, he or she must be regularly in attendance in some public or private school conducted by some authorized teacher during the other fourth.
>
> This lays the foundation for that wide-spread intelligence which prevails amongst the factory operatives of the United States; and though at first sight the manufacturer may appear to be restricted in the free use of the labour offered to him, the system re-acts to the permanent advantage of both employer and employed.
>
> The skill of hand which comes of experience is, notwithstanding present defects, rapidly following the perceptive power so keenly awakened by early intellectual training. Quickly learning from the skilful European artisans thrown amongst them by emigration, or imported as instructors, with minds, as already stated, prepared by sound practical education, the Americans have laid the foundation of a wide-spread system of manufacturing operations, the influence of which cannot be calculated upon, and are daily improving upon the lessons obtained from their older and more experienced compeers of Europe.[54]

The critical influence in American manufacturing development was not so much one or two strategic industries, but the general improvement of factor endowments for manufacturing. The most

---

[52] Zachariah Allen, *Science of Mechanics* (Providence: 1829), p. 349, as quoted in Gibb, *Saco-Lowell Shops*, p. 178.

[53] Whitworth and Wallis, *Industry of the United States*, Preface, ix.

[54] *Ibid.*, pp. 160-61.

striking fact is the broad variety of industrial activities which were growing up on every side. No one can read the studies of the British investigators without being impressed that this reflected a broadly based ability to produce profitably a vast range of finished goods. Certainly in the 1820's and 1830's the linkages associated with the textile industry were important when the Northeast was a marginal producer of manufactures. By the middle of the 1840's, however, when the surge of the expansion got under way, it was not one or two industries which were leading sectors, but a much more generalized ability to produce manufactures. The most important contrast between the 1840 Census figures on manufactures and the 1860 figures is not so much the rapid growth of output as the spread of manufacturing into new industries.

The development of manufacturing in the Northeast after the sharp readjustment following the War of 1812 centered around a few industries which had already been demonstrated to possess growing markets. Their location in the Northeast was dictated by prior developments there as well as by the natural resource endowment of abundant water power. The linkages associated with the textile industry were an important influence in the development of the 1820's and early 1830's. It was the growth in the size of the market as a consequence of regional specialization which led to acceleration in manufacturing development, and to the specialization of function of the firm in the 1830's. The cotton trade of the South and the decline in transport costs were the proximate influences in this growing regional specialization and the development of interregional trade.

If the growing size of the market made possible the development of manufacturing, it was the quality of entrepreneurial talent and the labor force that could effectively take advantage of these opportunities. The adaptation of foreign inventions, the variety of native innovations, particularly those which cut labor costs, and the rapid spread of new techniques were indicative of the *quality* of labor and entrepreneurial talent. While the underlying aspirations and motivations of people in American society were important, the investment in human capital was a critical factor both in innovations and in the relative ease with which they could spread. The primary source of this quality of the labor force and entrepreneurial talent was the widespread free education system in the Northeast, although the skills of English and German immigrants were an important supplement.

The surge of expansion that began in 1843 was an era in which the Northeast had ceased being a marginal manufacturing area and could successfully expand into a vast array of industrial goods. By 1860 the *problems* of industrialization were behind in the development of the United States.

XIII

THE ECONOMY 1815-1823

Preceding sections of this part of the study have set the scene for analyzing the economic growth which took place between 1815 and 1860. The statistical evidence of international and interregional flows, together with the structural characteristics of the three separate regions of the United States, provide the necessary evidence. In terms of overall analysis, the foreign sector is really considered as another region, but the greater immobilities and friction which characterized its relationship with those regions comprising the national economy during this period must be recognized.

I

Most Americans expected to pick up in 1815 where they had left off in 1807, and the news of peace in February of that year was sufficient to lead to a sharp drop in import prices. By May the first British ships laden with manufactured goods were coming into American ports, and the major seaports, particularly Baltimore, Philadelphia, and New York, were prosperous and thriving.[1] Yet as Chapter VI has made clear, both external and internal conditions had changed. The years between 1815 and 1818 can be most completely understood if this process of readjustment is examined.

The most significant external change was a world at peace, with all that it implied in terms of reimposed navigation laws and the comparative advantage of Britain in the production of finished goods, particularly textiles. While there were other important long run implications, these were the ones which most affected Ameri-

---

[1] W. E. Folz, *The Financial Crisis of 1819* (Urbana: University of Illinois Ph.D. Thesis, 1935), Chapter II. Hereafter cited as *Financial Crisis*.

can economic affairs during this period. The most important internal change was the evolution of three distinct regions, each increasingly specializing in goods and services produced for sale to the other regions, including the foreign region.

Immediately after the war, freight rates fell drastically, reviving only briefly at the height of the boom in 1818, while the demand for shipping during these years was good. Earnings, while less than half those of 1806–1807, were higher than they would be for many years to come.[2] Shipping earnings were again an important base for the New England economy in the face of the depression in manufacturing, due to the flood of English goods and the relative decline of New England's ports in the re-export and import trade.[3] While the re-export trade no longer constituted the major share of total exports, it accounted for as much as $19 million annually in the years 1817–1819. This was still a far cry from the tremendous trade of the Napoleonic War era, and New England's share in this trade declined. Domestic exports from New England were less in absolute terms in the years 1815–1819 than they had been from 1803–1807. The condition of New England during these years was one of painful readjustment, in which relative depression in some sectors was mixed with fairly prosperous activity in others.[4]

Conditions in the Middle Atlantic states resembled those in New England in some respects. Manufactures were depressed there, too. But a thriving trade in wheat and flour was an important advantage, particularly to Baltimore, which continued to grow rapidly.[5] The import trade and subsequent auction and distribution of imported goods were important to the economic activity of the

---

[2] See Table A-III, Appendix II.

[3] The large specie reserves New England had accumulated during the war (see Chapter V, above) also redounded against that region as a result of New England's note issue being at a premium compared to other regions. See Folz, *Financial Crisis*, p. 23, citing R. Hildreth, *Banks, Banking, and Paper Currencies* (Boston: Whipple and Damrell, 1840), p. 68, and Henry Adams, *History of the United States of America*, 9 Vols. (New York: Scribners, 1921), Vol. 9, *Second Administration of James Madison*, p. 18.

[4] Folz, *Financial Crisis*, p. 88.

[5] In contrast to New England domestic exports of the middle states were substantially greater than in the years 1803-07. They were approximately $88 million in the years of the Napoleonic Wars, and were $106 million for the years 1815-19. Folz, *Financial Crisis*, p. 88.

ports of Baltimore, Philadelphia and New York, although the latter was already getting the lion's share of this trade.

There was no question about the prosperity of the South and West during these years. While some western towns, such as Pittsburgh and Cincinnati, experienced a depression in manufactures from the effects of English imports, this was a relatively unimportant part of the area's economic activity. Western prosperity rested upon a rapidly expanding market for its produce from new settlers pouring into the region, and particularly from the opening of the river trade with upriver steam navigation in 1816. It was an era of substantial speculation of western lands, with rising prices of its agricultural staples. From 1815 to 1819, approximately 7.5 million acres of land were sold in the Northwest, and almost half of the $16 million for which the land was sold by the government was still outstanding in 1819.[6]

It was in the South that prosperity and expansion were most striking. The rapid growth in the value of exports in the postwar period reflected modest increases in flour and wheat shipments, but primarily it mirrored the expansion in southern staples. Tobacco exports, which had averaged about $6 million a year in the pre-Embargo years, were approximately $9 million annually in the years following the war, reaching a peak of $12.8 million in 1816.[7] Rice exports also showed an increase over the earlier years, albeit a modest one.[8] It was cotton, however, that dominated the scene. Cotton exports averaged about $9 million between 1803–1807, approximately 22 per cent of exports. From 1815–1819 they averaged over $23 million, almost 39 per cent of total exports. The spectacular rise in cotton prices during these years made cultivation of this fiber enormously rewarding. The profitability of cotton had already transformed the old southern states of Georgia and South Carolina from a rather diversified agriculture to dependence on cotton. In the years after the second war with England, cotton culture spread throughout the rest of the settled South and initiated

---

[6] Folz, *Financial Crisis*, p. 60, quoting *American State Papers, Public Lands*, III, 420.

[7] This led to the extension of tobacco cultivation into Kentucky during these years.

[8] Folz, *Financial Crisis*, p. 80.

a vast surge into new lands of Alabama, Louisiana, and other states
and territories where cotton could be grown.

II

The readjustment to the different international economic conditions after 1815 made these years ones of mixed prosperity. Distress
of the manufacturing areas, the decline in freight rates and of the
re-export trade were only partially compensated for in New England with full utilization of ships and some revival of the re-
export trade. To a lesser extent these conditions also applied to
the Middle Atlantic states, although the thriving export trade in
wheat and flour and the import trade more than made up for
them. It is easy to overemphasize the importance of manufacturing
to the United States economy in these years. A very substantial
part of manufacturing at this time existed only because of poor
transport facilities and isolation. It reflected a condition of backwardness, not one of development, since it depended on communities which were not integrated into a national and international economy. Internal improvements built in response to the
booming conditions before 1808 became, by 1815, a way to reduce
the isolation of small, almost self-sufficient communities and allow
cheap imports to be substituted for these inefficiently produced
local manufactures. The years between 1815 and 1819 represented
a shaking down of the heterogeneous manufacturing which had
grown up under the protection of Embargo and war. Those firms
which did go under were the relatively inefficient ones. The profitability of the Lowell Mills during these years indicated clearly
that large, efficient firms could compete with English textiles in
the production of coarse grades of cloth. The residue of manufacturing establishments that was left formed the nucleus for expansion in subsequent decades.

The expansion of the economy was far more significant than the
readjustments in manufacturing, and the export trade to the rest
of the world was the source of this growth. Wheat and flour, tobacco, and increasingly cotton, were at the base not only of expansion of southern and middle states, but also were indirectly
responsible for a large part of the boom in the West.

The rapid growth of export values in these years did not reflect increased volume so much as a tremendous rise in the price of exports (see Chart X-VIII). It was these high prices which encouraged the westward surge into new cotton land in Alabama and into western lands capable of producing wheat and tobacco. Western development was more a consequence of the opening up of the Mississippi and the growing market in the cotton South for western staples. The extension of cotton cultivation into the new South meant a growing market for flour, cornmeal, livestock products, and whiskey.

Accompanying the flow of people into the lands of the new South and the West was a flow of capital to develop these lands as well as to speculate in them, to create towns and transport facilities in the western river trade. This capital came partly from bank expansion in the West where, despite the resumption of specie,[9] western bank notes circulated at a substantial discount. In its early years, the Second United States Bank furthered this extension of credit, and did not press the state institutions in the West for specie payments.[10] Almost equally important was the extension of mercantile credit by British exporters, which financed the large import surplus of the period and eased, at least temporarily, the strictures of the domestic capital market. (See the Balance of Payments Section, Appendix I.)

There can be no doubt that these years were generally prosperous ones. One has only to look at the extremely favorable terms of trade resulting from the large rise in export prices and the much smaller relative rise of import prices to appreciate that, whatever the difficulties of the manufacturer, the consumer enjoyed very substantial improvements in real income.[11]

---

[9] Specie payments were resumed on February 20, 1817.

[10] Cf. Walter B. Smith, *Economic Aspects of the Second Bank of the United States.* Harvard Studies in Economic History (Cambridge: Harvard University Press, 1953), Chapter VII. Hereafter cited as *Second Bank;* Leon M. Schur, "The Second Bank of the United States and the Inflation after the War of 1812," *Journal of Political Economy* LXVIII (April 1960), 120. Hereafter cited as "Second Bank of the United States."

[11] Abramovitz (Joint Economic Committee, *Hearings, loc. cit.,* p. 439, Table 10 and p. 456), and Willard Thorp, *Business Annals* . . . (New York: National Bureau of Economic Research, 1926), both make 1815 a peak year followed by depression from 1816 through 1818 (and then severe depression thereafter). This is in error, and reflects an overweighting of series connected with manu-

III

The basis for the collapse in 1818–1819 may be found in the
forces which created the boom preceding it, augmented by monetary conditions in the country and the international economy. Rising
prices of our export staples induced a tremendous movement of
population into new lands, coupled with liberal credit policies to
finance their development. The consequences were inevitable, and
were to be repeated many times in our subsequent economic experience. Credit was extended under the optimistic conditions generated by the rising prices of these export commodities. As long
as prices were rising, or remained at a high level, the note issue
of banks and foreign mercantile credit appeared secure, although
this was not true for the financing of imports, where the price
was already falling. The surge of expansion induced a substantial
shift in supply, ultimately reflected in declining prices and a lengthy
period of depressed prices. Cotton played an important role here.
Cotton prices reached a low point in 1812 and then began to rise,
reflecting almost stable output within the context of continued expanding demand for cotton. Land sales began to rise concomitant
with the increase in the price of cotton, and after 1814 cotton output
also rose. By 1819 it was double that of 1814. Chart I-XIII illustrates
the monthly range of cotton prices at Charleston. By July 1819
prices were half that for the same month of the preceding year.
From November 1818 the break in prices is clearly evident. The
rising price of cotton induced an increased flow of resources into
cotton production, augmented by the optimistic speculation that

---

facturing (and to a lesser extent shipping) and reports from newspapers of the
Northeast. It was a mixed period for the Northeast, but it was also a booming
era in the South and the West.

The question of the date of the upturn is more conjectural. Both Abramovitz
and Thorp make it 1821, whereas I have made it 1823. There was a revival in
1821, but was followed by a large gold outflow in 1822 and a further sharp fall
in prices. Since the United States was geared to the international economy, it
seems most likely to me that the real beginning of recovery only took place
after this final adjustment had occurred. Again there were important regional
differences. The revival of manufacturing in the Northeast occurred in 1821,
but the recovery of the South and West did not take place until 1823. (See
Section IV, this chapter.)

accompanies rising prices, and led to credit extension predicated on 30 cent cotton. The consequence of this diversion of resources was that after the period of time required to clear land, and perhaps plant a crop or two of corn to break up the soil, there was a substantial increase in supply; [12] prices fell, and remained low for some time. The reasons for the decline in prices and for the lengthy period of depressed prices are discussed in Chapters I and VII. The development of vast new cotton lands can be viewed as having accomplished the same thing as plant expansion; that is,

CHART I-XIII

Monthly Range of Short Staple Cotton Prices in the Charleston Market: 1815–1820

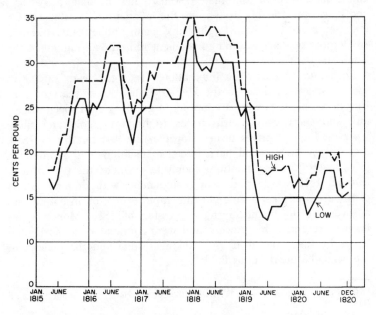

Source: Appendix II, Table A-XIII.

---

[12] The supply response to a price increase actually is of two sorts: (1) a planter can shift out of corn or other staple production to cotton during high prices of cotton and import his corn, or (2) it can come about by the method outlined above. The increase by the first method occurs much more rapidly, but it is not so substantial as by the second method.

capacity has been increased. With depressed prices the planter might decide to use some of the land to produce foodstuffs for his slaves rather than cotton, but at the first sign of rising prices he could redivert it back into cotton.

Monetary affairs also played a role in the 1819 depression, but they will be dwelt on only briefly here.[13] The expansion of note issue has already been noted, as has the attitude of the Second United States Bank during the period after specie resumption in February, 1817.[14] The speculative purchase of land in the South and West on credit was furthered by the Bank's policies. Only after eastern branches had refused the bills and notes of southern branches did the Bank attempt to do something about it, but its affairs in the South and the West had now become precarious, and it was inextricably drawn into the inflated credit extension for land purchases. In July, 1818, the bank began a policy of contraction. In October of that year the government retired $4.5 million of the Louisiana debt.

Economic affairs in the international economy were similar in some respects to those in the United States. After years of war, European countries were attempting to get back on a specie standard, and every country was trying to build up gold and silver reserves. English prices turned down in the first quarter of 1818, and this in itself would have forced a deflation in the American price level. For the Atlantic economy as a whole, the period 1815 through 1818 was a period of realignment, with dramatic shifts of resources into peacetime pursuits, rapid expansion in output and a severe readjustment in the depression of 1818. Monetary influences reflected this process, and were aggravated in the United States by the structure of the banking system and the policies of the Second United States Bank.

---

[13] Cf. Folz, *Financial Crisis;* W. B. Smith, *Second Bank;* and Schur, "Second Bank of the United States," *loc. cit.*

[14] Cf. Schur, "Second Bank of the United States," *loc. cit.*, for a thoughtful discussion of the inability of the Second Bank effectively to curb the western and southern bank note issue.

IV

As Chart II-XIII indicates, 1819–1823 were years of dramatic price deflation. Cotton prices, which had reached a peak of thirty-five cents a pound at Charleston in January 1818, dropped to eight and one-half cents by March 1823.[15] Freight rates fell by almost

CHART II-XIII

Prices and Freight Rates: 1815–1823
(Base 1830)

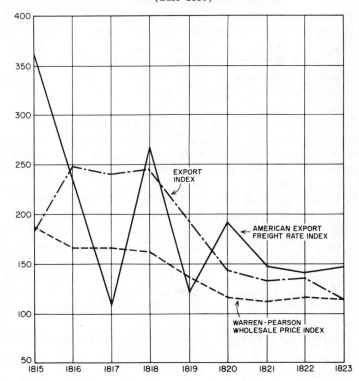

Source: Appendix II, Table B-XIII.

---

[15] A. G. Smith, *Economic Readjustment*, Appendix Table 1.

half during the period. The price decline was far more severe in agricultural commodities than in manufactures, primarily because the latter had already been subject to severe price competition from 1815 to 1818 while prices of agricultural commodities and freight rates had risen sharply during those years.[16]

The consequences of the price decline in the Northeast were to improve the position of manufacturing vis-à-vis alternative uses of capital. The drastic fall in ocean freight rates made shipping less profitable, while the drop in manufacturing prices made the tariff of 1815 a more effective protection to spinning. Moreover, the price decline had been much smaller. The result was that manufacturing, particularly in Massachusetts, recovered rather early and there was a renewal, from the Embargo days, of the shift of New England capital from shipping into manufacturing. The recovery of manufacturing was less striking in New York and Pennsylvania where smaller scale, less specialized firms [17] probably had higher costs than the Waltham type firms which were beginning to develop in Massachusetts.

In the old South the year 1819 marked the real beginning of a long and difficult era of readjustment.[18] The sharp fall in cotton prices led to severe economic distress. Nine cent cotton was unremunerative for most plantations in the old South at this time. Without a satisfactory alternative use of resources, the old South entered a period of relative decline which was mitigated only by interruptions in the secular fall of cotton prices and the profitability of slaves as an intermediate good for sale to the new South. Evidence of the old South's relative decline is seen from the condition of Charleston. Once the South's leading cotton port, in this era it was bypassed in the import trade and was a shipping point only for cotton from the tributary area. Its shipments increasingly went to New York for reshipment to England rather than enjoying direct trade.

The price decline brought to a halt the settlement on new lands

---

[16] Actually freight rates fell in 1817 and rose sharply in 1818. See North, "Ocean Freight Rates and Economic Development, 1815-1910," *loc. cit.*, Table 2.

[17] See the description of New York and Philadelphia manufacturing in Chapter XII.

[18] A. G. Smith, *Economic Readjustment*, Chapter I.

in Alabama, Mississippi and the other southwestern states. Unlike conditions in the old South, the longer run consequence—as opposed to the immediate distress resulting from monetary and credit stringency—was the consolidation and gradual development of new lands purchased between 1815 and 1818. With the development of steamboat traffic on the Mississippi, New Orleans was gradually emerging as the major entrepôt and cotton shipping center. Yet the short run distress was real enough. Credit extended on the basis of 20 to 30 cent cotton led to many bankruptcies, and the drying up of the credit flow from the Northeast still further aggravated conditions in the new South.

Conditions in the West, even more. than in the new South, were aggravated by the extensive note issue of banks. The depreciation of bank notes, the failure of many banks, and the spread of bankruptcy in 1821–1822 were all indicative of the monetary conditions of the period. Berry writes:

> Nevertheless, Cincinnati's future was clouded by the fact that facilities for credit were almost entirely lacking, prices of her exports were at rock bottom, and other leading sources of strength—sales of land and immigration—were at a low ebb.[19]

The antipathy generated during this deflationary period to banks in general, and to the Second United States Bank in particular, was to have lasting political consequences in the next decade.

International economic relations of the United States during these years were the decisive influence in the pattern of deflation. Relative readjustment of the price level in the United States vis-à-vis United Kingdom prices was the most important influence in the sharp decline of 1818–1820. Capital indebtedness dropped in these years, while in 1822 there was a sharp increase in the import trade and adverse trade balances of $18.5 million. There was also a gold outflow of $7.4 million that year, and a further fall in prices into 1823. Price inflation in the United Kingdom had not been as pronounced as in the United States, nor was the the the deflation as severe. This pattern was in many respects to be repeated as subsequent surges of United States expansion resulted in relatively greater rises and falls in the price level of this country than in the rest of the world. Such a pattern is only natural under the condi-

---

[19] Berry, *Western Prices*, p. 399.

tions of extensive expansion and the irregular pattern in which it occurred, the international mobility of capital, and the character of the monetary system.

The monetary structure of the economy, which was the proximate cause of the inflation and deflation of the years 1815 to 1823, was shaped by the political forces of the period. It is easy to blame the ineptitude of William Jones, yet political pressures on the Second Bank severely circumscribed its alternatives.[20] Given the expansionist spirit of Americans of the time and the boundless opportunities associated with the opening up of the new South and the West, it is hard to visualize the emergence of any different pattern. Even the painful experience of 1818 to 1823 had little effect, and the pattern was to be repeated again and again in the nineteenth century.

---

[20] Schur, "Second Bank of the United States," *loc. cit.*

XIV

THE ECONOMY 1823-1843

The twenty years between the trough of the precipitous depression of 1818 and that of the even more severe depression following 1839 were a critical period in American economic growth. If one were to date the beginning of acceleration in the economy's growth and the years when industrialization began, it would be during this period. It was also a period of tremendous westward expansion. Underlying both of these developments was the cotton trade. During this period, cotton played its greatest role in inducing growth in the size of the market for manufactures and in influencing the pace of the westward movement. When this era of expansion came to a close with the severe depression of the early 1840's, the cotton trade had irrevocably done its part as the proximate prime mover in quickening the pace of the country's growth.

I

The broad outlines of development during these years can be sketched out readily enough from the available statistics.[1] The remaining years of the 1820's were a period of declining prices, except for 1825, when a brief speculative flurry interrupted the decline. The decline was gradual compared to the very severe deflation of 1818–1821. The decade of the thirties was one of rising prices, with only brief interruptions in 1834 and 1837–1838. Another severe price deflation followed from 1839–1843. Domestic wholesale prices and export prices were more volatile than foreign domestic and import prices (see Charts I-VIII and III-VIII), and

---

[1] In addition to those used in the statistical chapters herein see Berry, *Western Prices*, Chapters XII, XIV, and Smith and Cole, *Fluctuations*, Section II.

the quotient of wholesale prices (Chart V-VIII) and the terms of trade turned extremely *favorable* in the 1830's. All of the relevant time series, both international and interregional, give evidence that the general rate of expansion in the economy was relatively slow in the twenties, picked up speed in the 1830's, and was capped by typical speculative excesses at the height of the boom in 1836–1837 and 1839. There is also abundant evidence that the depression from 1839 to 1843 was one of the most severe in our history. The flow of international capital and of people moved with the fortunes of the economy. The westward tide gradually accelerated with the step-up in economic activity, reached a peak in 1836, and then dwindled to a trickle in the early forties.

Diversities did exist among the three regions and the Atlantic economy. Where significant differences in regional activity occurred, they typically resulted from influences other than the interregional flows which are the central focus of this study, and such exogenous elements must be introduced to modify the general argument. The tariff act of 1824, the "bank war," the Specie Circular, to name but three political decisions, had important consequences for the economy and affected the several regions to different degrees. Yet the test of the framework of analysis is that it should reveal the broad underlying movements of the economy, and that such policies as must be brought into the explanation did not fundamentally alter the pattern of economic activity which began with England's industrial development in textile manufacturing and the growth of the cotton trade.

II

While cotton consumption by English textile mills grew in the 1820's, and United States cotton exports increased over the decade, their value did not show comparable gains because of a downward drift in cotton prices, interrupted briefly in 1824–1825, which lasted until 1831. The decline in prices was general throughout the decade, reflecting fundamental monetary and international economic conditions, but the drop in cotton prices was precipitous (see Chart X-VIII). Expansion into new lands in the period 1816–1818 resulted in a large increase in cotton acreage and a tendency for supply to increase readily with any rise in price. The existence of a larger increment of cleared land in Alabama and Louisiana meant that the relative or anticipated prices of cotton and alternative crops would dictate the acreage actually put into cotton. Any rise in the price of cotton greatly increased the supply. In the old South, with higher production costs of cotton, the alternative was to shift back to a more self-sufficient agriculture, but even a temporary rise in cotton prices was sufficient to "cause fields in which corn and other grains were already growing to be plowed up and replanted in cotton." [2]

Interruptions in the decline in cotton prices, as in 1825, readily brought forth a large increase in supply in the succeeding year. After 1826, cotton output actually declined for some years in South Carolina and some other states of the old South.[3]

There can be no doubt that the period of the twenties was one of serious readjustment for the old South, and it is likely that per capita incomes declined between 1819–1823. Emigration and plantation consolidation were the old South's answer to the low cotton prices of the 1820's. Smith estimates net emigration from South Carolina for the decade at 69,513. Small farmers with higher costs were the most affected and contributed largely to this migration, although some large planters migrated west with their slaves.[4] The engrossment of small farms into larger plantations led to improvements in production costs.

If the old South gave a clear indication of the relative decline that was to continue until the Civil War, the new South showed vitality throughout the decade, even in the face of declining prices of its key staple. It is true that there was little impetus to purchase new lands, but land already acquired was gradually put into cultivation. Equally significant for the vitality of the new South was investment in the variety of activities associated with the development of a new region.[5] This was particularly true of New

---

[2] A. G. Smith, *Economic Readjustment,* p. 54.

[3] *Ibid.,* pp. 47, 55.

[4] *Ibid.,* p. 22. It should be noted that emigration in the thirties was nearly twice this figure. With rising cotton prices, the lure of rich western lands attracted the large planters and their slaves.

[5] It should be remembered that such investment was much more limited in opening up the Southwest than in the West because of the structure of the southwestern economy. See Chapter XI herein.

Orleans, which was emerging not only as a major export port for cotton, but was becoming the entrepôt of the South.

This strengthening of the link between South and West not only gave greater economic vitality to the new South during the decade, but meant that the West was provided with an expanding market for its produce. The growing river trade meant increasing market orientation of western farmers and rapid growth of river ports such as Pittsburgh and Cincinnati. The latter in particular became a leading river port and the center of the early development of food processing for export to the new South. Berry's index of economic activity in the West shows expansion throughout the period 1823 to 1831, with only minor recessions in 1824, 1827, and 1830.[6] He notes that "Cincinnati clinched her position as the leading point of concentration for the export of surplus of the Ohio Valley. Her onward march appears hardly to have been affected by the price depression of 1821–27." [7] During the decade its population increased from 9,602 to 24,695. Even though the twenties were years of slower growth for the economy as a whole, the development of interregional dependence between West and South was sufficient to foster substantial investment in urban areas, river transport, warehousing, and the auxiliary services essential to facilitating this new interdependence. Greater than average expansion took place in those areas of the new South and West whose accessibility to the river trade gave them location advantages as entrepôts. While the opening of the Erie Canal in 1825 had an expansive influence on Lake Erie and other accessible areas, as Chart III-IX makes clear, its effect in the early years of its operation was felt far more in western New York State than in the West.

Economic activity in the Northeast was also mixed during the years 1823–1831. The old sources of expansion, shipping and mercantile pursuits, were severely hit by the depression of 1818. Freight rates fell sharply with the revival of world shipping competition, and shipping was not very prosperous during the decade.

Manufacturing, particularly textiles, which had faced a serious period of readjustment to foreign competition after 1815, recovered early from the 1818 crisis. The minimum duty on textiles imposed

---

[6] Berry, *Western Prices,* p. 427.
[7] *Ibid.,* p. 409.

in the tariff of 1816 had been ineffective with high textile prices, but with the introduction of the cost-reducing power loom and the price decline of 1818–1821, the minimum duty closed out coarser grades of foreign cotton cloth. Expansion was rapid, and throughout New England new manufacturing villages developed while older ones, such as the celebrated Waltham Mills, expanded. The Woodbury Report of 1836 cites a figure of 230,000 cotton spindles in 1821 and 800,000 in 1825.[8] There was marked improvement in distributive organization to take advantage of the growing markets of the South and West. Three methods were employed by New England textile mills: consignment to wholesale merchants on a commission basis, employment of a selling agent, and the auction system. This was essential, since the manufacturing growing up in New England textile and other industries had a national rather than a local market, and the fortunes of such manufacturing depended on the growth of population and income of the whole economy.[9]

The Northeast, like the West and South, was going through a decade of fundamental transformation in which manufactures were expanding and becoming well rooted in the region, with their fortunes tied to the evolving interregional dependence that marked the development of a national market. Shipping and foreign commerce, the old cornerstones of the region's prosperity, were characterized by a more painful period of readjustment. Packet lines began to run on regular schedules in 1818, and were a feature of New York's growing pre-eminence in foreign trade.[10] Increasing trade with the South meant the development of coastwise trade, yet shipping earnings in the twenties were much lower than in the years 1815–1818, and were no longer a source of expansion. The shift of capital from shipping into manufacturing reflected the change in relative rates of return during the decade.

Within the Northeast, the opening of the Erie Canal marked an

---

[8] Taussig, *Tariff History,* p. 51, citing *Executive Document No. 146,* 24th Congress, 1st Session. He makes clear that these figures are only rough estimates.

[9] Clark, *History of Manufactures,* I, 360.

[10] Robert G. Albion, *Square Riggers on Schedule; the New York Sailing Packets to England, France, and the Cotton Ports* (Princeton: Princeton University Press, 1938).

important change. It solidified New York's pre-eminence among the ports of the Northeast,[11] opening up an extensive and rich intraregional trade as well as providing a gateway to the West.

Contrasted with the structural changes and the mixed character of economic activity in the years 1823–1831 was the relative *neutrality* of our external economic relations. Variation between domestic and foreign prices and movements in the terms of trade was limited, except for 1825. Capital movements and immigration were of modest proportions and specie movements were not large. Only in 1825, when a speculative expansion and collapse occurred in England, was the United States drawn to any degree into economic conditions abroad, and even then this country was not as severely affected as some South American economies.

III

The quickening pace of economic activity was evident in 1831 and 1832. There was improvement in the terms of trade, the beginnings of capital inflow, and a striking rise in Berry's index of economic activity in the West.[12] The thirties were a decade of contrast to the preceding one. The surge in economic activity was evident on all sides and in all regions. The decade was also marked by sharp crises in 1834, 1837 and of course in 1839, which marked the onset of one of the most severe depressions in our economic history.

Cotton played the leading role. The previous decade had established a pattern of regional interdependence which ultimately rested on the cotton trade. Between 1831 and 1836 the value of cotton exports almost trebled, rising from $25 million to $71 million. While this expansion rested in part on increased acreage, it also reflected a rise in the price of cotton in the Charleston market from a range of six and one-half to twenty and one-half cents in 1836.[13] This was only partly attributable to general monetary conditions, since the rise of the domestic price index was smaller than that of the cotton

---

[11] Robert G. Albion, "New York Port and Its Disappointed Rivals, 1815-1860," *Journal of Economic and Business History* III (1930-31), 602-29.

[12] Berry, *Western Prices*, p. 427.

[13] A. G. Smith, *Economic Readjustment*, p. 221.

dominated export price index. The sharp rise in cotton prices reflected the gradual shift to the right in demand for cotton assimilating the acreage expansion of 1816–1818. The supply curve for cotton, which was elastic over a range of output within the limits of the acreage currently available, was increasingly inelastic as the available acreage was put into use. A shift to the right in the supply function involved the opening up of new acreage and a flow of capital and labor into these lands to clear and develop them. The rise in cotton prices set in motion both the internal and international factors essential to accomplishing this shift.

Internally the increased profitability of cotton led to a surge into virgin land in the new South and an unparalleled increase in government land sales. Chart X-IX shows these land sales in the five cotton states of Alabama, Mississippi, Louisiana, Arkansas and Florida. It was accompanied by a shift of planters and slaves from the old South to these new states. Net emigration from South Carolina alone was estimated at 65,031 whites and 56,683 Negroes; [14] the slave movement from Virginia was much greater.[15]

Plantation banks, in Mississippi and Louisiana in particular, expanded to finance the internal slave trade and to make loans for the purchase, clearing, and development of new cotton lands. The increased profitability of cotton and the investments associated with the cotton trade were particularly attractive to English investors, who participated through the securities of these plantation banks. The output of new cotton lands increased gradually during the 1830's and then rose sharply in 1840 (see Chart I-X), reflecting the long period between the initial move to take advantage of the increased profitability of cotton and the marked shift to the right in the supply function which led to depressed prices for the first half of the 1840's.

The value of produce shipped down the Mississippi to New Orleans showed no sustained increase in the last half of the 1820's, varying between $20 million and $22 million annually. In 1831 it began to increase rapidly, and by 1837, at $45.6 million, had more than doubled. Cotton shipments from Arkansas and Mississippi account for part of the rise, but a substantial part of the increase

[14] *Ibid.*, p. 22.
[15] The *Virginia Times* estimated the export of slaves from that state in 1836 at 40,000. Quoted in Callender, *Economic History,* p. 307.

was western foodstuffs for the plantation population of the expanding new South.

The southern demand for foodstuffs was the initial impetus to
westward expansion, but the consequence was more extensive than
a simple regional multiplier of an older settled area. Increasing
demand led to rising prices and a growing tide of western migrants
who had to be fed. Demand for foodstuffs and a wider variety of
necessities to supply the settler supplemented the demand for
staples from the South. The pattern of urbanization which evolved
in the West during this decade was located with reference to this
two-fold demand for its products.

Transportation costs limited the supply of western foodstuffs.
Once the areas near the navigable waterways of the Mississippi,
Ohio, and Illinois rivers and their tributaries had been settled, a
substantial increase in supply could only come from improved transportation. In the 1830's this meant improving the navigability of
rivers, particularly in the construction of canals. Ohio led the way,
with the completion of the 308 mile Ohio and Erie Canal connecting the Ohio river with Lake Erie in 1833, the Miami and Erie
Canal from Cincinnati to Dayton in 1832, and finally to Toledo
in 1845. A number of branch canals were also constructed. Indiana,
Michigan, and Illinois followed suit. These canals entailed large-
scale capital expenditures and necessitated state government par-
ticipation and underwriting, since both the limitations of private
saving and the primitive state of financial intermediaries made
private undertakings on such a scale impossible.[16] In many cases
banks provided the initial capital, but it was the flotation in England of the securities of the states which provided most of the funds.

The pattern of expansion in the West was similar to expansion
in the South in that the time between the initial impetus and the
actual shift to the right was lengthy because of the time involved
in building canals and improving waterways. It was dissimilar to
the South in that opening new areas was accompanied by large-
scale investment in a variety of economic activities. The development of towns, warehousing facilities, and a wide variety of resi-

---

[16] See Callender, "The Early Transportation and Banking Enterprises of the
States in Relation to the Growth of Corporations," *loc. cit.,* pp. 111-62.

dentiary industry was the typical pattern.[17] Increased demand for capital and labor in the West was met primarily by immigration from the East and to a lesser extent from the old South. The demand for labor had the important effect of pulling farmers out of self-sufficiency into the market; canal building attracted men from the self-sufficient farm. The era of western expansion had a dual effect: it redirected the labor force from consumer goods agricultural production into investment goods (canals) and expanded the *market* labor force by pulling labor out of a self-sufficient existence into a money economy.

The boom in the new South and West was paralleled by equal expansion in the Northeast. The financial, transport and marketing services associated with the cotton trade were prosperous, but more important was the growth in demand for northeastern manufactures in these booming areas. Demand for textiles, leather products, clothes, and shoes increased with the rising incomes in the new regions. The demand for machinery for farm implements, western steamboats, construction, and processing expanded in an equally dramatic fashion. This growing market for the manufactures of the Northeast resulted in increased specialization, and the development of the textile machinery industry and specialized production of steam engines for land and water transportation. Earlier developments in the capital market, initially associated with shipping, foreign trade, and cotton, were now available to facilitate the financing of manufactures.[18]

Our international economic relations provide the final, and in this period decisive, link in the pattern of economic expansion. The rising price of cotton, the improving turn of trade, and the anticipation of profits from the opening up of western lands through canal construction served to stimulate capital flow from Britain to the United States. The effect, as we have seen, was to direct real resources into plantation expansion and canal construction. An

---

[17] Dayton, Pittsburgh, Louisville, Nashville, Chicago, Detroit, and St. Louis were all rapidly growing urban areas during this period, with a wide range of residentiary industries developing for the western market. See Reginald C. McGrane, *The Panic of 1837; Some Financial Problems of the Jacksonian Era* (Chicago: University of Chicago Press, 1924), p. 29.

[18] Clark, *History of Manufactures,* I, 367-72.

equally important result was the provision of credits for a sizable increase in imports of both capital and consumer goods. It was the increased well-being of the populace in this prosperous period that led to the sharp increase in demand for these wares. The large import surplus made possible by capital flows provided the necessary consumer goods to *sop up* the increased income, rather than have it dissipated by a rapid rise in the price level. While domestic prices rose more rapidly than foreign prices, there can be little doubt that this rise was relatively dampened by the inflow of consumer goods.

The era of expansion between 1831 and 1839 may be summarized as follows: The initial expansion was set off by the conjunction of rising cotton prices and the structural changes in the three regions brought about by the development of regional interdependence. It took place at first with scant rise in prices because of the unemployed and underemployed resources available. Once under way, the actual or anticipated development of internal improvements implied a reduction in transfer costs, making it possible for vast new areas to market their commodities and accelerate further the westward movement and demand for land. Bank expansion played the most important role in supplying capital; foreign investment was selective and limited. The significant flow of foreign funds came later, as a result of increased opportunities with both staple commodities and regional expansion in the South and Northwest. The growth of facilities to market these commodities and supply the local needs of planters or settlers in new areas led to a construction boom. This expansion reacted in turn on the East in the form of demand for services and manufactured goods. The resultant widening of the market permitted greater specialization and increased efficiency in manufacturing. The inflow of capital sustained the expansion for a number of years by permitting a level of consumption goods imports which slowed down the domestic price rise.

This brief summary focuses upon the underlying real forces making for overall expansion but neglects the short run institutional, monetary, and international economic influences which affected the pace and timing of expansion and subsequent contraction. There is not space here to treat in any detail the Bank War, the Specie Circular, distribution of surplus revenues, the policies of the Bank of England, and so on, that made this a remarkable decade.[19] A brief characterization will serve to place them in context and evaluate their influence on the timing of economic events. With the gradual acceleration after 1830 of the pace of economic activity initiated by the cotton trade, there was sharp improvement in the terms of trade and an increase in capital imports. Commodity imports rose swiftly, and there was an inflow of specie. Commodity prices rose very slowly, because of the absorption of productive factors into the market economy. It was a period of real productive expansion which was interrupted in late 1833 by the Bank War. As the government allowed its deposits with the Bank to run down, the Second Bank began, in August, 1833, to contract its activities. In addition to curtailing loans and discounts, it accumulated $5.5 million in specie between August 1833 and September 1834. Although specie continued to be imported during the period, the Bank's policy sterilized this inflow. The result was a sharp recession in economic activity. It was short-lived, however, and expansion was under way again by mid-1834 at a sharply accelerated pace. With full utilization of resources, the result of the specie inflow and bank expansion was a sharp rise in commodity prices. The optimism of a booming period produced the customary speculation, nowhere more evident than in the new lands of the Southwest and Northwest. Land sales reached a peak in 1836, amidst outcries of small purchasers and the conviction of the federal government that both were being victimized. The result was the Specie Circular of July 11, 1836. It is impossible to separate the effects of this act from the act to distribute surplus revenues to the states.[20] Distribution was to be made in quarterly installments beginning January 1, 1837. Nicholas Biddle accurately stated the effect of these two acts.

> By this unnatural process the specie of New York and other commercial cities is piled up in Western States—not circulated; not

[19] For varying accounts see the studies by W. B. Smith, McGrane, and Macesich cited in this chapter. For a British view which suggests that the United States initiated the cyclical pattern which then spread abroad, see Robert C. O. Matthews, *A Study in Trade Cycle History* (Cambridge: The University Press, 1954).

[20] George Macesich, *Monetary Disturbances in the United States, 1834-45* (Chicago: University of Chicago Ph.D. Thesis, 1958), p. 72. Hereafter cited as *Monetary Disturbances.*

used but held as a defense against the Treasury—and while the
West cannot use it—the East is suffering from the want of it. The
result is, that the commercial intercourse between the West and
the Atlantic, is wholly suspended, and the few operations which
are made are burdened with most extravagant expenses . . .
while Europe is alarmed and the Bank of England itself uneasy
at the quantity of specie we possess . . . we are suffering because, from mere mismanagement, the whole ballast of the currency is shifted from one side of the vessel to the other. . . .[21]

The Bank of England was uneasy. In the second half of 1836,
specie reserves declined from £7.4 million to £4.25 million. A
significant part of this decline was in specie exports to the United
States. The bank rate was raised to 4.5 per cent on July 21, 1836,
and a short while later to 5 per cent. The Anglo-American merchant banking houses were part of the connection between speculation and credit extension in America, particularly in the cotton
belt, the flow of capital, and the discounting of American paper.
When the Bank of England refused to discount the bills of the
three W's in early 1837, it reacted back through the chain to the
other side of the Atlantic.

The disparity in English and American price levels, the flow of
specie, and the speculation in America combined as the forces
underlying the Panic of 1837. That spring was a dismal one in
economic affairs. Sterling bills sold at a 12.5 per cent premium,
domestic credit was severely restricted, and innumerable banks
and commercial establishments failed. General suspension of specie
payments went into effect in May. There was a sharp decline in
prices, and the fragmentary evidence indicates there was downward wage flexibility as well.[22] The panic was sharp, but its major
effects were financial and monetary, and the adjustment to it was
made through the price level of goods and productive factors.
Both the volume of trade [23] and employment indicate that the *real*
effect was much less, and one can agree with Walter B. Smith
that it was far less severe than the Panic of 1819.[24]

---

[21] Open letter from Nicholas Biddle to John Quincy Adams, November 11,
1836 in the New York *Spectator* of December 15, 1836, quoted in Macesich,
Monetary Disturbances, p. 73.

[22] W. B. Smith, *Second Bank,* p. 198.

[23] Macesich, *Monetary Disturbances,* p. 15.

[24] W. B. Smith, *Second Bank,* p. 194.

The Panic of 1837 was an interruption and not an end to the underlying expansive forces in the economy. The sharp drop in cotton prices reflected the readjustment in the American price level rather than any larger increase in supply as a result of new lands being put into cultivation. By the spring of 1838, cotton prices were again rising, the low point having been reached in early summer of 1837, and economic expansion was visible on all sides. The improving profitability of cotton and western staples again attracted foreign capital into plantation expansion and *productive* internal improvements. The revival of western regional expansion and the cotton trade provided the necessary stimulus for expansion of manufacturing in the East. Both domestic wholesale prices and export prices rose sharply.

The Second Bank, which had now become the United States Bank of Pennsylvania, began its celebrated (or notorious) speculation in cotton in July, 1837. The Bank had always been a leader in foreign exchange and a large purchaser of cotton bills. With the failure of a number of cotton brokerage firms in 1837, it was a simple step to extend its operations to the shipment of cotton.[25] While the early operations of the Bank were probably profitable with the rising price of that staple, their success depended on stable or rising cotton prices, and efforts at controlling supply ran into the wave of cotton from the vast plantation expansion of the previous five years. Chart I-X shows the sharp rise in cotton output in the five new cotton states in 1839–1840. The decline in cotton prices plummeted from a high of 17 cents a pound in April 1839 at Charleston to $7\frac{1}{2}$ cents a pound a year later.[26] The results were disastrous, and not only for the Bank. They also ushered in a depression whose severity can most accurately be compared to that of 1929. It was not merely the overexpansion of cotton, nor even the tremendous increase in capacity of western foodstuffs, which depressed prices. It was these factors in conjunction with the credit structure and the cessation of foreign investment, plus the necessary readjustment in American price levels vis-à-vis foreign prices, which triggered the depression. The difference between 1837 and 1839 was that the former panic had centered around temporary malad-

---

[25] *Ibid.*, p. 196.
[26] A. G. Smith, *Economic Readjustment,* Appendix 1, p. 221.

justments in internal monetary affairs and external influences, while
these monetary and external influences in the latter period were
combined with the real effects of a decade of uninhibited expansion of productive capacity, which necessarily entailed a long
period of readjustment.

IV

The period from the fall of 1839 to 1843 resembles a similar era
just ninety years later in that both were severe and prolonged drops
in economic activity. There was a precipitous decline in domestic
and export prices, a cessation of capital imports, and the return of
securities to the United States as Pennsylvania, Maryland and other
states defaulted on their interest payments. Both domestic and
foreign trade declined sharply,[27] with the West and South the
hardest hit. The cessation of capital imports halted the vast pro-
gram of internal improvements and accompanying investments in
the economic opportunities associated with a new region. The
stoppage of the flow of capital into the West from the Northeast
operated on the West in much the same way that it operated
between the United States and England. During the period of
capital inflow, western prices rose relative to those of the Northeast, but when this inflow ceased the readjustment in western price
levels meant a more drastic decline than for the economy as a
whole.[28] The same pattern held for the South, except that the fall
in cotton prices was even more severe. Cotton planters had little
incentive to expand production, and as the price continued to drop
the advantage of becoming more self-sufficient by putting available
acreage into corn and hogs became evident. While the depression
did not spare the Northeast and was perhaps harder on states like
Pennsylvania, with large commitments in internal improvements,

---

[27] Macesich's index of the volume of trade (*Monetary Disturbances*, p. 6)
shows no decline, and I have not had the opportunity of seeing his sources.
Yet on the evidence available (as well as contemporary qualitative description)
he is clearly in error. There was certainly a very substantial decline in the
volume of trade. See Berry's *Western Prices*, Chapter XIV, and Smith and
Cole, *Fluctuations*, p. 73.

[28] See Berry, *Western Prices*, pp. 466-67.

the decline in manufacturing prices was relatively less than that of agricultural products, and flexible money wages modified the employment effects.[29]

The precipitous price decline of 1839 leveled off, and prices actually rose slightly in late 1840 and 1841. Then the decline resumed, continuing until the beginning of 1843. By 1843, the depression had run its course, foreign and domestic price levels were in line, and a new era of expansion was slowly getting under way. But cotton was no longer king.

---

[29] Macesich, *Monetary Disturbances,* p. 15.

XV

THE ECONOMY 1843-1861

In some respects, the pattern of economic activity in this period resembles that of the previous era. Like the 1820's, the early 1840's were a period of slower growth and gradual reabsorption of unemployed resources into the market economy. The pace quickened in the last half of the 1840's and in the early 1850's, as it had in the 1830's. 1854, like 1834, was a recession year. 1857, like 1837, marked a sharp panic, although 1856–1857, unlike the previous period, was the peak of the long cycle.

In other important respects, the two periods were strikingly different. The 1840's and 1850's were an era of enormous land acquisition. Beginning with Texas in 1845, the Oregon territory in 1846, California and the Southwest in 1848, and the Gadsden Purchase in 1854, the continental boundaries of the country were rounded out, and a vast new area of rich resources was opened for exploitation. The gaudy California gold rush was only one of several surges of men and capital to take advantage of these new opportunities.

I

As important as the extensive territorial expansion was the growth of manufacturing. Economic growth during the long swing 1823–1839 had set the scene for an industrial society by widening the market. Manufacturing growth throughout the Northeast in the 1830's gave evidence that this development was under way. But it was during the 1840's and early 1850's that the pace of industrialization accelerated to the degree that the Northeast could unequivocally be called a manufacturing region. This manufacturing

204

was based on a wide range of finished commodities rather than being limited to a few highly developed industries. Gallman's figures provide evidence that the decade 1844–1854 was one of very rapid development in manufacturing output.[1] Value added per worker in manufacturing showed an equally rapid gain, indicating that productivity in manufacturing was also growing fast.[2]

Gallman's study of American commodity output suggests that the decade 1844–1854 was one of unusual growth compared to decade rates for the rest of the nineteenth century. His figures show a decennial rate of increase of 69 per cent in 1879 prices. This figure is exceeded slightly by only one other decade growth rate throughout the rest of the nineteenth century.[3] The quinquennial patterns of growth show that the rate of manufacturing output increased most rapidly between 1844 and 1849, while agriculture, mining, and construction output had their highest rate of increase between 1849 and 1854. The figures are given in Table 15. Gallman's figures suggest the sources of expansion in this period. Cotton had played the dominant role in the previous period; the fortunes of the cotton trade called the major turns in economic activity.

TABLE 15

VALUE ADDED BY AGRICULTURE, MINING, MANUFACTURING
AND CONSTRUCTION, 1839-1859, IN 1879 PRICES

Year	Agricul-ture	Mining	Manufac-turing	Construction		Total	
				Variant A	Variant B	Variant A	Variant B
1839	$ 787	$ 7	$190	$110	$ 87	$1,094	$1,071
1844	944	14	290	126	105	1,374	1,353
1849	989	17	488	163	143	1,657	1,637
1854	1,316	26	677	298	255	2,317	2,274
1859	1,492	33	859	302	277	2,686	2,661

Source: Gallman, "Commodity Output," loc. cit., p. 43.

[1] Robert E. Gallman, "Commodity Output, 1839-1899," *Trends in the American Economy in the Nineteenth Century*. Studies in Income and Wealth, Vol. 24 (Princeton University Press for the National Bureau of Economic Research, 1960), Table 3. Hereafter cited as "Commodity Output."

[2] Gallman, "Commodity Output," loc. cit., Table 7.

[3] Gallman, "Commodity Output," loc. cit., Table 1. The figure for 1874-84 was 70 per cent in 1879 prices. All other decade rates of growth are substantially below these figures.

In the 1840's and 1850's it is abundantly clear that, while cotton was still an important influence in the economy, it was no longer dominant. The manufacturing Northeast and the West no longer were so dependent on the southern market, and were more inter-dependent with each other. The market in the Northeast alone was large enough to support a substantial industrial base. It was, in addition, an ever growing market for western foodstuffs as canals and railroads bound East and West together. The California gold rush provided still another impetus to growth, both through its major export commodity, gold, which had important repercus-sions on our international economic relations, and through the stimulus it provided to the Northeast.

When expansion began again in 1843, the American economy had escaped from the limitations of being tied to a single agri-cultural export staple. Its future as a manufacturing nation was assured, and the pace of its westward movement was stimulated by the demand for foodstuffs in the East and in Europe.

II

Recovery in the Northeast was evident from the renewal of rail-road construction and expansion of manufacturing. The revival which began in 1843 was sharply accelerated the following year with rising manufacturing prices. Manufacturing growth was rapid during the rest of the decade. The Northeast had become a manu-facturing center and its burgeoning urban areas reflected this in-dustrialization and were themselves large concentrated markets. By 1860, New York's population exceeded one million, Philadelphia's nearly 600,000. The growth rate of the major cities in the Northeast substantially exceeded the national population increase of 85 per cent between 1840 and 1860. Immigration was a major contributing factor during this period. A stream of Irish and then German im-migrants swelled the cities of the Northeast and spilled over into the West. As noted in Chapter XII, the Irish were predominantly urban, and a large percentage of them remained in the industrial Northeast. In a society where the problem of relative labor scarcity was augmented by aspirations of the native born for independent employment, the supply of European labor provided a workforce ready and willing to enter industrial employment.

Recovery in the Northeast reflected the revival of manufacturing with the allied investments in urban development, construction, and transportation which accompanied the industrial development and inflow of immigrants. The depression was more severe and recovery slower in the West. Cessation of foreign capital from Britain and domestic capital from the Northeast brought the system of internal improvements to a halt, and it was not until the end of the 1840's that foreign investment again flowed into western developments—railroad construction this time instead of canals. Recovery began after 1843, but it was slow. The occasional completion of an improvement such as the Wabash Canal provided local expansion and renewal of interest in land settlement, but the first big impetus to westward expansion was the demand for wheat and corn resulting from the Irish famine. The shift in demand and the rising price of cereals called forth a wave of settlement on new western lands and a renewed interest in transport developments to tie the West and the eastern seaboard together. It is during this period (1845–1848) that shipments over the Erie Canal from the West (as distinguished from western New York state) grew substantially.

Recovery in the South did not begin until cotton prices turned the corner in 1845. Even in the rich lands of the Mississippi delta, six cent cotton was hardly profitable. Prices improved after the middle 1840's, although not at a rate calculated to induce large-scale investment in new lands.

The governing influence in our international economic relations was a reversal of the capital flow, with the repatriation of many defaulted American securities and a resulting favorable trade balance. Exports, which had fallen in value from 1840 through 1843 because of the price decline, rose gradually until 1847, when the export of cereals resulted in a dramatic increase. After reaching a nadir in 1843, imports rose more rapidly, but the import surplus was small and during most years there was a favorable trade balance. Aggregate foreign indebtedness of the United States fell from a peak of approximately $300 million in 1839 to less than $200 million a decade later.

By 1843, United States domestic prices had fallen well below international (specifically United Kingdom) prices, and a $20 million inflow of specie occurred that year. This expansion in the money supply was an important impetus to revival in the Northeast. A further large inflow occurred in 1847 to pay for the shipment of cereals to Ireland, and thereafter United States prices rose relative to foreign prices.

For the period 1843 through 1848, the growth of manufacturing in the Northeast was the main impetus to expansion. Gallman's figures show very rapid growth during this period, and they are supported by the monographic studies of individual industries, which show progressive specialization of function and increasing localization in the Northeast. The industrial base broadened during this period, reflecting the overall improvement in factor endowments for manufacturing in the New England and Middle Atlantic states. Railroad mileage in New England grew with marked rapidity. There were 527 miles of track in 1840 and 2508 miles of track in 1850.[4] Railroad construction was itself an impetus to this expansion. Equally important was the cost decline in transportation, which opened up new sites for manufacturing development and reduced transport costs for existing firms.

III

While 1848 was a year of turmoil throughout Europe, the depression was not felt severely in the United States. The Northeast's close financial ties with Europe made for some recession in that region in 1847–1848, but little effect was felt elsewhere. Gold outflow was not enough to influence the revival significantly, and the impetus provided by the growing trade between Northeast and West in many ways duplicated the pattern of trade between the South and West in the 1820's with the investment that accompanied the development of new urban trade centers.

The pace of economic activity in the South and West quickened after 1848. Recovery of cotton prices in late 1849, the renewal of railroad construction to the West, investment opportunities in

---

[4] Henry V. Poor, *Manual of Railroads of the United States for 1869-70* (New York: H. V. and H. W. Poor, 1869), p. xxvi.

the East associated with the western trade, the inflow of immigrants, and the gold discoveries in California all contributed to the revival.

Only the last of these was fortuitous and outside the intrinsic pattern of development. The recovery in cotton prices reflected the gradual shift to the right in demand for cotton as textile output grew. This increase eventually absorbed the increased potential supply of the previous boom, and rise in cotton prices ensued. The most striking feature of the economy from 1848 through 1854 was the growth that took place in the West. Gallman's figures show a 33 per cent growth in agricultural output between 1849 and 1854. Not only was there expansion into new lands, but also increasing efficiency, and a large number of new agricultural implements first achieved widespread use. This decade was perhaps the first in which there was a sharp increase in agricultural productivity.[5]

The initial impetus to this extensive expansion was the rising prices of agricultural commodities. Berry's index of western prices shows continual improvement throughout the period.[6] Chart I-XV shows the movement of corn and wheat prices. Both had risen sharply in 1846–1847. Wheat prices later declined, reflecting a short run readjustment after the end of the large scale exports to the United Kingdom, then renewed their rise in the early 1850's. Corn prices continued to improve throughout. It was the shift in demand, in this case from the Irish famine, which initiated rising prices. After the European demand subsided, the rapid pace of manufacturing development and urbanization in the East, along with large scale immigration, continued to maintain the higher prices. Demand in the middle of the 1850's was again influenced by external events, this time by the Crimean War which cut off Russian wheat and led to large scale exports.

The pace of public land sales in the West mirrored the improving profitability of western agriculture. Illinois, Wisconsin, Iowa, Minnesota, Michigan, and Missouri all had public land sales in

---

[5] Marvin Towne and Wayne Rasmussen, "Farm Gross Product and Gross Investment During the Nineteenth Century," *Trends in the American Economy in the Nineteeth Century*. Studies in Income and Wealth, Vol. 24 (Princeton University Press for the National Bureau of Economic Research, 1960).

[6] Berry, *Western Prices*, pp. 504-05.

excess of $1,000,000 in 1855, the peak year of the land boom and westward movement of this surge in expansion. The concomitant revival of interest in internal improvements was now centered on the railroad. It was not long before foreign capital was attracted, this time from Germany. The British followed in 1850–1851, and an era of railroad construction firmly uniting the East and the West in the 1850's was under way. The result not only reduced transfer costs between the two regions, but opened up vast new areas to farming, as the discussion of Illinois in Chapter XI has made clear.

Expansion in the Northeast was partly related to the western trade and to investment induced by western expansion. Textiles, shoes and leather, iron products, and light machinery were now firmly established. The burgeoning of the other regions provided a rapidly developing market, and the influx of immigrants provided an elastic supply of labor conducive to manufacturing growth.

This was to be the last decade of United States shipping prosperity. Freight rates rose in 1846–1848 with the demand for wheat, declined until 1851 and then rose again. Rising demand for ship-

CHART I-XV

Average Prices of Wheat and Corn at New York: 1845–1861

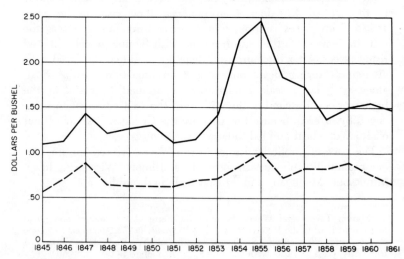

Source: Appendix II, Table A-XV.

ping from the growth of foreign trade and from the California trade (restricted to United States ships as coastwise trade) raised rates, and the Crimean War led to a further sharp advance. It was the era of the clipper ships; New England and Atlantic shipyards were heavily engaged in construction.

California provided an impetus to expansion similar to that of the West. It brought a growing demand for goods and services, and its export commodity, gold, was a basic influence upon international economic relations. United States gold exports climbed throughout the decade, and it was gold even more than foreign capital which permitted a large import surplus of consumer and capital goods, particularly railroad iron.

While capital imports were quantitatively as large in the 1850's as in the 1830's, their relative importance was far less. They did direct resources into railroad construction and provide credits for an import surplus. Of greater significance was the inflow of immigrants which began in 1845 and reached its peak from 1849–1854. In a period when increasing expansion could be achieved only by pulling more labor out of self-sufficiency (and then it was a net gain only by the difference in productivity), or by attracting it from without, the large immigration played an important role.

There was no fundamental change in American exports during this period. Cotton was still the most important commodity by a wide margin. Wheat and flour exports, which declined after the famine of 1847, expanded again during the Crimean War. Manufacturing exports showed a substantial absolute increase, although they were still a small percentage of the total. The total volume of exports increased dramatically. Consumer goods, particularly quality textiles, were still a large part of imports, but there was also a marked rise in capital goods associated with the railroad expansion.

The pattern of expansion from 1848 through 1856 was in many respects similar to that of the 1830's. Acceleration in development was evident in all regions in 1849. There was active railroad construction in the West, continued manufacturing growth in the East, feverish expansion in California, and a revival of cotton prices in the fall of that year. A shifting of people in the West out of self-sufficiency into the market economy, and the inflow of labor and capital, provided an important elasticity to the supply of productive factors during the expansion. The redirection of productive resources into railroad construction is indicated by the substantial railroad mileage added during the period (see Table 10). Immigrant labor and foreign capital played a large and complementary role in this expansion. The increase in domestic consumer and capital goods was again augmented by an import surplus, which was a tempering influence on the domestic price level as full employment was achieved.

The expansion of the 1850's was characterized by gradually rising prices, interrupted in 1851 and 1854. The latter marked a severe recession, particularly in the West. Recovery was rapid, however, and the economy continued to prosper until the downturn of 1857. The pace of the westward movement during these years was striking. In both 1855 and 1856 more than seventeen million acres were obtained from the federal government through purchase and military bounty warrants.[7] Taken in conjunction with the railroad extension of the period, the result was a very large increase in supply of agricultural commodities in later years.

IV

The crisis of 1857 reflected factors associated with rapid regional expansion, producing dislocations particularly in railroad finance and in the chain of dependence leading from the London money market. The pace of the westward movement was determined by the buoyant price of cereals, and with the end of the Crimean War and the revival of Russian grain exports, cereal prices fell and the westward movement slowed down more than a year before the downturn of 1857. The volume of internal trade also slackened.[8] It was only the buoyancy of eastern manufacturing, the cotton trade, and foreign trade which continued the prosperity and sustained the demand for western foodstuffs so that there was some upturn of western prices in 1857. The East and our external trade remained closely tied to European prosperity. The continuous demands of the Bank of France for specie were at the heart of the

---

[7] George Van Vleck, *The Panic of 1857* (New York: Columbia University Press, 1943), p. 32.

[8] Smith and Cole, *Fluctuations,* p. 104.

growing problem of stability.[9] The drain of specie to the Far East during and after the Crimean War led to strenuous efforts by the French to recoup specie from England. French success produced an ever growing strain on English banking and a rise in the rediscount rate. During the winter of 1856–1857, the rate of the Bank of England was between 6 per cent and 7 per cent, and the rate in the London money market was 8 per cent. English capital was increasingly rediverted to the domestic market.

Connections between the London money market, the financing of our external trade, and the New York money market put increasing strains on the United States banking structure. The failure of the Ohio Life Insurance and Trust Company was the spark that set off a four months' period of contraction, business failures and, with the flexible price structure, a sharp downward movement of prices. Rapid drain of specie from the New York banks to banks outside that city was quickly reversed by the rapid inflow of specie from California, and the net importation of over $2 million in specie to New York from foreign sources. Specie reserves increased from less than $8 million in October to $24 million in November, and to $31 million in January. New York banks, which had suspended specie payments in October, returned to that standard in December.

The worst of the crisis of 1857 was quickly over, but the years from 1858–1861 present no picture of booming expansion. Prices remained depressed, with little tendency to rise. There was some improvement in the middle of 1860, but there followed another sharp falling off of economic activity. Fundamentally, it was similar to the periods 1820–1823 and 1840–1843 which followed the sharp crises of 1818–1819 and 1839. In all three cases *capacity* had been substantially increased, so that even small price increases resulted in an increased supply and continually depressed prices. While the first period of assimilating extensive expansion was connected with cotton, and the second with both cotton and western foodstuffs, the third was exclusively connected with western agriculture.

The West was particularly affected during these years. Wheat prices remained low throughout the period. Economic activity, as

---

[9] For an extended account of the crisis and the influence of French specie movements see Van Vleck, *The Panic of 1857,* Chapter III.

shown in Berry's index, recovered from 144 in 1857 to 153 in 1858, then fell to 150 in 1860 and 140 in 1861.[10] A decline in land sales and western migration, a slowing down in railroad construction, and a diminution of eastern and foreign capital flowing into the West underlay conditions there.[11] Prices rose briefly in 1860, and economic affairs improved, only to decline sharply in 1861.[12]

Conditions in the South were in marked contrast to those in the West. The price of cotton during the previous decade had experienced no such rise as had western foodstuffs. It had improved gradually in the 1850's, but the price of slaves had also risen, and it is doubtful if profit expectations had improved very much. There was no speculative boom in cotton lands; supply had grown rather steadily and the South was not confronted by the problem of excess capacity which had occurred during the two previous periods of readjustment. Prices fell very little in the 1857 depression and remained relatively high during subsequent years.[13]

While the Northeast was affected by the depression in 1857, revival was rather rapid, and manufacturing appears to have experienced some prosperity in 1859 and early 1860. Stock prices of eastern railroads were in sharp contrast with those of western railroads. Like those of the West they fell in 1857, but thereafter they recovered and rose until the latter part of 1860, when the uncertainties of the election and the secession of South Carolina led to a break in stock prices.[14]

V

As the succession of events from Lincoln's election to the firing on Fort Sumter brought civil war from dark shadow to darker reality, the economy mirrored that growing uncertainty. For the rest of the Western World the nineteenth century continued as an era of progress, but the United States took time out to undergo

---

[10] Berry, *Western Prices*, p. 526.

[11] The course of western railroad stock prices mirrored the West's difficulties. See Smith and Cole, *Fluctuations*, pp. 110, 112.

[12] Conditions in the West were not paralleled in the Far West. California appears to have been little affected by the depression of 1857.

[13] The same conditions held for other southern staple commodities as well.

[14] Smith and Cole, *Fluctuations*, p. 112.

a fratricidal blood bath. It was costly on all scores. The political and social consequences are still in evidence a century later. The economic scars healed more rapidly. But the decade of the sixties was a real interruption of the accelerated economic growth which had gotten under way during the period of this study. In contrast to decade rates of growth in commodity output in excess of 60 per cent (in constant prices) for the 1850's and the 1870's, the rate for the 1860's was 23 per cent.[15] This painful break in United States economic expansion marked the end of an era, both socially and politically, but was only a pause in the economic expansion which was already deeply rooted in American society.

---

[15] Gallman, "Commodity Output," *loc. cit.*, Table 1.

APPENDIX I

INTERNATIONAL ECONOMIC RELATIONS—
STATISTICAL DATA

(Refers to Footnote 1, Chapter III.)

CALCULATION OF THE BALANCE OF PAYMENTS; FIVE-YEAR
MOVING AVERAGES, 1790-1794 TO 1818-1822; YEARLY 1820-1860
(millions of dollars)

Period	Merchandise Trade Balance	Specie Balance	Service and Current Items	Dividends and Interest	Annual Net Balance	Capital Accounts	Aggregate Indebtedness
1790-1794	− 7.3	1.9	8.4	−4.1	− 1.1	−0.1	70.0
1791-1795	−11.2	1.4	10.6	−4.2	− 3.4	−0.2	73.2
1792-1796	−12.1	0.8	13.3	−4.4	− 2.3	−0.3	75.9
1793-1797	−13.8	0.4	14.9	−4.6	− 3.0	−0.3	79.3
1794-1798	−14.3	− 0.2	15.6	−4.8	− 3.7	−0.3	83.3
1795-1799	−14.2	− 0.5	17.1	−5.0	− 2.6	−0.2	86.2
1796-1800	−14.0	0.2	18.5	−5.2	− 0.5	−0.1	86.8
1797-1801	−14.7	0.2	20.2	−5.2	0.5		84.3
1798-1802	−11.8	0.6	20.5	−5.2	4.2		82.1
1799-1803	−12.1	1.2	22.0	−4.9	6.1	−2.2	78.2
1800-1804	−13.5	1.4	22.5	−4.7	5.7	−2.2	74.8
1801-1805	−15.0	0.6	23.0	−4.5	4.1	−2.2	73.0
1802-1806	−18.2	1.2	23.5	−4.4	2.1	−2.2	73.1
1803-1807	−24.3	0.6	27.8	−4.4	− 0.3	−2.2	75.7
1804-1808	−29.3	0.8	27.6	−4.5	− 5.4		81.0
1805-1809	−29.2	0.8	27.7	−4.8	− 5.5		86.6
1806-1810	−27.7	0.8	29.9	−5.2	− 2.2		88.8
1807-1811	−20.0	− 0.2	31.9	−5.3	6.4		82.4
1808-1812	−20.7	− 0.8	29.8	−4.9	3.3		79.1
1809-1813	−12.5	− 1.2	28.1	−4.7	9.6		69.5
1810-1814	−11.9	− 2.2	23.8	−4.2	5.4		64.1
1811-1815	−14.0	− 1.4	20.3	−3.8	1.0		63.0
1812-1816	−28.6	− 0.6	15.3	−3.8	−17.7		76.7
1813-1817	−23.4	0.4	11.9	−4.6	−15.6	4.0	84.3
1814-1818	−31.3	0.4	12.3	−5.0	−23.7	8.0	94.0
1815-1819	−34.8	1.2	14.5	−5.6	−24.7	14.0	98.7
1816-1820	−29.2	0.8	12.6	−5.8	−21.6	20.0	100.3
1817-1821	−15.3	1.1	11.1	−5.8	− 8.9	16.0	93.2
1818-1822	−16.2	2.4	10.6	−5.3	− 8.5	12.0	89.7
1820	− 4.7		10.2	−4.8	0.7		86.7
1821	0.1	2.4	7.3	−4.8	5.0		81.7
1822	−18.5	7.4	7.2	−4.5	− 8.3		90.1
1823	− 4.2	1.3	9.8	−5.0	2.0		88.1
1824	− 3.2	− 1.4	10.4	−4.8	1.0		87.1
1825	0.5	2.6	8.4	−4.8	6.8		80.3
1826	− 5.2	− 2.2	9.2	−4.5	− 2.6		82.9
1827	3.0	− 0.1	11.7	−4.6	10.0		72.9
1828	−17.0	0.8	8.9	−4.0	−11.4		84.3
1829	0.3	− 2.5	8.2	−4.6	1.5		82.3
1830	9.0	− 6.0	9.5	−4.6	7.9		74.9
1831	−23.6	1.7	11.9	−4.1	−14.1		89.0
1832	−15.5	− 0.3	13.9	−4.9	− 6.8		95.7
1833	−15.5	− 4.5	11.8	−5.3	−13.5		109.2
1834	− 8.5	−15.8	11.6	−6.0	−18.0		128.0
1835	−24.3	− 6.7	8.0	−7.0	−30.0		158.1

TABLE A-III (continued)

CALCULATION OF THE BALANCE OF PAYMENTS; FIVE-YEAR
MOVING AVERAGES, 1790-1794 TO 1818-1822; YEARLY 1820-1860
(millions of dollars)

Period	Merchandise Trade Balance	Specie Balance	Service and Current Items	Dividends and Interest	Annual Net Balance	Capital Accounts	Aggregate Indebtedness
1836	−55.8	− 9.1	11.3	− 8.7	−62.2		220.3
1837	−21.6	− 4.5	12.4	− 8.8	−22.6		242.9
1838	6.1	−14.2	12.6	− 9.7	− 5.3		248.1
1839	−47.4	3.2	8.8	−13.6	−49.1		297.2
1840	23.4	− 0.5	19.7	−11.9	30.8		266.4
1841	−13.6	5.0	9.0	− 8.0	− 7.6	12.0	262.0
1842	1.9	0.7	11.5	− 7.9	6.2	12.0	243.8
1843	39.6	−20.8	10.8	− 7.3	22.2		221.6
1844	1.1	0.4	9.9	− 6.6	4.7		216.8
1845	− 9.4	4.5	17.4	− 8.7	3.8		213.0
1846	−13.0	0.1	22.2	− 8.5	0.8		212.2
1847	29.4	−22.2	27.9	− 8.5	26.6	−8.0	193.7
1848	−16.4	9.5	24.2	−11.6	5.7	−8.0	196.0
1849	− 6.5	− 1.2	27.8	−11.8	8.3	−5.5	193.2
1850	−36.1	2.9	20.2	−11.6	−24.6	−4.3	222.1
1851	−30.3	24.0	15.5	−13.3	− 4.1	−3.4	229.6
1852	−48.8	37.2	13.5	−14.9	−13.0	−3.2	245.8
1853	−70.8	23.3	8.0	−16.0	−55.6		301.3
1854	−72.7	34.4	22.7	−19.6	−35.1	−7.0	343.4
1855	−49.2	52.6	6.1	−22.3	−12.9		356.3
1856	−41.6	41.5	12.5	−23.2	−10.7		366.9
1857	−68.5	56.7	10.1	−14.7	−16.4		383.3
1858	− 1.9	33.4	6.9	−15.3	23.1		360.2
1859	−51.7	56.5	−7.6	−23.4	−26.2		386.5
1860	−34.2	58.0	8.6	−25.1	7.3		379.2

Source: North, "Balance of Payments," loc. cit., pp. 578,581.

TABLE B-III

(Refers to Chart I-III)

VALUE OF EXPORTS AND RE-EXPORTS 1790-1815
(thousands of dollars)

Year	Exports	Re-Exports	Year	Exports	Re-Exports
1790	20,205	300	1803	55,800	13,594
1791	19,012	500	1804	77,699	36,232
1792	20,753	1,000	1805	95,566	53,179
1793	26,110	1,750	1806	101,537	60,283
1794	33,044	6,500	1807	108,343	59,644
1795	47,989	8,300	1808	22,431	12,997
1796	67,064	26,300	1809	52,203	20,798
1797	56,850	27,000	1810	66,758	24,391
1798	61,527	33,000	1811	61,317	16,023
1799	78,666	45,523	1812	38,527	8,495
1800	70,972	49,131	1813	27,856	2,848
1801	94,116	46,643	1814	6,927	145
1802	72,483	35,775	1815	52,558	6,583

Source: North, "Balance of Payments," loc. cit., pp. 591-592.

TABLE C-III

(Refers to Chart II-III)

EXPORT PRICE INDEX 1790-1815

Year	Index number	Year	Index number
1790	100	1805	156.4
1791	85.8	1806	142.0
1792	81.7	1807	136.2
1793	97.8	1808	115.3
1794	103.6	1809	116.2
1795	153.6	1810	128.6
1796	172.6	1811	128.6
1797	174.8	1812	127.1
1798	207.4	1813	126.5
1799	220.3	1814	127.3
1800	145.9	1815	182.9
1801	154.1		
1802	131.6		
1803	132.8		
1804	147.7		

Source: Derivation for the figures in the above table is found in the charts and explanation of Appendix III.

TABLE D-III

(Refers to Chart IV-III)

FREIGHT RATES OF A NUMBER OF COMMODITIES ON DIFFERENT ROUTES 1790-1815

TIMBER: RIGA TO LONDON			TIMBER: MEMEL TO LONDON		
Date	Average Rate*	Rate Relative to 1790	Date	Average Rate*	Rate Relative to 1790
1790	18	100	1790	15	100
1791	18	100	1791	15	100
1792	18	100	1792	15.5	103
1793	32.5	181	1793	28.75	192
1794	32.5	181	1794	28.75	192
1795	36	200	1795	34.25	228
1796	40	222	1796	32.5	217
1797	25	139	1797	21	140
1798	35	194	1798	27.5	183
1799	50	278	1799	44	293
1800	55	306	1800	43	287
1801	40	222	1801	35	233
1802	24	133	1802	19	127
1803	47.5	264	1803	37.5	250
1804	40	222	1804	33	220
1805	40	222	1805	33	220
1806	38	211	1806	30.5	201
1807	50.05	278	1807	--	--
1808	132.33	735	1808	--	--
1809	--	--	1809	--	--
1810	--	--	1810	--	--
1811	--	--	1811	--	--
1812	55	306	1812	55	367
1813	--	--	1813	--	--
1814	--	--	1814	--	--
1815	--	--	1815	--	--

*Rate includes hat money & port charges, Shillings per load (50 cu. ft.)

*Shillings per load (50 cu. ft.), rate includes port charges

Sources: Riga to London: Collection of Interesting and Important Reports and Papers, Printed by the Order of the Ship Owners' Society of Great Britain (London: 1807). Great Britain, Parliament. Parliamentary Papers, 1835, Vol. 15 (No. 519), pp. 348-50; Parliamentary Papers, 1839, Vol. 46 (No. 240), p. 127.

Memel to London: Collection of Interesting and Important Reports and Papers. Parliamentary Papers, 1839, Vol. 46 (No. 240), p. 127.

TABLE D-III

FREIGHT RATES OF A NUMBER OF COMMODITIES ON DIFFERENT ROUTES 1790-1815 (cont.)

GENERAL COMMODITIES: ENGLAND TO OPORTO			GENERAL COMMODITIES: ENGLAND TO LISBON		
Date	Average Rate*	Rate Relative to 1790	Date	Average Rate*	Rate Relative to 1790
1790	1.12	100	1790	1.12	100
1791	1.12	100	1791	1.12	100
1792	1.12	100	1792	1.12	100
1793	1.69	151	1793	2.25	201
1794	1.69	151	1794	2.25	201
1795	1.69	151	1795	2.25	201
1796	--	--	1796	--	--
1797	--	--	1797	--	--
1798	--	--	1798	--	--
1799	--	--	1799	--	--
1800	1.69	151	1800	2.25	201
1801	1.69	151	1801	2.25	201
1802	1.69	151	1802	1.5	134
1803	3.0	268	1803	1.5	134
1804	3.0	268	1804	2.5	223
1805	2.0	179	1805	2.5	223
1806	2.0	179	1806	2.5	223
1807	--	--	1807	--	--
1808	--	--	1808	--	--
1809	--	--	1809	--	--
1810	--	--	1810	--	--
1811	--	--	1811	--	--
1812	--	--	1812	--	--
1813	--	--	1813	--	--
1814	--	--	1814	--	--
1815	--	--	1815	--	--

* £ per ton   * £ per ton

Source: Collection of Interesting and Important Reports and Papers, p. 167.

Appendix I

TABLE D-III

FREIGHT RATES OF A NUMBER OF COMMODITIES ON
DIFFERENT ROUTES 1790-1815 (cont.)

GENERAL COMMODITIES: OPORTO TO ENGLAND			GENERAL COMMODITIES: LISBON TO ENGLAND		
Date	Average Rate*	Rate Relative to 1790	Date	Average Rate*	Rate Relative to 1790
1790	2	100	1790	2.5	100
1791	2	100	1791	2.5	100
1792	2	100	1792	2.5	100
1793	5	250	1793	4.5	180
1794	5	250	1794	4.5	180
1795	5	250	1795	4.5	180
1796	--	--	1796	--	--
1797	--	--	1797	--	--
1798	--	--	1798	--	--
1799	--	--	1799	--	--
1800	6.5	325	1800	5	200
1801	6.5	325	1801	5	200
1802	3	150	1802	2.5	100
1803	6	300	1803	2.5	100
1804	6	300	1804	5	200
1805	5	250	1805	4.5	180
1806	5	250	1806	4.5	180
1807	--	--	1807	--	--
1808	--	--	1808	--	--
1809	--	--	1809	--	--
1810	--	--	1810	--	--
1811	--	--	1811	--	--
1812	--	--	1812	--	--
1813	--	--	1813	--	--
1814	--	--	1814	--	--
1815	--	--	1815	--	--

* £ per ton   * £ per ton

Source: Collection of Interesting and Important Reports and Papers, p. 167.

TABLE D-III

FREIGHT RATES OF A NUMBER OF COMMODITIES ON DIFFERENT ROUTES 1790-1815 (cont.)

RUM: JAMAICA TO ENGLAND			RUM: LEEWARD IS. TO ENGLAND		
Date	Average Rate*	Rate Relative to 1790	Date	Average Rate*	Rate Relative to 1790
1790	.5	100	1790	.5	100
1791	.5	100	1791	.5	100
1792	.5	100	1792	.5	100
1793	.66	132	1793	.5	100
1794	1.0	200	1794	.83	166
1795	1.0	200	1795	.83	166
1796	1.0	200	1796	.83	166
1797	1.0	200	1797	.83	166
1798	1.0	200	1798	.83	166
1799	1.0	200	1799	.83	166
1800	1.0	200	1800	.83	166
1801	1.0	200	1801	.83	166
1802	.66	132	1802	.5	100
1803	.50	100	1803	.5	100
1804	.83	166	1804	.66	132
1805	1.0	200	1805	.83	166
1806	1.0	200	1806	.83	166
1807	.92	184	1807	.83	166
1808	--	--	1808	--	--
1809	--	--	1809	--	--
1810	--	--	1810	--	--
1811	--	--	1811	--	--
1812	--	--	1812	--	--
1813	--	--	1813	--	--
1814	--	--	1814	--	--
1815	--	--	1815	--	--

*Shillings per gallon   *Shillings per gallon

Source: Great Britain. Parliament. Parliamentary Papers, 1808, Vol. 4, p. 376, Report from the Committee on the Distillation of Sugar and Molasses.

TABLE D-III

FREIGHT RATES OF A NUMBER OF COMMODITIES ON DIFFERENT ROUTES 1790-1815 (cont.)

HEMP: PETERSBURG TO LONDON			SUGAR: JAMAICA TO ENGLAND		
Date	Average Rate*	Rate Relative to 1790	Date	Average Rate*	Rate Relative to 1790
1790	1.62	100	1790	4	100
1791	1.62	100	1791	4	100
1792	1.62	100	1792	5	125
1793	3.25	201	1793	8	200
1794	3.25	201	1794	9	225
1795	4.0	247	1795	9	225
1796	4.12	254	1796	9	225
1797	3.0	185	1797	9	225
1798	3.38	209	1798	10	250
1799	5.38	332	1799	10	250
1800	5.0	309	1800	10	250
1801	4.5	278	1801	10	250
1802	2.38	147	1802	6	150
1803	4.75	293	1803	5	125
1804	3.75	231	1804	9	225
1805	3.75	231	1805	9.5	238
1806	4.25	262	1806	9.5	238
1807	--	--	1807	9.75	244
1808	--	--	1808	--	--
1809	30.0	1852	1809	--	--
1810	30.0	1852	1810	--	--
1811	30.0	1852	1811	--	--
1812	30.0	1852	1812	--	--
1813	--	--	1813	--	--
1814	--	--	1814	--	--
1815	--	--	1815	9.5	244

* £ per ton   *Shillings per cubic weight

Sources: Hemp. Collection of Interesting and Important Reports and Papers, Supplement, p. 166. Thomas Tooke, A History of Prices and the State of the Circulation of Trade from 1793 to 1837 (London: Longman, Orme, Brown, Green and Longman, 1838-1857), I, 309.

Sugar. Great Britain, Parliament. Parliamentary Papers, 1808, Vol. 4, p. 376. Parliamentary Papers, 1831-32, Vol. 20 (No. 318), n.p., Report from the Select Committee on the Commercial State of the West Indian Colonies.

TABLE D-III

FREIGHT RATES OF A NUMBER OF COMMODITIES ON DIFFERENT ROUTES 1790-1815 (cont.)

WAINSCOT LOGS: RIGA TO LONDON			TALLOW: PETERSBURG TO LONDON		
Date	Average Rate*	Rate Relative to 1790	Date	Average Rate*	Rate Relative to 1790
1790	7.25	100	1790	1.25	100
1791	7.25	100	1791	1.25	100
1792	7.25	100	1792	1.25	100
1793	11.08	153	1793	2.19	175
1794	17.50	241	1794	2.25	180
1795	13.66	188	1795	2.50	200
1796	8.83	122	1796	2.50	200
1797	12.25	169	1797	2.0	160
1798	18.75	259	1798	2.25	180
1799	18.33	253	1799	3.31	265
1800	7.33	101	1800	3.0	240
1801	10.66	147	1801	2.75	220
1802	16.08	221	1802	1.63	130
1803	14.5	200	1803	2.62	210
1804	16.66	230	1804	2.50	200
1805	16	221	1805	2.50	200
1806	19.83	274	1806	2.75	220
1807	42	579	1807	--	--
1808	--	--	1808	--	--
1809	42	579	1809	20.0	160
1810	--	--	1810	20.0	160
1811	--	--	1811	20.0	160
1812	--	--	1812	20.0	160
1813	--	--	1813	--	--
1814	--	--	1814	--	--
1815	--	--	1815	--	--

*Shillings per log   * £ per ton

Sources: Wainscot logs. Great Britain, Parliament. Parliamentary Papers, 1835, Vol. 15 (No. 519), n.p.
Tallow. Collection of Interesting and Important Reports and Papers. Tooke, History of Prices, I, 309.

TABLE E-III

(Refers to Chart V-III)

VALUE OF IMPORTS AND VALUE OF IMPORTS FOR CONSUMPTION,
1790-1815

Date	Value of Imports	Value of Imports for Consumption
1790	23,800,000	23,500,000
1791	30,500,000	30,000,000
1792	32,500,000	31,500,000
1793	32,550,000	30,800,000
1794	36,000,000	29,500,000
1795	71,300,000	63,000,000
1796	82,936,164	56,636,164
1797	77,379,406	50,379,406
1798	70,551,700	37,551,700
1799	81,069,148	35,546,148
1800	93,252,768	44,121,891
1801	113,363,511	66,720,790
1802	78,333,333	42,558,362
1803	65,666,666	52,072,594
1804	87,000,000	50,768,403
1805	125,525,175	72,346,156[a]
1806	136,561,730	76,278,496
1807	144,740,342	85,096,784
1808	58,101,023	45,103,609
1809	61,029,726	40,232,195
1810	89,366,069	64,974,774
1811	57,887,952	41,865,162
1812	78,788,540	70,293,413
1813	22,177,812	19,329,967
1814	12,967,859	12,822,690
1815	85,356,680	78,773,330

[a] Value of imports for consumption 1805-1815, Table A-2, Column 7 minus Column 2.

Source: North, "Balance of Payments," loc. cit., Table A-2, Appendix A.

TABLE F-III

(Refers to Chart VI-III)

IMPORT PRICE INDEX 1790-1815
Base 1790

Year	Index Number	Year	Index Number
1790	100	1805	139.5
1791	109.8	1806	129.8
1792	118.8	1807	124.7
1793	108.4	1808	124.3
1794	129.2	1809	129.1
1795	124.3	1810	129.8
1796	132.8	1811	121.1
1797	139.9	1812	131.7
1798	127.6	1813	179.7
1799	135.5	1814	232.3
1800	124.6	1815	191.3
1801	119.9		
1802	111.8		
1803	118		
1804	134.7		

Source: Derivation for the figures in the above table is found in the charts and explanation of Appendix III.

TABLE G-III

(Refers to Chart VII-III)

UNITED STATES TERMS OF TRADE 1790-1815
Base 1790

Year	Index Number	Year	Index Number
1790	100	1805	112.1
1791	78.1	1806	109.4
1792	68.8	1807	109.2
1793	90.2	1808	92.8
1794	80.2	1809	90
1795	123.6	1810	99.1
1796	130	1811	106.2
1797	124.9	1812	96.5
1798	162.5	1813	70.4
1799	162.6	1814	54.8
1800	117.1	1815	95.6
1801	128.5		
1802	117.7		
1803	112.5		
1804	109.7		

Source: Calculated from import and export price indices found in Charts II-III and VI-III.

TABLE A-IV

(Refers to Chart I-IV)

VOLUME OF EXPORTS IN POUNDS 1792-1814: COCOA, COFFEE, PEPPER AND SUGAR

Year	Cocoa	Coffee	Pepper	Sugar, brown & other clayed
1792	6,000	2,136,742	5,040	1,176,156
1793	234,875	17,580,049	14,361	4,539,809
1794	1,188,302	33,720,983	23,886	20,721,761
1795	525,432	47,443,179	301,692	21,377,747
1796	928,107	62,385,117	491,330	34,848,644
1797	875,334	44,521,887	1,901,130	38,366,262
1798	3,146,445	49,580,927	501,982	51,703,963
1799	5,970,590	31,987,088	441,312	78,821,751
1800	4,925,518	38,597,479	635,849	56,432,516
1801	7,012,155	45,106,494	3,153,139	97,565,732
1802	3,878,526	36,501,998	5,422,144	61,061,820
1803	367,177	10,294,693	2,991,430	23,223,849
1804	695,135	48,312,713	5,703,646	74,964,366
1805	2,425,680	46,760,294	7,559,224	123,031,272
1806	6,846,758	47,001,662	4,111,983	145,837,320
1807	8,540,524	42,122,573	4,207,166	143,136,905
1808	1,896,990	7,325,448	1,709,978	28,974,927
1809	2,029,336	24,364,099	4,722,098	45,248,128
1810	1,286,010	31,423,477	5,946,336	47,038,125
1811	2,221,442	10,261,136	3,057,456	18,383,673
1812	752,148	10,073,722	2,521,003	13,927,277
1813	108,188	6,568,527	99,660	7,347,038
1814	27,386	220,594	--	762

Source: Timothy Pitkin, A Statistical View of the Commerce of the United States of America, Chapter III, Table IV.

TABLE B-IV

(Refers to Chart II-IV)

VOLUME OF COTTON EXPORTS, 1791-1815

Year	Thousands of pounds	Year	Thousands of pounds
1791	189	1804	38,118
1792	138	1805	40,383
1793	488	1806	37,491
1794	1,602	1807	66,213
1795	6,276	1808	12,064
1796	6,107	1809	53,210
1797	3,788	1810	93,874
1798	9,360	1811	62,186
1799	9,532	1812	28,953
1800	17,790	1813	19,400
1801	20,911	1814	17,806
1802	27,501	1815	82,999
1803	41,106		

Source: Matthew B. Hammond, The Cotton Industry, an Essay in American Economic History, Part I, The Cotton Culture and the Cotton Trade (New York: MacMillan, for the American Economic Association, 1897).

TABLE C-IV

(Refers to Chart III-IV)

UNITED STATES SHIPPING ACTIVITY INDEX

Year	Activity* Index	Year	Activity* Index
1790	91	1803	120
1791	91	1804	113
1792	93	1805	114
1793	117	1806	121
1794	115	1807	125
1795	106	1808	68
1796	114	1809	64
1797	100	1810	90
1798	87	1811	106
1799	96	1812	77
1800	105	1813	32
1801	115	1814	9
1802	125	1815	76

*Obtained by dividing net tonnage capacity entered (from Historical Statistics, p. 216) into gross registered tonnage and calculating upon base of 1796-1800 equals 100.

Source: North, "Balance of Payments," loc. cit., Appendix A, Table A-3.

TABLE A-VII

(Refers to Chart II-VII)

COTTON PRICES
(AVERAGE NEW YORK PRICES FOR MIDDLING UPLANDS)

AND

COTTON PRODUCTION & LAND SALES
(ALABAMA, ARKANSAS, FLORIDA, LOUISIANA & MISSISSIPPI)

1833-1842

Year	Price (cents)	Production (bales)	Land Sales (acres)
1833	12.32	559,210	1,816,083
1834	12.90	641,435	2,388,146
1835	17.45	760,923	5,522,474
1836	16.50	788,013	5,805,180
1837	13.25	916,960	1,259,814
1838	10.14	747,227	821,600
1839	13.36	911,913	851,586
1840	8.92	1,538,904	401,394
1841	9.50	1,231,334	228,699
1842	7.85	1,160,389	238,079

Source: M. B. Hammond, The Cotton Industry, an Essay in American Economic History. Part I. The Cotton Culture and the Cotton Trade (New York: Mac-Millan. published for the American Economic Association, 1897), pp. 72 and Appendix I.

TABLE A-VIII

(Refers to Chart I-VIII)

VALUE OF TOTAL EXPORTS AND COTTON EXPORTS 1815-1860

Year	Total Exports	Cotton Exports
1815	52,557,753	17,529,000
1816	81,920,452	24,106,000
1817	87,671,569	22,627,614
1818	93,281,133	31,334,258
1819	70,142,521	21,081,760
1820	69,692,000	22,308,667
1821	54,596,000	20,157,484
1822	61,350,000	24,035,058
1823	68,326,000	20,445,520
1824	68,972,000	21,947,401
1825	90,738,000	36,846,649
1826	72,891,000	25,025,214
1827	74,310,000	29,359,545
1828	64,021,000	22,487,229
1829	67,435,000	26,575,311
1830	71,671,000	29,674,883
1831	72,296,000	25,289,492
1832	81,521,000	31,724,682
1833	87,529,000	36,191,105
1834	102,260,000	49,448,402
1835	115,216,000	64,961,302
1836	124,339,000	71,284,925
1837	111,443,000	63,240,102
1838	104,979,000	61,556,811
1839	112,252,000	61,238,982
1840	123,669,000	63,870,307
1841	111,817,000	54,330,341
1842	99,878,000	47,593,464
1843	82,826,000	49,119,806
1844	105,746,000	54,063,501
1845	106,040,000	51,739,643
1846	109,583,000	42,767,341
1847	156,742,000	53,415,848
1848	138,191,000	61,998,294
1849	140,351,000	66,396,967
1850	144,376,000	71,984,616
1851	188,915,000	112,315,317
1852	166,984,000	87,965,732
1853	203,489,000	109,456,404
1854	237,044,000	93,596,220
1855	218,910,000	88,143,844
1856	281,219,000	128,382,351
1857	293,824,000	131,575,859
1858	272,011,000	131,386,661
1859	292,902,000	161,434,923
1860	333,576,000	191,806,555

Sources: Total exports: North, ''Balance of Payments,'' loc. cit., Table 1, and Table B-1, Appendix B. Cotton exports: U.S. Congress, House, Miscellaneous Document No. 49, 48th Congress, 1st Session, 1884, Part 2, Tables 2 and 7.

TABLE B-VIII

(Refers to Chart II-VIII)

NET U.S. SHIPPING EARNINGS AND EARNINGS OF FOREIGN SHIPS
CARRYING U.S. IMPORTS, 1815-1860 [1]
(in millions of dollars)

Year	American earnings	Foreign earnings	Year	American earnings	Foreign earnings
1815	20.6		1838	18.5	1.0
1816	16.9		1839	11.5	1.6
1817	10.8		1840	26.2	1.4
1818	16.3		1841	12.5	1.4
1819	15.2		1842	12.8	1.1
1820	13.9	.6	1843	15.0	1.5
1821	10.5	.5	1844	13.4	1.3
1822	10.0	.6	1845	18.8	1.4
1823	13.4	.6	1846	16.6	1.5
1824	13.5	.6	1847	18.5	2.9
1825	11.6	.4	1848	16.0	2.4
1826	12.6	.4	1849	15.6	2.5
1827	14.2	.5	1850	8.6	3.2
1828	10.1	.7	1851	26.4	4.7
1829	9.8	.5	1852	15.9	5.5
1830	10.5	.4	1853	20.5	8.9
1831	14.2	1.0	1854	25.8	10.2
1832	11.5	1.2	1855	21.2	3.9
1833	9.1	1.0	1856	26.4	4.0
1834	9.5	1.3	1857	16.1	7.1
1835	8.8	1.5	1858	21.6	4.1
1836	10.1	1.6	1859	22.2	9.8
1837	12.8	1.8	1860	32.5	10.2

TABLE C-VIII

(Refers to Chart III-VIII)

VALUE OF IMPORTS 1815-1860 [2]

Year		Year		Year	
1815	85,356,680	1831	95,885,000	1847	127,321,000
1816	151,448,644	1832	97,024,000	1848	154,585,000
1817	101,652,436	1833	103,069,000	1849	146,854,000
1818	127,120,105	1834	110,782,000	1850	180,450,000
1819	93,501,200	1835	139,499,000	1851	219,202,000
1820	74,450,000	1836	180,111,000	1852	215,738,000
1821	54,521,000	1837	133,082,000	1853	274,328,000
1822	79,872,000	1838	97,889,000	1854	309,716,000
1823	72,481,000	1839	159,627,000	1855	268,121,000
1824	72,169,000	1840	100,224,000	1856	322,849,000
1825	90,189,000	1841	125,417,000	1857	362,365,000
1826	78,094,000	1842	97,997,000	1858	273,873,000
1827	71,333,000	1843	43,282,000	1859	344,586,000
1828	81,094,000	1844	104,657,000	1860	367,760,000
1829	67,089,000	1845	115,448,000		
1830	62,721,000	1846	122,630,000		

Source: North, "Balance of Payments," loc. cit., (1) Table A-3, Appendix A,
and Table B-2, Appendix B; (2) Table 1, and Table B-1, Appendix B.

TABLE D-VIII

(Refers to Chart IV-VIII)

IMMIGRANTS FROM THE UNITED KINGDOM, 1844-1860, GRAPHED
AGAINST IMMIGRANT REMITTANCES TO THE UNITED KINGDOM
1847-1863

Year	Number of Immigrants	Remittances in thousands of dollars
1844	47,843	
1845	64,031	
1846	73,932	
1847	128,838	1,363
1848	148,093	2,240
1849	214,530	2,630
1850	215,089	4,661
1851	272,740	4,821
1852	200,247	6,837
1853	200,225	7,008
1854	160,253	8,425
1855	97,199	4,252
1856	99,007	4,631
1857	112,840	2,883
1858	55,829	2,304
1859	61,379	2,532
1860	78,374	2,601
1861		1,800
1862		1,800
1863		1,900

Sources: Number of Immigrants, Historical Statistics, Series B306-307, p. 34;
Remittances, 1847-1860, North, "Balance of Payments," loc. cit., Table B-3,
Appendix B; 1861-1863, Matthew Simon, "Statistical Estimates of the Balance
of International Payments and the International Capital Movements of the United
States, 1861-1900," 24th Conference on Income and Wealth of the National Bureau of Economic Research (Princeton: Princeton University Press, forthcom-
ing), Table XXI, p. 88.

TABLE E-VIII

(Refers to Chart V-VIII)

QUOTIENT OF UNITED STATES WHOLESALE PRICE INDEX (BASE 1830)
DIVIDED BY ENGLISH WHOLESALE PRICE INDEX (BASE 1830)
GRAPHED AGAINST SPECIE FLOWS, 1815-1860

Year	Quotient of Wholesale Prices	Specie Flows (in thousands of dollars)	Year	Quotient of Wholesale Prices	Specie Flows (in thousands of dollars)
1815	138	2,000	1838	111	− 14,239
1816	146	1,000	1839	109	3,181
1817	113	1,000	1840	92	− 466
1818	98	1,000	1841	92	5,046
1819	98	1,000	1842	90	727
1820	90	--	1843	90	− 20,799
1821	97	2,413	1844	92	376
1822	105	7,440	1845	96	4,534
1823	100	1,275	1846	94	128
1824	93	− 1,364	1847	94	− 22,214
1825	88	2,647	1848	106	9,480
1826	99	− 2,177	1849	111	− 1,248
1827	102	− 137	1850	108	2,894
1828	101	753	1851	110	24,013
1829	103	− 2,480	1852	114	37,169
1830	100	− 5,977	1853	102	23,286
1831	102	1,709	1854	106	34,438
1832	107	− 252	1855	109	52,587
1833	104	− 4,459	1856	105	41,539
1834	100	− 15,834	1857	106	56,675
1835	109	− 6,654	1858	102	33,359
1836	112	− 9,077	1859	100	56,453
1837	121	− 4,540	1860	94	57,996

Sources: Quotients of wholesale prices calculated from wholesale price indices found in G. F. Warren and F. A. Pearson, Wholesale Prices for 213 Years, 1720 to 1932 (Ithaca: Cornell University Press, 1932), Part I, pp. 8, 9, 17. Specie movements, from North, "Balance of Payments," loc. cit., Table A-4, Appendix A, and Table B-1, Appendix B.

TABLE F-VIII

(Refers to Chart VI-VIII)

INTEREST AND DIVIDENDS ON FOREIGN INDEBTEDNESS 1815-1860
(in thousands of dollars)

Year		Year	
1815	5,000*	1838	9,715
1816	5,600*	1839	13,648
1817	5,800*	1840	11,888
1818	5,800*	1841	7,993
1819	5,300*	1842	7,860
1820	4,807	1843	7,313
1821	4,770	1844	6,648
1822	4,495	1845	8,674
1823	4,955	1846	8,490
1824	4,845	1847	11,621
1825	4,792	1848	11,759
1826	4,416	1849	11,594
1827	4,559	1850	13,326
1828	4,011	1851	14,978
1829	4,637	1852	19,589
1830	4,557	1853	21,870
1831	4,121	1854	22,677
1832	4,894	1855	22,320
1833	5,268	1856	23,156
1834	6,007	1857	14,677
1835	7,042	1858	15,332
1836	8,693	1859	23,416
1837	8,812	1860	25,122

*five year moving averages

Source: North, "Balance of Payments," loc. cit., p. 575, and Table B-4, Appendix B.

TABLE G-VIII

(Refers to Chart VIII-VIII)

RESIDUAL BALANCE OF PAYMENTS 1790-1860
(millions of dollars)

Year	Balance	Year	Balance	Year	Balance	Year	Balance
1790	− 1.1	1808	−16.8	1826	− 2.6	1844	4.7
1791	− 8.0	1809	11.6	1827	10.0	1845	3.8
1792	− 7.5	1810	6.8	1828	−11.4	1846	0.8
1793	1.7	1811	35.4	1829	1.5	1847	26.6
1794	9.4	1812	−20.7	1830	7.9	1848	5.7
1795	−12.4	1813	15.0	1831	−14.1	1849	8.3
1796	− 2.9	1814	− 9.3	1832	− 6.8	1850	−24.6
1797	−11.0	1815	−15.2	1833	−13.5	1851	− 4.1
1798	− 1.5	1816	−58.1	1834	−18.0	1852	−13.0
1799	14.6	1817	−10.5	1835	−30.0	1853	−55.6
1800	− 1.8	1818	−25.2	1836	−62.2	1854	−35.1
1801	2.3	1819	−14.7	1837	−22.6	1855	−12.9
1802	7.2	1820	0.7	1838	− 5.3	1856	−10.7
1803	8.4	1821	5.0	1839	−49.1	1857	−16.4
1804	12.4	1822	− 8.3	1840	30.8	1858	23.1
1805	−10.0	1823	2.0	1841	− 7.6	1859	−26.2
1806	− 7.4	1824	1.0	1842	6.2	1860	7.3
1807	− 5.1	1825	6.8	1843	22.2		

Source: North, "Balance of Payments," loc. cit., pp. 581, 600.

TABLE H-VIII

(Refers to Chart IX-VIII)

AGGREGATE FOREIGN INDEBTEDNESS, 1815-1860
(in millions of dollars)

Year		Year		Year	
1815	94.0*	1831	89.0	1846	212.2
1816	98.7*	1832	95.7	1847	193.7
1817	100.3*	1833	109.2	1848	196.0
1818	93.2*	1834	128.0	1849	193.2
1819	89.7*	1835	158.1	1850	222.1
1820	86.7	1836	220.3	1851	229.6
1821	81.7	1837	242.9	1852	245.8
1822	90.1	1838	248.1	1853	301.3
1823	88.1	1839	297.2	1854	343.3
1824	87.1	1840	266,4	1855	356.3
1825	80.3	1841	262.0	1856	366.9
1826	82.9	1842	243.8	1857	383.3
1827	72.9	1843	221.6	1858	360.2
1828	84.3	1844	216,8	1859	386.5
1829	82.8	1845	213.0	1860	379.2
1830	74.9				

*five year moving averages

Source: North, "Balance of Payments," loc. cit., p. 575; Table B-5, Appendix B.

TABLE I-VIII

(Refers to Chart X-VIII)

EXPORT INDEX AND THE PRICE OF COTTON, 1815-1860 (BASE 1830)

Year	Exports	Cotton Price relatives
1815	182.98	213.1
1816	248.22	297.0
1817	240.35	266.7
1818	245.46	342.4
1819	294.74	242.4
1820	144.17	175.8
1821	127.92	162.6
1822	136.32	167.7
1823	114.37	119.2
1824	126.16	155.6
1825	152.47	211.1
1826	114.78	123.2
1827	102.53	101.0
1828	102.10	108.1
1829	107.07	101.0
1830	100.00	100.0
1831	98.77	91.9
1832	104.63	100.0
1833	115.08	112.1
1834	127.01	129.3
1835	149.81	169.7
1836	155.37	169.7
1837	142.57	143.4
1838	115.87	104.0
1839	155.85	149.5
1840	99.73	86.9
1841	110.19	103.0
1842	93.84	81.8
1843	75.83	62.6
1844	89.20	81.8
1845	78.32	59.6
1846	92.79	78.8
1847	112.79	102.0
1848	94.29	76.8
1849	84.17	65.7
1850	120.72	123.2
1851	123.72	122.2
1852	96.30	81.8
1853	93.50	99.0
1854	116.74	96.0
1855	119.04	87.9
1856	124.43	96.0
1857	141.90	127.3
1858	128.29	118.2
1859	126.46	117.2
1860	119.81	109.1

Sources: Export index - see Chart XV, this chapter; cotton price relatives calculated from cotton prices found in U.S. Congress, House, Miscellaneous Document No. 49, 48th Congress, 1st Session, 1884, Part 2, Tables 2 and 7.

TABLE J-VIII

(Refers to Chart XI-VIII)

EXPORT PRICE INDEX &WARREN AND PEARSON WHOLESALE
PRICE INDEX. 1815-1860 (BASE 1830)

Year	Export Index	Warren-Pearson Index
1815	182.98	187
1816	248.22	166
1817	240.35	166
1818	245.46	162
1819	194.74	137
1820	144.17	116
1821	127.92	112
1822	136.32	116
1823	114.37	113
1824	126.16	108
1825	152.47	113
1826	114.78	109
1827	102.53	108
1828	102.10	107
1829	107.07	105
1830	100.00	100
1831	98.77	103
1832	104.63	104
1833	115.08	104
1834	127.01	99
1835	149.81	110
1836	155.37	125
1837	142.57	126
1838	115.87	121
1839	155.85	123
1840	99.73	104
1841	110.19	101
1842	93.84	90
1843	75.83	82
1844	89.20	85
1845	78.32	91
1846	92.79	91
1847	112.79	99
1848	94.29	90
1849	84.17	90
1850	120.72	92
1851	123.72	91
1852	96.30	97
1853	93.50	107
1854	116.74	119
1855	119.04	121
1856	124.43	115
1857	141.90	122
1858	128.29	102
1859	126.46	104
1860	119.81	102

Sources: Export Index, see Chart XI-VIII; Warren-Pearson Index, G. R. Warren
and F. A. Pearson, <u>Wholesale Prices for 213 Years, 1720-1932</u> (Ithaca: Cornell
University Press, 1932), Part I, pp. 8-9.

TABLE K-VIII

(Refers to Chart XII-VIII)

VOLUME INDEX, U. S. EXPORTS, 1815-1860
(BASE 1830)

Year	Index	Year	Index
1815	42.93	1838	140.92
1816	44.60	1839	111.42
1817	48.57	1840	191.31
1818	51.41	1841	160.71
1819	44.73	1842	167.15
1820	61.26	1843	175.05
1821	58.34	1844	190.66
1822	62.51	1845	214.80
1823	70.45	1846	187.31
1824	68.60	1847	228.11
1825	75.02	1848	235.95
1826	78.08	1849	267.38
1827	96.46	1850	190.94
1828	83.64	1851	246.69
1829	87.91	1852	274.90
1830	100.00	1853	346.98
1831	102.45	1854	315.17
1832	100.81	1855	276.68
1833	103.86	1856	365.88
1834	108.46	1857	335.85
1835	114.58	1858	334.78
1836	117.20	1859	376.16
1837	113.00	1860	451.02

Source: Obtained by dividing yearly components of export price index (see Chart XV, this chapter) into corresponding yearly export values (taken from series M52, "Exports of U.S. Merchandise," Historical Statistics), which gives a series in constant dollars. This series expressed as relatives to the base 1830 of 100 gives the above volume index.

TABLE L-VIII

(Refers to Chart XIII-VIII)

IMPORT PRICE INDEX AND INDICES OF ITS COMPONENT PARTS
1815-1860 (BASE 1830)

Year	Imports	Raw Mat. & Crude Food	Manufactured Foods	Manufacturers & Semi-mfgs
1815	222.7	170.9	275.5	239.6
1816	194.9	169.2	222.3	203.7
1817	176.8	148.7	201.1	186.9
1818	189.7	160.6	195.6	203.7
1819	171.9	162.3	173.6	177.3
1820	151.2	150.4	148.8	153.3
1821	134.0	145.3	129.5	131.8
1822	133.6	151.8	129.0	129.4
1823	127.7	151.4	121.3	122.3
1824	119.8	134.1	100.8	119.8
1825	127.1	138.0	124.8	125.1
1826	121.6	133.1	129.2	116.6
1827	111.1	113.5	127.4	106.9
1828	112.3	113.3	129.0	108.3
1829	105.9	112.3	112.7	102.7
1830	100.0	100.0	100.0	100.0
1831	95.8	100.6	98.4	93.8
1832	93.6	109.8	103.7	86.5
1833	100.0	122.3	116.7	89.7
1834	103.3	129.1	117.2	92.4
1835	101.3	118.4	116.8	92.9
1836	109.6	118.5	147.8	99.6
1837	104.1	117.1	129.9	95.1
1838	90.8	97.9	81.5	90.3
1839	97.8	102.5	123.0	91.4
1840	94.0	102.4	106.3	89.0
1841	91.3	104.9	104.8	84.7
1842	82.8	95.2	84.2	78.5
1843	79.4	88.7	82.8	75.7
1844	78.2	80.9	95.4	74.2
1845	80.9	85.9	106.3	74.9
1846	81.6	75.9	103.3	79.0
1847	82.3	77.7	100.5	80.0
1848	74.1	77.0	91.9	70.0
1849	72.0	75.0	85.2	68.6
1850	74.2	79.0	90.2	69.7
1851	78.8	95.9	90.7	71.1
1852	75.5	88.2	85.8	69.6
1853	83.3	98.6	90.3	77.4
1854	83.2	101.2	89.6	76.6
1855	84.7	95.4	99.2	78.8
1856	89.8	100.6	125.2	79.9
1857	95.8	103.1	158.8	81.7
1858	91.7	103.1	135.6	80.0
1859	90.2	106.0	127.7	78.3
1860	92.2	97.5	133.3	78.0

Source: See chart XV-VIII, and the discussion of the export and import price indices in Appendix III.

TABLE M-VIII

(Refers to Chart XIV-VIII)

REAL VALUE OF IMPORTS
(Value of imports deflated by Import Price Index)

Year		Year		Year		Year	
1815	38,328	1827	64,206	1839	163,218	1851	278,175
1816	77,706	1828	72,212	1840	106,621	1852	285,746
1817	57,496	1829	63,351	1841	137,368	1853	329,325
1818	67,011	1830	62,721	1842	118,354	1854	372,255
1819	54,393	1831	100,089	1843	54,511	1855	316,554
1820	49,239	1832	103,658	1844	133,832	1856	359,520
1821	40,687	1833	103,069	1845	142,704	1857	378,252
1822	59,784	1834	107,243	1846	150,282	1858	298,662
1823	56,759	1835	137,709	1847	154,704	1859	382,024
1824	60,241	1836	164,335	1848	208,617	1860	398,872
1825	70,959	1837	127,841	1849	203,964		
1826	64,222	1838	107,807	1850	243,194		

Source: Calculated from Imports and Price Index, see Charts XII-VIII and
XV-VIII, and Appendix III.

TABLE N-VIII

(Refers to Chart XV-VIII)

EXPORT AND IMPORT PRICE INDICES 1815-1860
(BASE 1830)

Year	Exports	Imports	Year	Exports	Imports
1815	182.98	222.7	1838	115.87	90.8
1816	248.22	194.9	1839	155.85	97.8
1817	240.35	176.8	1840	99.73	94.0
1818	245.46	189.7	1841	110.19	91.3
1819	194.74	171.9	1842	93.84	82.8
1820	144.17	151.2	1843	75.83	79.4
1821	127.92	134.0	1844	89.20	78.2
1822	136.32	133.6	1845	78.32	80.9
1823	114.37	127.7	1846	92.79	81.6
1824	126.16	119.8	1847	112.79	82.3
1825	152.47	127.1	1848	94.29	74.1
1826	114.78	121.6	1849	84.17	72.0
1827	102.53	111.1	1850	120.72	74.2
1828	102.10	112.∴	1851	123.72	78.8
1829	107.07	105.9	1852	96.30	75.5
1830	100.00	100.0	1853	93.50	83.3
1831	98.77	95.8	1854	116.74	83.2
1832	104.63	93.6	1855	119.04	84.7
1833	115.08	100.0	1856	124.43	89.8
1834	127.01	103.3	1857	141.90	95.8
1835	149.81	101.3	1858	128.29	91.7
1836	155.37	109.6	1859	126.46	90.2
1837	142.57	104.1	1860	119.81	92.2

Sources: For derivation of table, see Appendix III.

TABLE O-VIII

(Refers to Chart XVI-VIII)

TERMS OF TRADE, 1815-1860
(Base 1830)

Year		Year		Year		Year		Year	
1815	82	1825	120	1834	123	1843	96	1852	128
1816	127	1826	94	1835	148	1844	114	1853	112
1817	136	1827	92	1836	142	1845	97	1854	140
1818	129	1828	91	1837	137	1846	114	1855	141
1819	113	1829	101	1838	128	1847	137	1856	139
1820	95	1830	100	1839	160	1848	127	1857	148
1821	95	1831	103	1840	106	1849	117	1858	140
1822	102	1832	112	1841	121	1850	163	1859	140
1823	90	1833	115	1842	113	1851	157	1860	130
1824	105								

Source: Calculated from Export & Import Price Indices, see Chart XV-VIII, and Appendix III.

TABLE P-VIII

(Refers to Chart XVII-VIII)

TERMS OF TRADE AND THE RESIDUAL OF THE BALANCE OF PAYMENTS
1815-1860

Year	Terms of Trade (Base 1830)	Residual Balance (in millions of dollars)	Year	Terms of Trade (Base 1830)	Residual Balance (in millions of dollars)
1815	82	−15.2	1838	128	− 5.3
1816	127	−58.1	1839	160	−49.1
1817	136	−10.5	1840	106	30.8
1818	129	−25.2	1841	121	− 7.6
1819	113	−14.7	1842	113	6.2
1820	95	.7	1843	96	22.2
1821	95	5.0	1844	114	4.7
1822	102	− 8.3	1845	97	3.8
1823	90	2.0	1846	114	.8
1824	105	1.0	1847	137	26.6
1825	120	6.8	1848	127	5.7
1826	94	− 2.6	1849	117	8.3
1827	92	10.0	1850	163	−24.6
1828	91	−11.4	1851	157	− 4.1
1829	101	1.5	1852	128	−13.0
1830	100	7.9	1853	112	−55.6
1831	103	−14.1	1854	140	−35.1
1832	112	− 6.8	1855	141	−12.9
1833	115	−13.5	1856	139	−10.7
1834	123	−18.0	1857	148	−16.4
1835	148	−30.0	1858	140	23.1
1836	142	−62.2	1859	140	−26.2
1837	137	−22.6	1860	130	7.3

Sources: Calculated from Export and Import Price Indices, Chart XV-VIII; residual balance of payments, North, "Balance of Payments," loc. cit., Table 3.

TABLE Q-VIII

(Refers to Chart XVIII-VIII)

FREIGHT RATE INDEX, UNITED STATES EXPORTS, 1815-1860
(BASE 1830)

Year	Index	Year	Index	Year	Index
1815	363.3	1831	124.9	1847	117.0
1816	238.0	1832	99.7	1848	73.7
1817	109.2	1833	87.8	1849	68.6
1818	266.9	1834	88.1	1850	57.4
1819	122.2	1835	87.0	1851	60.2
1820	191.7	1836	99.8	1852	76.1
1821	148.3	1837	110.7	1853	93.5
1822	140.8	1838	124.3	1854	100.7
1823	147.1	1839	108.5	1855	75.9
1824	127.2	1840	134.9	1856	86.0
1825	134.1	1841	82.6	1857	67.0
1826	127.9	1842	81.5	1858	73.1
1827	125.0	1843	95.9	1859	75.6
1828	106.7	1844	85.7	1860	97.3
1829	100.1	1845	90.6		
1830	100.0	1846	97.8		

Source: Freight series on seven commodities (cotton, tobacco, rice, naval stores, flour, wheat and ashes) weighted by decennial moving averages of quantities converted to standard units by stowage factors.

TABLE R-VIII

(Refers to Chart XIX-VIII)

IMMIGRATION TO THE UNITED STATES 1815-1860

Year	Number	Year	Number	Year	Number
1815		1831	22,633	1847	234,968
1816		1832	60,482	1848	226,527
1817		1833	58,640	1849	297,024
1818		1834	65,365	1850	369,980
1819		1835	45,374	1851	379,466
1820	8,385	1836	76,242	1852	371,603
1821	9,127	1837	79,340	1853	368,645
1822	6,911	1838	38,914	1854	427,833
1823	6,354	1839	68,069	1855	200,877
1824	7,912	1840	84,066	1856	200,436
1825	10,199	1841	80,289	1857	251,306
1826	10,837	1842	104,565	1858	123,126
1827	18,875	1843	52,496	1859	121,282
1828	27,382	1844	78,615	1860	153,640
1829	22,520	1845	114,371		
1830	23,322	1846	154,416		

Source: Historical Statistics, Series B304, p. 34.

TABLE S-VIII

(Refers to Chart XX-VIII)

UNITED STATES TERRITORIAL EXPANSION
1790-1860

Year	Acquisition in Sq. Miles		Total U.S. Sq. Miles
1790			888,811
1803	Louisiana Purchase	827,192	1,716,003
1819	By treaty with Spain:		1,788,006
	Florida	58,560	
	Other Areas	13,443	
1845	Texas	390,144	2,178,150
1846	Oregon	285,580	2,463,730
1848	Mexican Cession	529,017	2,992,747
1853	Gadsden Purchase	29,640	3,022,387

Source: Historical Statistics, p. 25.

APPENDIX II

INTERREGIONAL ECONOMIC RELATIONS—
STATISTICAL DATA

(Refers to footnote 1, Ch. II)

POPULATION OF THE WESTERN STATES AND TERRITORIES, 1790, 1800, 1810

State	1790	1800	1810
Kentucky	73,677	220,955	406,511
Tennessee	35,691	105,602	261,727
Ohio		45,365	230,760
Indiana		5,641	24,520
Illinois			12,282
Mississippi		8,850	40,352
Louisiana (Missouri)			20,845
Territory of Orleans (Louisiana)			76,556
Michigan			4,762

Source: E. R. Johnson and collaborators, History of Domestic and Foreign Commerce of the United States, Table 12.

TABLE A-III

(Refers to Chart III-III)

NET FREIGHT EARNINGS OF THE UNITED STATES CARRYING TRADE
1790-1815
(Millions of Dollars)

Year	Earnings	Year	Earnings	Year	Earnings
1790	5.9	1799	24.2	1808	23.0
1791	6.2	1800	26.2	1809	26.2
1792	7.4	1801	31.0	1810	39.5
1793	11.9	1802	18.2	1811	40.8
1794	15.5	1803	23.7	1812	29.0
1795	19.0	1804	26.9	1813	10.2
1796	21.6	1805	29.7	1814	2.6
1797	17.1	1806	34.6	1815	20.6
1798	16.6	1807	42.1		

Source: North, "Balance of Payments," loc. cit., p. 595.

TABLE B-III

(Refers to Chart VIII-III)

TONNAGE PASSING THROUGH LOCKS ON THE POTOMAC

Year		Year		Year	
1800	129,414.00	1805	340,334.18	1811	925,074.80
1801	328,445.32	1806	86,790.40	1812	515,525.75
1802	163,916.00	1807	551,896.47	1813	423,340.32
1803	345,472.82	1808	337,007.47	1814	312,093.72
1804	284,040.60	1809	365,628.00	1815	489,498.15
		1810	318,237.62		

Source: American State Papers, XXI, 997 (Washington: 1834).

TABLE C-III

(Refers to Chart IX-III)

TONNAGE ENGAGED IN COASTWISE AND INTERNAL TRADE

Year	Tons	Year	Tons	Year	Tons
1790	103,775	1799	246,640	1808	420,819
1791	106,494	1800	272,492	1809	405,163
1792	120,957	1801	274,551	1810	405,347
1793	122,071	1802	289,623	1811	420,362
1794	162,578	1803	299,060	1812	477,972
1795	184,398	1804	317,537	1813	471,109
1796	217,841	1805	332,663	1814	466,159
1797	237,403	1806	340,540	1815	475,666
1798	251,443	1807	349,028		

Source: Historical Statistics, Series K 94-104, p. 208.

TABLE A-IX

(Refers to Chart I-IX)

VALUE OF RECEIPTS OF PRODUCE FROM THE INTERIOR AT NEW ORLEANS, 1815-1860

Year ending September 30	Receipts in Dollars	Year ending September 30	Receipts in Dollars
1815-16	9,749,253	1838-39	42,263,880
1816-17	8,773,379	1839-40	49,763,825
1817-18	13,501,036	1840-41	49,822,115
1818-19	16,771,711	1841-42	45,716,045
1819-20	12,637,079	1842-43	53,782,054
1820-21	11,967,067	1843-44	60,094,716
1821-22	15,126,420	1844-45	57,199,122
1822-23	14,473,725	1845-46	77,193,464
1823-24	15,063,820	1846-47	90,033,256
1824-25	19,044,640	1847-48	79,779,151
1825-26	20,446,320	1848-49	81,989,692
1826-27	21,730,887	1849-50	96,897,873
1827-28	22,886,420	1850-51	196,924,083
1828-29	20,757,265	1851-52	108,051,708
1829-30	22,065,518	1852-53	134,233,735
1830-31	26,044,820	1853-54	115,336,798
1831-32	21,806,763	1854-55	117,106,823
1832-33	28,238,432	1855-56	144,256,081
1833-34	29,820,817	1856-57	158,161,369
1834-35	37,566,842	1857-58	167,155,546
1835-36	39,237,762	1858-59	172,952,664
1836-37	43,515,402	1859-60	185,211,254
1837-38	45,627,720		

Source: U. S. Congress, House, Report on the Internal Commerce of the United States, 50th Congress, 1st Session, 1888, House Executive Document No. 6, Part 2.

TABLE B-IX

(Refers to Chart II-IX)

TONNAGE OVER ERIE CANAL TO TIDEWATER FROM WESTERN STATES
AND FROM NEW YORK, 1836-1860

Year	From Western States	From New York
1836	54,219	364,906
1837	56,255	331,251
1838	83,233	336,016
1839	121,761	264,596
1840	158,148	309,167
1841	224,176	308,344
1842	221,477	258,672
1843	256,376	378,969
1844	308,025	491,791
1845	304,551	655,039
1846	506,830	600,440
1847	812,840	618,412
1848	650,154	534,183
1849	768,659	498,065
1850	841,501	530,358
1851	1,045,820	462,857
1852	1,151,978	492,726
1853	1,213,690	637,748
1854	1,094,391	602,167
1855	1,092,876	327,839
1856	1,212,550	374,580
1857	1,019,998	197,201
1858	1,273,099	223,588
1859	1,036,634	414,699
1860	1,896,975	379,086

Source: U. S. Congress, Senate, Preliminary Report of the Inland Waterways
Commission, 60th Congress, 1st Session, 1908, Senate Document No. 325,
p. 226.

TABLE C-IX

(Refers to Chart III-IX)

TONNAGE OF VESSELS ON THE WESTERN RIVERS, 1816-1860; AND TONNAGE EMPLOYED IN THE LAKE TRADE, 1830-1860*

Year	Western Rivers	Lake Trade	Year	Western Rivers	Lake Trade	Year	Western Rivers	Lake Trade
1816	9,930		1831	43,852	8,879	1846	214,550	101,545
1817	12,946		1832	55,755	12,738	1847	241,448	134,659
1818	24,512		1833	59,589	15,226	1848	277,331	160,250
1819	25,192		1834	(1)	19,044	1849	286,476	177,077
1820	27,269		1835	72,697	29,709	1850	302,829	186,790
1821	27,160		1836	79,395	32,000	1851	317,950	200,507
1822	19,665		1837	90,786	37,480	1852	348,207	221,235
1823	17,719		1838	108,814	49,159	1853	266,427	251,492
1824	18,477		1839	(1)	46,935	1854	304,672	286,564
1825	19,393		1840	117,952	48,262	1855	346,032	339,193
1826	23,988		1841	137,260	54,569	1856	269,466	369,950
1827	21,942		1842	142,918	58,808	1857	294,676	398,709
1828	39,403		1843	152,329	66,938	1858	320,119	395,140
1829	(1)		1844	174,408	73,124	1859	331,633	422,381
1830	32,664	7,728	1845	187,740	86,071	1860	369,004	450,726

* Official record of tonnage existing at all ports of the Great Lakes and St. Lawrence river.

1 No returns reported.

Sources: Tonnage in the Lake trade, U. S. Congress, Senate, Statistics of Foreign and Domestic Commerce, 38th Congress, 1st Session, 1864, Senate Executive Document no. 55, p. 143; Tonnage on Western Rivers, 1816-1851, U. S. Commerce Department, Bureau of Marine Inspection and Navigation, Merchant Marine Statistics, 1936 (Washington: Government Printing Office, 1937), 1852-1860, Annual Reports of the Secretary of the Treasury on Commerce and Navigation. Note: while Merchant Marine Statistics, 1936 provides data for the entire period, 1816-1860, it does not appear to be a continuous series of comparable data. A sharp break occurs in 1854 when tonnage drops from 281,582 to 110,602. This may be a consequence of changes in the method of admeasurement or clearance of tonnage for vessels lost, abandoned, transferred etc., however an explanation is not offered. Reconstruction of the series from data drawn from the reports on Commerce and Navigation reveals that the tonnage reported for 1850 and 1851 are the sum of the "enrolled and liscenced tonnage" for the ports of Pittsburgh, Wheeling, Mobile, Pearl River, Vicksburg, New Orleans, Teche, Nashville, Louisville, St. Louis, Cincinnati, and Miami. For subsequent years aggregation of the same data (with addition of new river ports: Memphis, Alton, Galena, New Albany, Knoxville, Paducah, and St. Paul) gives tonnage totals which differ significantly from those reported in Merchant Marine Statistics, 1936. Substitution of these tonnage totals for the years 1852-1860 gives a continuous series which better reveals the development of commerce on the western rivers. Even so, this series must be interpreted with caution, for example the decline in 1856 may be largely a consequence of clearance from tonnage accounts, vessels lost, abandoned, transferred, etc., over the period 1855-1858 (Historical Statistics, p. 191).

TABLE D-IX

(Refers to Chart IV-IX)

RECEIPTS ON ALL OHIO CANALS, 1827-1860

Year	Receipts in Dollars	Year	Receipts in Dollars
1827	1,500	1844	490,818
1828	12,043	1845	452,394
1829	47,941	1846	576,409
1830	60,576	1847	754,196
1831	101,508	1848	754,508
1832	116,830	1849	694,824
1833	187,026	1850	711,022
1834	214,530	1851	799,025
1835	237,581	1852	629,758
1836	261,940	1853	595,539
1837	356,262	1854	485,774
1838	464,999	1855	442,192
1839	506,201	1856	321,074
1840	532,689	1857	327,819
1841	495,439	1858	279,866
1842	463,728	1859	234,679
1843	433,582	1860	267,729

Source: Ernest L. Bogart, Internal Improvements and State Debt in Ohio; an Essay in Economic History (London: Longmans, Green and Co., 1924), p. 146.

TABLE E-IX

(Refers to Chart V-IX)

RECEIPTS OF FLOUR AND GRAIN AT BUFFALO FROM THE WEST
1836-1860

Year	Flour in barrels	Grain in bushels*	Year	Flour in barrels	Grain in bushels*
1836	139,178	543,461	1849	1,207,435	8,628,013
1837	126,805	550,660	1850	1,103,039	6,635,905
1838	277,620	974,751	1851	1,258,224	11,449,661
1839	294,125	1,117,262	1852	1,299,513	13,892,919
1840	597,142	1,075,888	1853	975,557	15,574,741
1841	730,040	1,852,325	1854	739,756	18,512,465
1842	734,308	2,015,928	1855	936,761	20,788,673
1843	917,517	2,055,025	1856	1,126,048	20,129,467
1844	915,030	2,335,568	1857	845,953	15,348,930
1845	746,750	1,848,040	1858	1,536,109	20,005,044
1846	1,374,529	6,493,342	1859	1,420,333	15,229,060
1847	1,857,000	9,868,187	1860	1,122,335	31,441,440
1848	1,249,000	7,396,012			

* includes wheat, corn, oats, barley and rye.

Source: U. S. Congress, Senate, Statistics of Foreign and Domestic Commerce, 38th Congress, 1st Session, 1864, Senate Executive Document No. 55, p. 161.

TABLE F-IX

(Refers to Chart VI-IX)

TONNAGE GOING TO WESTERN STATES BY ERIE CANAL
1836-1860

Year	Tons of Merchandise	Year	Tons of Merchandise
1836	38,893	1849	87,899
1837	25,291	1850	115,045
1838	34,629	1851	177,623
1839	34,197	1852	219,799
1840	22,055	1853	261,752
1841	31,040	1854	331,879
1842	24,063	1855	220,466
1843	37,335	1856	183,513
1844	42,415	1857	108,125
1845	49,618	1858	76,890
1846	58,330	1859	98,876
1847	75,883	1860	119,682
1848	84,872		

Source: U. S. Congress, Senate, Statistics of Foreign and Domestic Commerce, 38th Congress, 1st Session, 1864, Senate Executive Document No. 55, p. 133.

TABLE G-IX

(Refers to Chart VII-IX)

TONNAGE IN COASTING TRADE, 1816-1860

Year	Gross Tons	Year	Gross Tons	Year	Gross Tons
1816	507,018	1831	486,792	1846	1,010,278
1817	505,218	1832	577,588	1847	1,113,123
1818	518,561	1833	667,932	1848	1,233,791
1819	538,374	1834	-- -- *	1849	1,310,375
1820	553,274	1835	707,790	1850	1,313,761
1821	580,335	1836	764,046	1851	1,386,260
1822	597,875	1837	831,551	1852	1,483,648
1823	592,775	1838	882,029	1853	1,598,964
1824	614,176	1839	-- -- *	1854	2,050,492
1825	614,441	1840	1,010,144	1855	2,207,974
1826	689,049	1841	912,026	1856	2,101,319
1827	758,414	1842	841,496	1857	1,958,174
1828	793,258	1843	857,620	1858	1,999,441
1829	-- -- *	1844	862,756	1859	2,010,690
1830	471,132	1845	949,581	1960	2,014,005

U. S. Commerce Department, Bureau of Marine Inspection and Navigation, Merchant Marine Statistics, 1936 (Washington: Government Printing Office, 1937), pp. 25-29. Above series derived by subtracting tonnage on Northern Lakes and Western Rivers from series on Coasting Trade which also included tonnage in internal commerce.

* Data for the years 1829, 1834, & 1839 not available owing to the absence of returns for the Northern Lakes and Western Rivers.

TABLE H-IX

(Refers to Chart VIII-IX)

CALIFORNIA GOLD PRODUCTION AND GOLD EXPORTS, 1848-1860

Year	Total Production[1]	Manifested in San Francisco for export[2]	Year	Total Production[1]	Manifested in San Francisco for export[2]
1848	$ 245,301	-- --	1855	$55,485,395	$45,182,631
1849	10,151,360	$ 4,921,250	1856	57,509,411	48,880,543
1850	41,273,106	27,676,346	1857	43,628,172	48,976,697
1851	75,938,232	42,582,695	1858	46,591,140	47,548,025
1852	81,294,700	46,588,434	1859	45,846,599	47,649,462
1853	67,613,487	57,330,034	1860	44,095,163	42,203,345
1854	69,433,931	51,328,653			

[1] ". . . [C]ompiled by Louis A. Garnett, for many years manager of the San Francisco refinery, who had abundant opportunity to eliminate some of the inaccuracies which have crept into published statements, and which have been adopted and repeated by subsequent statisticians."

[2] ". . . [F]rom U. S. Mining Commissioner J. Ross Browne's Report of 1867, p. 50, shows only the amount of treasure actually manifested for exportation from San Francisco in the respective years."

Source: California State Mining Bureau, Thirteenth Report of the State Mineralogist for the Two Years Ending September 15,1896 (Sacramento: Superintendent State Printing, 1896), table inserted between pp. 64 and 65.

TABLE I-IX

(Refers to Chart IX-IX)

WESTERN STATES TERMS OF TRADE
BASE 1824-1846

Year		Year		Year	
1816	57	1831	103	1846	118
1817	64	1832	105	1847	134
1818	61	1833	99	1848	128
1819	62	1834	96	1849	134
1820	47	1835	122	1850	136
1821	42	1836	131	1851	158
1822	47	1837	126	1852	165
1823	67	1838	119	1853	140
1824	70	1839	130	1854	150
1825	67	1840	121	1855	189
1826	70	1841	105	1856	151
1827	69	1842	92	1857	163
1828	71	1843	105	1858	156
1829	82	1844	113	1859	176
1830	82	1845	142	1860	167

Source: Thomas S. Berry, Western Prices Before 1861; a Study of the Cincinnati Market (Cambridge: Harvard University Press, 1943), Appendix B, Table 19.

TABLE J-IX

(Refers to Chart X-IX)

RECEIPTS FROM PUBLIC LAND SALES, 5 SOUTHERN STATES* 1815-1860

Year	Receipts in thousands of dollars	Year	Receipts in thousands of dollars	Year	Receipts in thousands of dollars
1815	332	1830	750	1846	496
1816	899	1831	1,016	1847	601
1817	2,016	1832	677	1848	445
1818	9,063	1833	1,544	1849	413
1819	4,441	1834	3,256	1850	664
1820	1,096	1835	7,159	1851	776
1821	564	1836	7,170	1852	357
1822	353	1837	1,568	1853	1,023
1823	228	1838	817	1854	1,363
1824	283	1839	1,297	1855	927
1825	539	1840	497	1856	685
1826	452	1841	299	1857	808
1827	590	1842	315	1858	862
1828	357	1843	481	1859	1,164
1829	830	1844	368	1860	1,089
		1845	299		

* Alabama, Arkansas, Florida, Louisiana and Mississippi.

Source: Arthur H. Cole, "Cyclical and Sectional Variations in the Sale of Public Lands, 1816-1860," Review of Economic Statistics, IX, No. 1 (January 1927), 52.

TABLE K-IX

(Refers to Chart XI-IX)

RECEIPTS FROM PUBLIC LAND SALES, 7 WESTERN STATES* 1815-1860

Year	Receipts in thousands of dollars	Year	Receipts in thousands of dollars	Year	Receipts in thousands of dollars
1815	2,078	1830	1,658	1846	2,386
1816	2,741	1831	2,350	1847	2,672
1817	3,068	1832	2,127	1848	2,088
1818	4,556	1833	2,628	1849	1,328
1819	4,540	1834	2,807	1850	1,124
1820	640	1835	9,007	1851	1,797
1821	714	1836	17,765	1852	1,031
1822	663	1837	5,374	1853	3,970
1823	580	1838	3,195	1854	9,771
1824	1,217	1839	5,192	1855	9,215
1825	743	1840	2,251	1856	3,453
1826	677	1841	1,212	1857	1,895
1827	814	1842	1,137	1858	765
1828	862	1843	1,568	1859	450
1829	1,331	1844	1,872	1860	248
		1845	2,163		

* Illinois, Indiana, Iowa, Michigan, Missouri, Ohio, Wisconsin.

Source: Arthur H. Cole, "Cyclical and Sectional Variations in the Sale of Public Lands, 1816-1860," loc. cit., p. 52.

TABLE L-IX

(Refers to Chart XII-IX)

UNITED STATES POPULATION DISTRIBUTION BY REGIONS
1810-1860

Year	South*		West*		Northeast*		Total U.S. Population (does not include territories)
	Population	% of total pop.	Population	% of total pop.	Population	% of total pop.	
1810	2,314,556	32.1	961,407	13.3	3,939,895	54.6	7,215,858
1820	2,918,198	30.4	1,845,863	19.2	4,836,722	50.4	9,600,783
1830	3,774,405	29.4	2,980,294	23.2	6,066,169	47.3	12,820,868
1840	4,749,875	27.9	4,960,580	29.1	7,309,186	42.9	17,019,641
1850	6,271,237	27.2	7,494,608	32.5	9,301,417	40.3	23,067,262
1860	7,993,531	25.6	11,796,680	37.8	11,393,533	36.5	31,183,744

*South—Alabama, Arkansas, Florida, Georgia, Louisiana, Mississippi, North Carolina, South Carolina, Texas and Virginia; West—Illinois, Indiana, Iowa, Kansas, Kentucky, Michigan, Minnesota, Missouri, Nebraska, Ohio, Tennessee, Wisconsin, California, Nevada and Oregon; Northeast—Connecticut, Delaware, Maine, Maryland, Massachusetts, New Hampshire, New Jersey, New York, Pennsylvania, Rhode Island, and Vermont.

Source: U. S. Census Bureau, A Compendium of the Ninth Census, June 1, 1870, by Francis A. Walker, Superintendent of Census (Washington: Government Printing Office, 1872), pp. 8-9.

TABLE A-X

(Refers to Chart I-X)

PUBLIC LAND SALES FIVE SOUTHERN STATES (ARKANSAS, ALABAMA, MISSISSIPPI, LOUISIANA, FLORIDA) AND COTTON PRICES
(AVERAGE NEW YORK PRICES FOR MIDDLING UPLANDS), 1814-1860
(thousands of dollars and cents)

Year	Sales	Prices	Year	Sales	Prices	Year	Sales	Prices
1814	101	15.0	1830	750	10.04	1846	496	7.87
1815	332	21.0	1831	1,016	9.71	1847	601	11.21
1816	899	29.5	1832	677	9.38	1848	445	8.03
1817	2,016	26.5	1833	1,544	12.32	1849	413	7.55
1818	9,063	24.0	1834	3,256	12.90	1850	664	12.34
1819	4,441	24.0	1835	7,159	17.45	1851	776	12.14
1820	1,096	17.0	1836	7,170	16.50	1852	357	9.50
1821	564	14.32	1837	1,568	13.25	1853	1,032	11.02
1822	353	14.32	1838	817	10.14	1854	1,363	10.97
1823	228	11.40	1839	1,297	13.36	1855	927	10.39
1824	283	14.75	1840	497	8.92	1856	685	10.30
1825	539	18.59	1841	299	9.50	1857	808	13.51
1826	452	12.19	1842	315	7.85	1858	862	12.23
1827	590	9.26	1843	481	7.25	1859	1,164	12.08
1828	357	10.32	1844	368	7.73	1860	1,089	11.00
1829	830	9.88	1845	299	5.63			

Source: Land Sales, Arthur H. Cole, "Cyclical and Sectional Variations in the Sale of Public Lands, 1816-1860," loc. cit., p. 52; Cotton Prices, Matthew B. Hammond, The Cotton Industry; an Essay in American Economic History, Part I, The Cotton Culture and the Cotton Trade (New York: MacMillan, published for the American Economic Association, 1897).

TABLE B-X

(Refers to Chart II-X)

**FREIGHT RATES, COTTON, NEW YORK TO LIVERPOOL AND
NEW ORLEANS TO LIVERPOOL, 1820-1860***
(Pence per pound)

Year	New York to Liverpool	New Orleans to Liverpool	Year	New York to Liverpool	New Orleans to Liverpool
1820	---	1.25	1841	.38	.50
1821	---	1.00	1842	.31	.50
1822	.62	1.12	1843	.38	.62
1823	.75	1.00	1844	.38	.50
1824	.50	----	1845	.31	.47
1825	.68	1.00	1846	.31	.50
1826	.62	.96	1847	.25	.62
1827	.62	.80	1848	.19	.46
1828	.44	.62	1849	.19	.46
1829	.38	.56	1850	.19	.37
1830	.50	.62	1851	.16	.44
1831	.56	.75	1852	.22	.46
1832	.44	.68	1853	.25	.56
1833	.44	.62	1854	.28	.69
1834	.41	.62	1855	.22	.48
1835	.38	.50	1856	.19	.50
1836	.44	.62	1857	.16	.47
1837	.56	.75	1858	.19	.48
1838	.68	.88	1859	.19	.48
1839	.62	.70	1860	.25	.56
1840	.68	.88			

*

Source: New York Shipping and Commercial List, and New Orleans Price
Current, issues for the years 1820-1860. Weekly rates were weighted by
volume shipped to arrive at an annual rate.

TABLE C-X

(Refers to Chart III-X)

URBAN POPULATION—A PERCENT OF TOTAL POPULATION

Area	\ Year							
	1790	1800	1810	1820	1830	1840	1850	1860
New England	7.5	8.2	10.1	10.5	14.0	19.4	28.8	36.6
Middle Atlantic	8.7	10.2	11.5	11.3	14.2	18.1	25.5	35.4
East North Central	*	0	0.9	1.2	2.5	3.9	9.0	14.1
West North Central	*	*	0	0	3.5	3.9	10.3	13.4
South Atlantic	2.3	3.4	4.5	5.5	6.2	7.7	9.8	11.5
East South Central	0	0	0.6	0.8	1.5	2.1	4.2	5.9

*No figures reported

Source: U. S. Census Bureau, Sixteenth Census of the United States, Population,
Vol. I (Washington: Government Printing Office, 1942), Table 8, p. 20.

TABLE A-XI

(Refers to Chart I-XI)

LAND SALES, 7 WESTERN STATES, 1815-1860
(OHIO, ILLINOIS, INDIANA, MICHIGAN, IOWA, WISCONSIN, MISSOURI)
(in thousands of dollars)

Year	Ohio	Illinois	Indiana	Michigan	Iowa	Wisconsin	Missouri
1815	1656*	53	369	---	---	---	---
1816	1332	207	1202	---	---	---	---
1817	1416	572	1080	---	---	---	---
1818	881	1491	1272	119	---	---	793
1819	958	611	458	52	---	---	2461
1820	142	87	272	11	---	---	128
1821	155	64	363	9	---	---	123
1822	236	35	326	26	---	---	40
1823	158	76	203	38	---	---	105
1824	243	58	724	94	---	---	98
1825	194	82	223	136	---	---	108
1826	169	110	250	75	---	---	73
1827	215	81	263	55	---	---	200
1828	208	121	315	33	---	---	185
1829	277	282	490	90	---	---	192
1830	199	402	604	185	---	---	268
1831	442	420	713	403	---	---	372
1832	544	261	685	323	---	---	314
1833	695	381	692	563	---	---	297
1834	599	440	843	623	---	21	281
1835	828	2688	2078	2272	---	317	824
1836	1665	4003	4063	5242	---	720	2072
1837	590	1271	1571	969	---	153	820
1838	305	983	756	122	344	40	645
1839	316	1421	778	175	373	822	1307
1840	41	492	150	33	661	161	713
1841	64	440	120	28	93	128	339
1842	54	544	73	36	64	165	201
1843	19	520	64	17	179	214	555
1844	48	616	137	29	139	333	570
1845	289	611	99	34	264	551	315
1846	151	600	146	36	330	885	238
1847	195	615	348	67	344	800	303
1848	115	374	708	94	195	345	257
1849	77	319	277	63	123	260	209
1850	53	313	135	93	141	97	292
1851	81	421	150	193	250	92	610
1852	58	492	49	49	42	37	304
1853	106	1218	104	331	1015	393	803
1854	95	1562	78	668	4605	1529	1234
1855	14	897	6	410	4310	2039	1539
1856	3	473	18	160	735	760	1304
1857	2	155	11	45	588	121	973
1858	2	12	1	24	97	62	567
1859	5	12	1	37	18	52	325
1860	2	---	31	46	11	41	117

*In a small degree estimated.

Source: Arthur H. Cole. "Cyclical and Sectional Variations in the Sale of Public Lands, 1816-60," loc. cit., p. 52.

TABLE B-XI

(Refers to Chart II-XI)

PRICES OF PORK, LARD, WHISKEY AND CORN
(9 yr. Moving Averages)
PHILADELPHIA, 1815-1857

Year	Lard (¢ per lb.)	Pork ($ per Bbl.)	Corn (¢ per bu.)	Whiskey (¢ per gal.)
1815	16.4	23.22	86.2	61.7
1816	16.1	22.58	85.0	60.6
1817	15.9	22.19	77.3	58.4
1818	15.5	21.80	73.1	52.0
1819	14.7	20.61	72.2	46.6
1820	13.7	19.14	69.6	41.0
1821	13.1	18.03	64.6	36.3
1822	11.8	16.03	56.5	32.8
1823	10.6	14.22	52.9	30.4
1824	9.9	13.47	49.3	29.1
1825	9.6	13.19	48.2	28.0
1826	8.9	13.19	48.6	27.2
1827	8.7	13.33	48.3	27.6
1828	8.7	13.18	48.0	28.0
1829	8.3	13.10	50.2	28.2
1830	8.2	13.21	51.8	28.4
1831	8.5	13.68	52.2	28.4
1832	9.0	15.12	54.4	30.2
1833	9.1	15.93	59.1	32.1
1834	9.9	16.40	61.7	34.1
1835	9.9	17.46	66.9	34.0
1836	9.8	17.63	66.9	32.9
1837	9.5	17.51	65.8	31.3
1838	9.2	16.82	64.8	30.7
1839	9.0	16.21	64.1	29.8
1840	8.6	15.53	61.9	28.4
1841	8.5	14.29	58.2	27.6
1842	8.4	13.24	55.6	24.3
1843	7.9	13.09	54.6	23.0
1844	7.7	11.74	52.3	22.4
1845	7.6	11.16	53.1	22.9
1846	7.9	10.93	54.6	23.5
1847	8.3	11.70	55.5	23.5
1848	8.9	12.83	58.9	23.8
1849	9.4	13.54	60.4	24.3
1850	9.7	13.71	63.8	25.9
1851	10.0	14.43	67.5	28.0
1852	10.6	14.57	69.9	28.6
1853	11.0	16.06	70.3	28.7
1854	11.7	16.88	70.4	28.5
1855	12.0	17.79	72.5	28.6
1856	12.2	18.21	74.1	28.2
1857		18.02		27.8

Source: Thomas S. Berry, Western Prices Before 1861, a Study of the
Cincinnati Market (Cambridge: Harvard University Press, 1943), p. 106.

TABLE C-XI

(Refers to Chart III-XI)

ANNUAL INCORPORATIONS, OHIO, 1803-1851, 1856-1860

Year	No.	Year	No.	Year	No.	Year	No.	Year	No.	Year	No.
1803	2	1812	2	1821	0	1830	17	1839	67	1848	80
1804	0	1813	1	1822	1	1831	8	1840	10	1849	103
1805	0	1814	3	1823	0	1832	37	1841	9	1850	192
1806	0	1815	1	1824	2	1833	14	1842	11	1851	170
1807	0	1816	18	1825	3	1834	31	1843	10	1856	64
1808	2	1817	18	1826	8	1835	38	1844	29	1857	47
1809	3	1818	3	1827	7	1836	71	1845	53	1858	49
1810	1	1819	2	1828	8	1837	92	1846	49	1859	97
1811	1	1820	2	1829	12	1838	55	1847	22	1860	36

Source: George H. Evans, Jr., Business Incorporations in the United States, 1800-1943, (New York: National Bureau of Economic Research, Inc., 1948), pp. 160-161.

TABLE D-XI

(Refers to Chart IV-XI)

CINCINNATI, NEW ORLEANS WHOLESALE COMMODITY PRICES, AVERAGE ABSOLUTE DIFFERENCES BY FIVE-YEAR PERIODS[1]

Year	Lard (lb.)	Mess Pork (Bbl.)	Flour (Bbl.)	Corn (bu.)
1816-20	$.051	$7.57	$2.16	$ --
1821-25	.027	2.81	2.37	.59
1826-30	.024	2.41	1.75	.59
1831-35	.017	2.03	1.29	.64
1836-40	.014	2.67	1.66	.49
1841-45	.006	1.66	.61	.14
1846-50	.005	1.31	.60	.20
1851-55	.006	1.24	.59	.16
1856-60	.007	1.27	.63	.21

TABLE E-XI

(Refers to Chart V-XI)

CINCINNATI, NEW YORK WHOLESALE COMMODITY PRICES, AVERAGE ABSOLUTE DIFFERENCES BY FIVE-YEAR PERIODS[2]

Year	Lard (lb.)	Mess Pork (Bbl.)	Flour (Bbl.)	Corn (bu.)
1816-20	$.048	$9.53	$2.48	$.48
1821-25	.031	4.46	2.81	.39
1826-30	.026	4.18	1.78	.36
1831-35	.025	3.48	1.43	.38
1836-40	.020	3.11	2.02	.42
1841-45	.011	2.25	1.37	.30
1846-50	.010	1.06	1.68	.36
1851-55	.007	1.56	1.36	.31
1856-60	.004	1.18	.28	.27

[1,2]Source: Thomas S. Berry, Western Prices Before 1861, a Study of the Cincinnati Market (Cambridge: Harvard University Press, 1943), p. 106.

TABLE F-XI

(Refers to Chart VI-XI)

SHIPMENTS OF FLOUR AND GRAIN FROM CHICAGO
1839-1861

Year	Total, Flour and Grain (in bushels)	Year	Total, Flour and Grain (in bushels)	Year	Total, Flour and Grain (in bushels)	Year	Total, Flour and Grain (in bushels)
1839	3,678	1845	1,024,620	1851	4,646,521	1857	18,032,678
1840	10,000	1846	1,599,819	1852	5,873,141	1858	20,040,178
1841	40,000	1847	2,243,201	1853	6,422,181	1859	16,768,857
1842	586,907	1848	3,001,740	1854	12,902,320	1860	31,109,059
1843	688,907	1849	2,895,959	1855	16,633,645	1861	50,511,862
1844	923,494	1850	1,858,928	1856	21,583,221		

Source: Eighth Census of the United States, 1860, Agriculture, Introduction, p. cxlix, Table H.

TABLE A-XIII

(Refers to Chart I-XIII)

MONTHLY RANGE OF SHORT STAPLE COTTON PRICES IN THE
CHARLESTON MARKET, 1815-1820
(cents per pound)

	1815	1816	1817
Jan.		24 – 28	$24\frac{1}{2} - 25\frac{1}{2}$
Feb.		$25\frac{1}{2} - 28$	$25 - 26\frac{1}{2}$
Mar.		25 – 28	25 – 29
Apr.	17 – 18	26 – 28	27 – 29
May	16 – 18	$28 - 31\frac{1}{4}$	27 – 30
June	17 – 20	30 – 32	27 – 30
July	20 – 22	30 – 32	27 – 30
Aug.	20 – 22	30 – 32	26 – 30
Sept.	21 – 25	25 – 28	26 – 30
Oct.	25 – 28	23 – 27	$26 - 31\frac{1}{2}$
Nov.	26 – 28	21 – 24	$30 - 33\frac{1}{2}$
Dec.	26 – 28	24 – 26	$32\frac{1}{2} - 35$

	1818	1819	1820
Jan.	33 – 35	25 – 27	15 – 17
Feb.	30 – 33	$23 - 25\frac{1}{2}$	$15 - 16\frac{1}{2}$
Mar.	29 – 33	17 – 25	$13 - 16\frac{1}{2}$
Apr.	$29\frac{1}{2} - 33$	14 – 18	$14 - 17\frac{1}{2}$
May	29 – 34	13 – 18	$15 - 17\frac{1}{2}$
June	31 – 34	$12\frac{1}{2} - 17\frac{1}{2}$	16 – 20
July	31 – 33	14 – 18	18 – 20
Aug.	30 – 33	14 – 18	18 – 20
Sept.	30 – 33	14 – 18	18 – 19
Oct.	30 – 32	$15 - 18\frac{1}{2}$	$15\frac{1}{2} - 20$
Nov.	26 – 32	$15 - 18\frac{1}{2}$	15 – 16
Dec.	24 – 27	15 – 16	$15\frac{1}{2} - 16\frac{1}{2}$

Source: Alfred G. Smith, Jr., Economic Readjustment of an Old Cotton State; South Carolina, 1820-1860 (Columbia: University of South Carolina Press, 1958).

TABLE B-XIII

(Refers to Chart II-XIII)

PRICES AND FREIGHT RATES, 1815-1823
(BASE 1830)

	Warren-Pearson Wholesale Price Index	Export Index	American Export Freight Rate Index
1815	187	183	363
1816	166	248	238
1817	166	240	109
1818	162	245	267
1819	137	195	122
1820	116	144	192
1821	112	128	148
1822	116	136	141
1823	113	114	147

Sources: G. F. Warren and F. A. Pearson, Wholesale Prices for 213 Years, 1720-1932 (Ithaca: Cornell University Press, 1932), Part I, pp. 8-9; Export Index, see discussion in Appendix III. Freight Rate Index, North, "Ocean Freight Rates and Economic Development, 1750-1913," loc. cit.

TABLE A-XV

(Refers to Chart I-XV)

AVERAGE PRICES OF WHEAT AND CORN AT NEW YORK[1]
1845-1861

	Corn[2]	Wheat[3]
1845	.56	1.08
1846	.70	1.12
1847	.87	1.42
1848	.64	1.21
1849	.63	1.26
1850	.63	1.29
1851	$.62\frac{1}{2}$	1.10
1852	.68	1.13
1853	$.71\frac{1}{2}$	1.41
1854	.85	2.25
1855	1.00	2.46
1856	.72	1.83
1857	$.82\frac{1}{4}$	1.72
1858	.82	1.37
1859	$.88\frac{1}{2}$	1.50
1860	.75	1.54
1861	.64	1.47

[1]Data for highest price in the range of average prices
[2]Corn, Northern
[3]Quoted prices for Wheat, Western for years 1845-48 and Wheat, Genesee for years 1849-61.

Source: U.S. Congress, House, Report of the Secretary of the Treasury, on the State of the Finances, for the Year Ending June 30, 1863, 38th Congress, 1st Session, 1864, Document No. 3, pp. 382-398.

APPENDIX III

EXPORT AND IMPORT
PRICE INDICES 1790-1860

I. Method and Sources of Data Used in Construction of Export Price Index, 1790–1815

A. *Calculation of Export Index:* As the first step in the calculation of the export price index a basic Laspeyres price relative index is calculated for the eleven commodities covered during the period 1790–1815. The bases used for this index are the years 1790, 1795, 1800, 1805, and 1810. Second, these eleven series of price relatives are weighted by the annual export value of each commodity in relation to its percentage of the value of exports of all commodities included in the index. For example, in the year 1797, the basic Laspeyres index calculated for flour to the base 1795 stood at 79.0, and the value of flour as a percentage of the value of total exports of the eleven commodities stood at 24.8 per cent. By multiplying the index by the relative percentage determined, the weighted price relative for flour is obtained for the year 1797. This process is repeated for each commodity and for each year. These weighted price relatives are then summed over all commodities for any given year. The result of this summation is the unlinked weighted index of price relatives. The final export index is obtained by linking the weighted index of price relatives to the base 1790.

B. *Sources of Data:* Prices used in the derivation of these relatives with few exceptions, as noted below, originate in Arthur Harrison Cole's study of wholesale prices in five cities, Boston, Charleston, New York, New Orleans, and Philadelphia: *Wholesale Prices in the United States.* In calculation of weights the annual quantities of each commodity exported were multiplied by those prices selected for use in the construction of the index. The export quantities which were used originate, with one exception noted below, in Charles H. Evans' compilations from the Annual Reports on Commerce and Navigation.

Insofar as was possible, the prices selected for each commodity are those from the city of its most likely export; however, since many series are incomplete or comprise varying quantities of the commodity, Philadelphia prices have been used contrary to what the general pattern of export traffic would suggest. The series employed along with the commodities comprising the index as well as difficulties peculiar to inclusion of these commodities are as

follows: (1) Wheat—Philadelphia, does not enter into the calcula-
tions for 1814 for want of reliable data on quantity exported;
(2) Flour—Philadelphia; (3) Rice—Charleston, data on quantities
exported reported in tierces and on prices in units of one hundred
pounds; on the strength of a study published by the United States
Department of Agriculture Bureau of Statistics, Circular 34, (Rice
Crop in the United States 1712–1911) by George K. Holmes, a
tierce of six hundred pounds was used in converting tierces to
pounds; (4) Beef—Philadelphia, quality of beef in price quotations changed from *Boston* (1790–1794) to *mess* (1795–1815) in
1795; (5) Fish (dried cod)—Philadelphia, quantities used in com-
puting annual weights include all dried and smoked fish exported;
(6) Cotton (upland)—Boston 1790–1795, Charleston 1796–1815,
quantities exported for the years 1793–1795 were taken from
Timothy Pitkin's *A Statistical View of the Commerce of the United
States of America* rather than from the compilations of Charles H.
Evans, and the value of cotton exports for the year 1790 by which
the index for that year is weighted was taken from the compilations
of Charles H. Evans; (7) Tobacco (James River)—Philadelphia,
data on the quantities exported reported in hogsheads and on prices
in units of one hundred pounds; on the strength of the findings of
Joseph Clarke Robert reported in *Tobacco Kingdom* weights of
1,000, 1,100, and 1,400 pounds were used in converting hogsheads
to pounds for the periods 1790–1799, 1800–1810, and 1811–1815,
respectively; (8) Whale Oil—Philadelphia, quantities exported used
in the calculation of annual weights do not include sperm oil;
(9) Boards, pine—Philadelphia, quantities exported used in the
calculation of annual weights include all boards, planks and
scantling exported; (10) Staves—Philadelphia, quantities used in
calculating annual weights include all staves and heading exported;
(11) Turpentine—Philadelphia, quantity exported for the year 1795
estimated to be 40,000 barrels.

As a measure of the coverage of the index, listed below are the
annual percentages of total exports which the above eleven exports
comprise. While the actual coverage is far from ideal, the fragmentary information of the period suggests that the price behavior
of these commodities was representative of price movements for
exports during the period.

Year	Percentage of Total Exports
1790	89.9
1791	70.9
1792	73.0
1793	64.7
1794	50.2
1795	45.8
1796	38.4
1797	32.5
1798	39.8
1799	35.0
1800	34.1
1801	35.5
1802	36.7
1803	56.7
1804	38.7
1805	32.5
1806	29.5
1807	33.5
1808	25.5
1809	43.1
1810	50.7
1811	54.0
1812	62.5
1813	65.5
1814	76.0
1815	82.1

II. Method and Sources of Data Used in Construction of Import Price Index 1790–1815

A. *Problems:* For the period 1790 to 1815, the problems involved in the construction of an import index are considerably greater than for construction of an export index. This is owing to a number of things, particularly the larger number of significantly important commodities entering into the import trade and the lack of good statistical series on prices and quantities of goods imported. The problem is particularly acute with regard to manufactured commodities. For the most part these goods entered the country under ad valorem duties, and as contrasted to those goods entering under specific duties the quantities imported are indistinguishable by commodity in customs records. Also, the quality of manufactured commodities has been more inclined to change, which heightens the problem of finding useable price and quantity data. As a consequence, it has been necessary to resort to judgments of a sometimes arbitrary nature where suitable data has not been available.

For *ten* commodities, primarily foodstuffs, suitable data was adequate for construction of an index using the method employed in construction of the export index for this same period. However, inasmuch as the commodities are primarily foodstuffs, the index can hardly be considered representative of American imports. To make it more representative, three additional series of prices were combined with the ten-commodity index. These consist of an English series on yarn, an English series on cloth and stockings and Anne Bezanson's textile series taken from *Wholesale Prices in Philadelphia 1784–1861*. In the final index, the three textile series were given a combined weight of forty and the ten-commodity index a weight of sixty.

B. *Sources of Data:* Prices used in the derivation of these relatives originate in Arthur Harrison Cole's study of wholesale prices in five cities, Boston, Charleston, New York, New Orleans and Philadelphia: *Wholesale Prices in the United States* and *Prices and Wages in England from the Twelfth to the Nineteenth Century* by W. H. Beveridge and others. For calculation of weights, annual quantities of each commodity imported were multiplied by the corresponding commodity's price (the price selected for use in the index). The export quantities which were used originate in the *American State Papers*.

The commodities comprising the index, along with the name of the city in which the prices were recorded (for those prices taken from Cole) or Greenwich Hospital (for those prices taken from Beveridge), as well as difficulties peculiar to inclusion of these commodities, are as follows: (1) Sugar (brown)—Philadelphia; (2) Coffee (St. Domingo)—Philadelphia; (3) Tea (hyson)—New York, for want of a New York unit price tea not included in the index for 1792; (4) Wine (Madeira)—Philadelphia, quality of wine in price quotations changed from unspecified (1790–1795) to *best London particular* (1796–1815) in 1796; (5) Molasses—Philadelphia, quality of molasses in price quotations was as follows: unspecified 1790–May 1800, *West India* July 1800–October 1802, *Havana* November 1802–1813, and *West India* 1814–1815; (6) Steel (English blistered)—Philadelphia, steel not included in calculation of index for 1795 owing to an unreliable import quantity reported in the *American State Papers* (5,411,123 cwt. as against 10,805 cwt. and 7,024 cwt. for the preceding and following years, respectively); (7) Nails (assorted sizes)—Philadelphia 1790–1813, 1815 and New York 1814, spikes included with nails for all years excepting 1793–1794; (8) Salt—Philadelphia, not included in the calculation of the index for the years 1809–1813 owing to the un-availability of data on quantities imported; (9) Shoes (men and women)—Greenwich Hospital, prices recorded at Greenwich for *shoes common;* (10) Bar and Other Lead—Greenwich Hospital, quantities imported reported changed from *Bar and Other Lead* (1790–1803) to *Lead and Manufactures of Lead* (1804–1815) in 1804 while the prices used are for *sheet and cast lead* for the entire period with the exception of 1806 for which a unit price was not reported, and hence lead is not included in the index of 1806.

C. *Method of Calculation:* As the first step in the calculation of the import index a basic Laspeyres price relative index is calculated for ten commodities imported during the period 1790–1815. The bases used for this index are the years 1790, 1795, 1800, 1805, and 1810. Second, these ten series of price relatives are weighted by the annual import values of each commodity in relation to its per-centage of the value of imports of all commodities included in this index. The final sub-index is obtained by linking the weighted index of price relatives to the base 1790.

The English yarn series was taken from G. R. Porter's *Progress of the Nation.* Price relatives were calculated from the unit prices in five year series with respective bases of 1790, 1795, 1800, 1805, and 1810, and were subsequently combined with the series of relatives for cloth and stockings and Bezanson's textiles, each receiving equal weight, and linked to give a single textile series with a base of 1790.

The cloth and stocking series was derived from Beveridge and consists of stocking prices as recorded at Greenwich Hospital, blue cloth—Greenwich Hospital, choristers cloth—Winchester College, and students cloth—Eton College. Price relatives for each of these commodities were calculated as outlined above, combined into a single series, each receiving equal weight, and subsequently com-bined with the yarn and Bezanson series and linked as outlined above.

The Bezanson series is comprised of both domestic and imported textile fabrics: checks—domestic, cordage—domestic and imported, diaper (linen)—domestic, duck (ravens) and (bear ravens)—imported, and sheeting (Russian brown) and (Russian white)—imported. From the Bezanson data, price relatives were calculated (in this case from other price relatives rather than from actual unit prices) and combined with the other two textile series and linked as indicated above.

In arriving at the final index, the linked relatives series for textiles was combined with the linked relatives series for the ten commodities in accordance with the aforementioned weights of forty and sixty, respectively.

As a measure of coverage of the index, listed below are the annual percentages of total imports which the above listed ten commodities comprise. As in the case of the export index, the coverage is far from satisfactory, but the price behavior of the commodities covered does appear to be representative of the behavior of import prices for the period.

Year	Percentage of Total Imports
1790	28.6
1791	21.9
1792	24.8
1793	44.3
1794	45.6
1795	32.8
1796	35.3
1797	35.5
1798	40.4
1799	28.6
1800	30.0
1801	23.8
1802	30.8
1803	23.5
1804	44.2
1805	37.4
1806	32.1
1807	30.8
1808	40.3
1809	30.1
1810	20.5
1811	29.8
1812	24.6
1813	51.2
1814	96.2
1815	23.5

III. Method and Sources of Export and Import Price Indices, 1815–1860

A

The basic source of quantity and value data from which the export and import price indices are constructed is the annual publication of the United States Treasury, Commerce and Navigation of the United States, 1821–1860.[1] Deficient coverage for the purposes of the index in this source has led to the use of the following sources.

In construction of the Export Price Index: U. S. Bureau of Labor Statistics, Bulletin No. 376, Appendix F. *Wholesale Prices in the United States, 1801–1840.* U. S. Congress, *Report of the Secretary of the Treasury on the State of the Finances, for the Year Ending June 30, 1863,* 38th Congress, 1st Session, 1864, Document No. 3.

In construction of the Import Price Index: Monthly Summary of Commerce and Finance, Vol. 7, Pt. 3, p. 2636. Great Britain, Parliament, *Annual Reports on Foreign Trade, 1850–1854.*

Remarks: (1) The question of under-reporting and under-valuation in American statistics has been explored in D. C. North's "Balance of Payments," *loc. cit.,* p. 575-576. (2) Considerations of qualitative changes in the commodities entering into trade have been ignored in preparation of the indices.

Economic Classes: Economic classification follows the principles employed by the Foreign Trade Division of the Bureau of the Census in the construction of the current "Schedule B," Statistical Classification of Domestic and Foreign Commerce Exported from the United States, Part II, Numerical classification and articles included (January 1, 1945 Ed.), and "Schedule D," Imports, etc. The basis of this classification is labor added to the produce of the forest, the sea, the field and the mine, and was adopted by the Bureau of the Census in 1906. Discussion of this principle of classification is to be found in *Foreign Commerce and Navigation of the*

---

[1] U.S. Congress, House, *Domestic Exports, 1789–1883.* House Miscellaneous Document No. 2236, compiled by C. H. Evans. 48th Congress, 1st Session, 1883–1884 (Washington: Government Printing Office, 1884).

U. S., (Washington: U. S. Government Printing Office, 1906), pp. 15-16. The five economic classes as found in *Historical Statistics of the United States, 1789–1945*, Series M. 56-67, are used for class weighting for the period of 1850–1860. For imports, betwen 1821 and 1850 three classes have been used: (1) Raw materials and crude foods, (2) Processed foods, and (3) Manufactures and semi-manufactures. Annual values are calculated from *Foreign Commerce and Navigation of the U. S.*, Imports, and are presented in Table 7. For exports, all five economic classes are calculated from 1820–1850, from data in *Domestic Exports, 1789–1883* and are presented in Table 5.

B

The Sample: The index sample of the population represented by the trade statistics is largely limited to those commodities for which both value and quantity data are given. Since few quantity series are given with textile manufacturing values, it is primarily here that outside sources have been used to improve the sample. See Table IX for coverage of the sample.

Construction of the Export and Import Indices: The import and export indices for 1815–1820 and 1820–1850 can be characterized as price-value indices constructed by linking five-year period indices from 1815–1820 and ten-year period indices from 1820–1860. Sixth and eleventh years are calculated on the base of the period indices to permit linking. In the periods, sub-indices are calculated for economic classes and combined according to the proportion that the aggregate value of the class represents the aggregate value of exports or imports. Commodity prices, in the determination of the class indices, are weighted by the aggregate value of the commodity relative to the aggregate value of the class sample. Alternatively, this weighting procedure may be expressed as the weighting of commodity prices in each class by the average value of the commodity in the period.

Exceptions in practice to the above formulation are: Because of the lack of quantitative data for imports in 1820, the sub-indices for the period 1815 to 1820 run on to 1821 and the subsequent index is calculated from 1821 to 1830 (1821 and 1830 being the extra years). The 1815–1821 index is weighted by average values of commodities from 1815 to 1819; the 1821–1830 index by average values from 1821 to 1829. Averages after 1820 are determined for the ten years including the decade years, 1820, 1830, 1840, 1850, with the exception noted above, and eleven year averages are employed for the period 1850–1860.

As the first step in the calculation of the export-import price indices for 1815–1820 and 1820–1860, the individual class indices are calculated for five and ten year periods. Letting $C_{t1}{}^{(K)}$ = the k'th class index number for the t'th year, the computational formula is:

$$(1) \quad C_{t1}^{(K)} = 100 \left\{ \frac{\sum_{i=1}^{m} \left[\frac{P_t^{(i)}}{P_1^{(i)}} (P_1^{(i)} Q_1^{(i)} + P_2^{(i)} Q_2^{(i)} + \ldots + P_N^{(i)} Q_N^{(i)}) \right]}{\sum_{i=1}^{m} (P_1^{(i)} Q_1^{(i)} + P_2^{(i)} Q_2^{(i)} + \ldots + P_N^{(i)} Q_N^{(i)})} \right\}$$

where N equals 10 for 1820–1860, 5 for 1815–1820 and $P^i{}_1$ the price of the i'th commodity in the first year of the five or ten year period.

The overall index I_{t1} = the index number for the t'th year. The overall index is calculated by the same method, the class indices being weighted by the average value of the class of commodities over the five year or ten year period. Letting I_{t1} represent the final index number for the t'th year, the computational formula is:

$$(2) \quad I_{t1} = \frac{\sum_{k=1}^{K} V^{(k)} C_{t1}^{(k)}}{\sum_{k=1}^{k} V^{(k)}}$$

where K equals the number of classes and $V^{(k)} =$

$$\sum_{i=1}^{m'} (P_1^{(i)} Q_1^{(i)} + P_2^{(i)} Q_2^{(i)} + \ldots + P_N^{(i)} Q_N^{(i)})$$

all p's and q's are drawn from the k'th class of commodities. m' equals the total number of commodities in the k'th class.

C

Class Reweighting: The decision to reweight class indices by the proportions of actual class values of the total values is taken because certain commodities could not be included in the class indices.

Periodization: Two reasons underly the decision to employ the five- and ten-year periodization in the construction of the indices. (1) Within economic classes, commodity proportions of totals change radically. For example, cotton rises from a small fraction of raw materials exported in 1790 to almost half the value of total exports in 1860. Wheat and flour, important in the era of the Napoleonic Wars, dwindle to relative unimportance in the three succeeding decades, and with the Irish famine and the abolition of the corn laws again increase to percentages as high as 10 and 12 per cent of exports. (2) The second reason for periodization arises from the character of the data. Only a few usable series are available in early years. In the later years, as greater attention was paid by the government to the extent and quality of its statistical reporting, many more series are usable. Through periodization, the period indices can be constructed from data available in the period; and in a subsequent period when more data is available, larger samples may be used.

Weighting by Averages of Period Value: In the context of the decision to use a price value index there appear to be two major alternatives: (1) Base year weighting or given year weighting, (2) Weighting by an average of base and given years. (Weighting by averages is in effect weighting the sum of values in base and given years, and since comparability within periods rather than only between two years is sought, for the purpose of the index averages (totals) of values of all years are used.)

Considering the radical fluctuations of values around trends in the periods and the decision to periodize the index by half-decades before 1820 and by decades after 1820, provision can be made for highly significant occurrences, such as the change of demand for wheat in the 1840's, the exploitation of Californian gold in the 1850's or the shifts in demand consequent upon repeal of the corn laws and the Crimean War, by averaging all of the values in the period. Under these random fluctuations, the period indices could be carried substantially out of relationship to the realities of trade in the period if either beginning year or end year values were employed as weights. In averaging, it is further attempted to avoid distortions due to periodization where beginning or end years of periods fall at one time in the prosperous phase of the cycle and at another in a depressed phase.

The considerations above generally refer to a choice between single year weighting and weighting by the total of values in the period. Both of these methods, because we are dealing with a price-value index, involve the multiplication of the price in the year for which the index number is being determined with the price or the prices that appear in the weight. There is subsequently division of the result of weighting by a similar weighting required in determination of the value of the weighted relatives of the base year. This applies not to the commodity but to the index, and must occur because the significance of weighting lies in the distribution of some total, for example, one, over a number of price relatives, and observing the variations effected in the total derived from variations of the relative multiplied against the parts of the distributed weight.

It is to be expected, because of the relation of commodity relatives and commodity quantities alone, that, with the use of a single year weight, the conditions of that year which have led to either large or small quantities will affect the values of the index for subsequent years. When, however, commodity relatives are combined with commodity quantities and prices (or values), a further element appears to affect subsequent values of the index. If in the base year prices are high and quantities are small, or the position of average of all commodities is high on the demand curve and in subsequent years supply shifts so that prices fall and quantities increase, the index will understate or overstate what might be expected to be the true level of prices depending on whether the aggregate demand curve has an elasticity greater or less than unity. The tendency here will be offset by the relation of base year price to subsequent prices caused by the division through of weighted and aggregated relatives by the base year weighted aggregate.

If now, rather than base year weights—or for that matter given year weights—averages of the period are used, there will be a multi-

plication in each value of the index of the price of each commodity
with all other prices of the commodity in the period. This, coupled
with the previous argument, will prevent the biases to be expected
from single year weighting but will have a tendency to accentuate
the fluctuations in the index. Fluctuations will be exaggerated because if price is initially low and then rises, high relatives in the
later period will be multiplied with a total including these high
prices, and then divided, in reduction of weighted relatives to an
index, by the total multiplied with the initially low price of the
base year and conversely. Also there will be a squaring of prices
both in the numerator and in the denominator of the ratio giving
rise to the index value. If, again, prices are low initially and high in
the later period, given the character of a sum of squares, reduction
of the series of weighted relatives to index numbers will involve
the division of the square of a small number by the square of a
large number, the result of which can be expected to be relatively
high, relative to the result of division of the given year price by
the base year price. This process too would seem to accentuate
fluctuation, but possibly only on the upward side. In the attempt to
determine the terms of trade in the years of the period, exaggera-
tion of fluctuations in the indices employed will amplify the result.
Upon the number of observations in the period, the number of
values of individual years that are averaged, will depend the
degree of amplification. The extreme case is weighting relatives
by annual values.

Consideration of Weighting and Periodization: Examining the
three decisions—(1) to employ a price-value index, (2) to periodize
and (3) to weight—together, it may be observed that periodization
will, if the period chosen happens to be on the average prosperous
or on the average poor, be accentuated in the period index, if not
compensated, by particular circumstances of the movements of
prices and quantities in the period. Considering their effect, the
rationale of the periods chosen may be investigated. In the case of
the indices developed in section B, the reasons for periodization
already given must be weighted against the probability of the element of amplification suggested here.

*Relationship of the Economic Class Index (Equation (1) to the
Paasche and Laspeyres Index Numbers:* If, in the weights shown
in equation (1), all terms except the $P^i_t \, Q^i_t$ are dropped, it is seen

that the Paasche index is obtained. Also of the weights shown in equation (1), if all terms except $P^i_1 Q^i_1$ are dropped, the Laspeyres index results.

Problems Arising Through Use of the Laspeyres Index: If the price relatives are correlated with the weights used, then the choice of a base year will influence the results. For example, if commodities with falling prices are commodities whose weights increase, the use of initial year weights will yield an index underweighting the commodities whose prices are declining.

The economic class indices derived in the previous section attempt to avoid this difficulty in that the weights used are average weights for the period. The simple interpretation given to the Paasche and Laspeyres indices may no longer be applied to the index derived in section B, nor may the standard tests, such as factor reversal, conformity to the ideal index, and so on. However, weights applied are average weights and most likely yield a result intermediate between the Laspeyres and Paasche indices.

TABLE I

UNITED STATES EXPORT AND IMPORT PRICE INDEXES, 1815-1860
1830 - 100

Year	Exports	Imports
1815	182.98	222.7
1816	248.22	194.9
1817	240.35	176.8
1818	245.46	189.7
1819	194.74	171.9
1820	144.17	151.2
1821	127.92	134.0
1822	136.32	133.6
1823	114.37	127.7
1824	126.16	119.8
1825	152.47	127.1
1826	114.78	121.6
1827	102.53	111.1
1828	102.10	112.3
1829	107.07	105.9
1830	100.00	100.0
1831	98.77	95.8
1832	104.63	93.6
1833	115.08	100.0
1834	127.01	103.3
1835	149.81	101.3
1836	155.37	109.6
1837	142.57	104.1
1838	115.87	90.8
1839	155.85	97.8
1840	99.73	94.0
1841	110.19	91.3
1842	93.84	82.8
1843	75.83	79.4
1844	89.20	78.2
1845	78.32	80.9
1846	92.79	81.6
1847	112.79	82.3
1848	94.29	74.1
1849	84.17	72.0
1850	120.72	74.2
1851	123.72	78.8
1852	96.30	75.5
1853	93.50	83.3
1854	116.74	83.2
1855	119.04	84.7
1856	124.43	89.8
1857	141.90	95.8
1858	128.29	91.7
1859	126.46	90.2
1860	119.81	92.2

Sources: For derivation of table, see Appendix III.

TABLE II

EXPORT PRICE INDEXES BY ECONOMIC CLASSES, 1815-1860

Base 1830

Year	Raw Materials	Raw Foods	Processed Foods	Semi-manufactures	Manufactures
1815	196.1	150.9	172.7	136.3	184.5
1816	300.8	197.7	202.1	146.9	178.3
1817	260.4	221.6	240.6	129.3	178.3
1818	294.2	232.0	204.7	122.5	170.9
1819	223.8	173.9	166.3	118.6	193.9
1820	169.6	146.3	101.2	102.8	172.9
1821	155.5	104.7	88.4	94.0	165.5
1822	156.2	120.5	118.4	99.3	148.3
1823	114.3	118.9	123.0	105.1	133.5
1824	143.4	104.7	112.9	96.0	130.0
1825	192.0	122.5	105.7	96.8	135.5
1826	125.3	119.3	97.2	94.6	120.3
1827	101.1	126.1	105.0	90.9	117.4
1828	102.7	96.3	102.5	96.0	116.2
1829	100.5	100.0	126.4	103.4	109.8
1830	100.0	100.0	100.0	100.0	100.0
1931	92.3	118.6	110.0	92.2	108.6
1932	99.5	118.6	112.9	89.7	108.1
1833	112.7	125.1	115.0	85.7	106.3
1834	129.1	117.9	106.1	89.0	102.8
1835	155.0	132.7	114.9	95.6	114.1
1836	115.9	129.7	146.4	112.5	126.3
1837	137.7	150.6	170.6	106.8	116.4
1838	106.2	159.4	152.7	100.6	110.6
1839	155.7	173.2	147.9	105.7	121.9
1840	93.6	123.6	110.7	92.4	101.6
1841	107.9	127.0	99.3	93.5	102.8
1842	84.2	124.1	100.2	92.4	90.2
1843*	65.4	98.3	83.9	84.7	81.3
1844	82.7	109.0	85.8	88.1	96.4
1845	62.9	112.0	95.7	93.2	88.3
1846	80.8	137.7	98.3	97.0	95.9
1847	101.8	179.7	119.7	90.9	95.4
1848	79.0	152.1	113.6	86.7	87.9
1849	59.3	134.6	100.1	87.1	83.5
1850	156.2	133.1	98.3	101.8	93.7
1851	127.5	123.1	100.2	100.8	105.4
1852	87.1	124.3	101.0	107.1	91.6
1853	76.8	141.4	111.9	114.1	98.6
1854	101.5	183.5	132.0	114.8	103.6
1855	95.2	200.1	161.7	107.1	110.4
1856	103.7	198.3	156.4	112.0	119.2
1857	113.9	171.5	145.3	116.5	132.4
1858	124.2	135.2	121.2	125.8	119.8
1859	121.4	134.2	126.5	123.6	107.1
1860	112.5	135.0	123.8	113.4	112.6

*Based on 9 months only

TABLE III

IMPORT CLASS PRICE INDEXES, 1815-1860
Bases 1830

Year	Raw Mat. and Crude Food	Manufactured Foods	Manufactures and Semi-mfg.
1815	170.9	275.5	239.6
1816	169.2	222.3	203.7
1817	148.7	201.1	186.9
1818	160.6	195.6	203.7
1819	162.3	173.6	177.3
1820	150.4	148.8	153.3
1821	145.3	129.5	131.8
1822	151.8	129.0	129.4
1823	151.4	121.3	122.3
1824	134.1	100.8	119.8
1825	138.0	124.8	125.1
1826	133.1	129.2	116.6
1827	113.5	127.4	106.9
1828	113.3	129.0	108.3
1829	112.3	112.7	102.7
1830	100.0	100.0	100.0
1831	100.6	98.4	93.8
1832	109.8	103.7	86.5
1833	122.3	116.7	89.7
1834	129.1	117.2	92.4
1835	118.4	116.8	92.9
1836	118.5	147.8	99.6
1837	117.1	129.9	95.1
1838	97.9	81.5	90.3
1839	102.5	123.0	91.4
1840	102.4	106.3	89.0
1841	104.9	104.8	84.7
1842	95.2	84.2	78.5
1843*	88.7	82.8	75.7
1844	80.9	95.4	74.2
1845	85.9	106.3	74.9
1846	75.9	103.3	79.0
1847	77.7	100.5	80.0
1848	77.0	91.9	70.0
1849	75.0	85.2	68.6
1850	79.0	90.2	69.7
1851	95.9	90.7	71.1
1852	88.2	85.8	69.6
1853	98.6	90.3	77.4
1854	101.2	89.6	76.6
1855	95.4	99.2	78.8
1856	100.6	125.2	79.9
1857	103.1	158.8	81.7
1858	103.1	135.6	80.0
1859	106.0	127.7	78.3
1860	97.5	133.3	78.0

*Based on 9 months only

Note: The series 1850-1860 represents a combination of 2 series each under Raw Materials and Crude Foods, and Manufactures and Semi-manufactures. The individual series are weighted by their per cent of value in the grouping.

TABLE IV

EXPORTED COMMODITIES INCLUDED IN ECONOMIC CLASSES IN
SUBPERIODS 1815-1860; INCLUSION INDICATED BY WEIGHT
GIVEN IN CALCULATION OF SUBPERIOD CLASS INDEXES.
WEIGHTS ARE ANNUAL AVERAGE VALUE OF
COMMODITY IN THOUSANDS OF DOLLARS

	1815-20	1820-30	1830-40	1840-50	1850-60
Class 1					
Raw Materials					
Cotton	15,673	25,655	52,881	55,341	123,606
Tobacco	5,966	5,589	7,466	8,166	14,177
Hops	14	34	65	71	185
Ginseng	72	150	106	174	115
Class 2					
Crude Foods					
Rice	2,302	2,006	2,223	2,359	2,178
Wheat	162	182	255	1,564	7,503
Indian Corn	850	389	268	3,303	3,750
Class 3					
Manufactured Foods					
Wheat Flour	9,712	4,904	5,658	10,043	18,014
Sugar, refined	9	43	300	314	325
Pickled Pork	763	772	987	1,926	3,196
Bacon and Hams	102	170	150	1,209	2,424
Lard	264	525	785	2,173	3,471
Butter	157	144	159	437	634
Cheese	60	43	62	560	716
Dry Fish	722	733	671	581	441
Pickled Fish	261	249	225	149	154
Class 4					
Semi-Manufactures					
Boards	1,203	883	1,093	1,265	1,763
Staves	1,101	585	723	549	1,157
Ashes	961	1,159	713	726	541
Whale Oil	259	301	980	1,057	515
Sperm Oil	51	44	116	521	1,279
Naval Stores	435	408	618	812	1,681
Furs	403	595	775	796	1,019
Whale Bone	5	48	206	452	937
Class 5					
Manufactures					
Cotton Mfgs.			2,520	3,955	5,565
Nails		63	96	134	193
Gun Powder	102	144	160	129	327
Soap	361	745	520	381	468
Sperm Candles	165	226	277	231	92
Tallow Candles	125	250	282	325	689
Tobacco Mfgs.	261	195	443	594	1,953

TABLE V

VALUE OF DOMESTICALLY PRODUCED EXPORTS BY ECONOMIC CLASS
1820-1860

(in thousands of dollars)

Year	Raw Materials	Crude Foods	Processed Foods	Semi-Manufacture	Manu-facture	Total
1820	30,914	2,284	9,851	5,611	2,924	51,684
1821	26,498	1,894	8,077	3,682	3,521	43,672
1822	30,096	2,092	9,221	3,843	3,622	49,874
1823	27,308	2,447	8,725	4,652	3,813	47,155
1824	27,853	2,441	9,963	4,893	5,502	50,650
1825	43,755	2,557	9,061	5,317	6,255	66,945
1826	31,029	2,482	8,805	4,057	6,077	52,450
1827	36,402	3,108	8,624	3,606	6,078	57,878
1828	28,211	2,819	8,738	4,033	6,176	49,977
1829	32,011	3,226	9,800	4,111	5,939	55,087
1830	35,745	2,387	9,671	4,337	6,385	58,525
1831	30,772	3,141	14,393	4,579	6,334	59,219
1832	38,159	2,661	9,752	4,831	6,323	61,726
1833	42,639	3,300	10,907	5,128	7,977	69,951
1834	56,823	2,496	8,986	4,696	7,623	80,624
1835	74,173	3,008	8,973	5,550	8,755	100,459
1836	82,197	2,819	7,790	6,240	7,526	106,571
1837	69,671	2,660	6,932	6,484	8,533	94,280
1838	69,448	2,065	7,537	6,585	9,926	95,561
1839	71,733	2,926	11,234	5,838	9,895	101,626
1840	74,185	4,138	14,947	6,352	12,039	111,661
1841	67,753	3,418	13,766	6,973	11,727	103,837
1842	57,610	3,462	13,421	7,364	9,942	91,799
1843*	54,383	2,362	8,814	4,260	7,868	77,687
1844	62,976	3,344	14,611	7,180	11,421	99,532
1845	59,966	3,291	13,343	9,022	12,834	98,456
1846	52,306	6,211	21,477	8,267	13,457	101,718
1847	61,269	25,852	42,849	7,368	12,910	150,248
1848	770,001	9,390	28,829	6,164	15,820	130,204
1849	72,615	12,608	26,546	6,028	13,913	131,710
1850	82,390	7,413	19,259	7,306	18,532	134,900
1851	124,519	5,369	19,702	6,203	22,799	178,620
1852	100,687	7,237	19,837	6,075	21,095	154,931
1853	124,292	8,019	26,620	6,451	24,488	189,869
1854	107,590	22,153	46,688	10,878	26,677	213,985
1855	108,685	10,920	33,009	11,304	28,833	192,751
1856	145,375	28,578	53,325	8,041	31,118	266,438
1857	158,052	31,207	48,559	11,304	30,052	278,907
1858	155,248	17,545	38,534	9,866	30,158	251,351
1859	190,114	10,147	32,437	10,672	35,023	278,392
1860	216,998	12,166	38,625	12,642	35,811	316,242

*Based on nine months only.

Class values for the years 1820-1850 calculated from HMD No. 2236, Evans Report, Table 3, pp. 61-71, showing the values of the produce of the Sea, Forest, Agriculture, and Manufactures, 1803-1850. Class values for 1851-1860 are taken from <u>Historical Statistics</u>, series M 56-61. <u>Historical Statistics</u> also gives class values for 1820—wrongly given as 1821—1830, 1840, and 1850.

TABLE V (cont.)

Comparisons in these years of the values above show slight variations due to differing classifications underlying both sets of figures. The HS classification is the 1906 classification described in text above; the classification adopted to reorganize the data as presented in Evans is the current Schedule B, (1958). Since the 1906 classification is the forerunner of Schedule B, discrepancy exists only with respect to minor commodities. A further difficulty arises from heading inclusions in Table 3 that do not allow for separation of commodities in conformity with the requirements of either the 1906 schedule or Schedule B. As a consequence of this manufactures from 1820 to 1829 have been calculated as a residual after the other four classifications have been determined.

Included in the series, value of all manufactures, in the original table, is exports of gold and silver coin from 1826 to 1850. These values have been deducted both from the class manufactures and the total series as given in the table.

The following commodities are included in the classes above:

Raw Materials
  Ginseng
  Horses and Mules
  Sheep
  Wool
  Tobacco
  Cotton
  Wax
  Hemp
  Indigo
  Flaxseed
  Hops

Crude Foods
  Wheat
  Indian Corn
  Rye, Oats, and other small grains
  Potatoes
  Apples
  Rice

Processed Foods
  Dried fish or Cod Fisheries
  Pickled Fish or River Fisheries
    Herring, Shad, Salmon,
    Mackerel
  Beef, Tallow, Hides and Horned
    Cattle
  Butter and Cheese
  Pork (Pickled), Bacon, Lard and
    Live Hogs
  Flour
  Indian Meal
  Rye Meal
  Biscuits and Ships Bread
  Sugar (Brown)

Semi-Manufactures
  Whale and other Fish Oil
  Whalebone
  Spermaceti Oil
  Stave, Shingles, Boards and Hewn
    Timber
  Other Lumber
  Masts and Spars
  Oak Bark and other Dye
  Naval Stores, Tar, Pitch, Rosin and
    Turpentine
  Ashes, Pot and Pearl
  Articles, Uncertain, other

Manufactures
  Spermaceti Candles
  All Manufactures of Food
  Skins and Furs
  Value of all Manufactures
  Articles, Uncertain, Manufactures

The items above following the headings in Table III.

TABLE VI

IMPORTED COMMODITIES INCLUDED IN ECONOMIC CLASSES IN SUB-
PERIODS 1815-1860, INCLUSION INDICATED BY WEIGHT GIVEN IN
CALCULATION OF SUBPERIOD CLASS INDEXES.
WEIGHTS ARE ANNUAL AVERAGE VALUE OF COMMODITY
IN THOUSANDS OF DOLLARS

	1815-21	1821-30	1830-40	1840-50	1850-60
Class 1					
Raw Materials					
Coal	98	131	250	423	680
Hemp		627	540	305	276
Guano					359
Opium				156	349
Wool		225	900	894	2,500
Grass and Sisal					788
Cotton		62			
Jute				134	
Class 2					
Raw Foods					
Tea	1,800	2,446	4,002	4,526	6,922
Coffee	5,100	5,137	8,538	7,976	17,685
Nutmegs			154	161	266
Pepper			197	110	321
Spices, generally		495			
Raisins			771	631	1,089
Fruits, generally		360			
Cocoa		350	211	130	190
Class 3					
Processed Foods					
Wines, generally		1,500	1,591		6,647
Champagne					978
Port			392	195	
Brandy				900	
Other Spirits		1,510	1,117		
Sugar	5,100	4,328	5,866	6,168	20,564
Molasses	3,100	2,264	3,072	2,650	4,461
Butter			6	5	76
Beer		74			
Fish		23			
Class 4					
Semi-manufactures					
Pig Lead, Inc., Mfgs.	202[2]	207	109	12	2,033[4]
Pig Iron		90	249	457	1,309
Rags				477	1,132
Paints		194			
Ocher			22	27	19
Linseed Oil*[1]			386	240	829
Linseed Oil, incl. Olive		90			
Skins, Tanned and Dressed				200	860
Leather					1,251
Soda Ash					1,092
Saltpeter, Crude*				200	998
Camphor, Crude*			36	59	44
Coppers		6			

TABLE VI (cont.)

	1815-21	1821-30	1830-40	1840-50	1850-60
Class 4 (cont.)					
Indigo*[1]		1,362	820	859	1,078
Bristles*			102	97	291
Bristles and Glue*		63			
Class 5					
Manufactures					
Cotton Print Piece Goods }	40,800	{ 5,502[3]	7,572	7,578	15,881
White Cotton Piece Goods }		{ 2,581	2,223	1,561	1,500
Cotton Thread		191	521	546	1,249
Silk Piece Goods					21,628
Woolen Mfgs.					3,000
Linen Mfgs.					1,500
Carpeting			443	340	1,535
Baize			82	68	125
Flannel			207	55	123
Floor Cloth			24	7	30
Furniture Cloth and Oil Cloth			17	2	9
Sail Duck					36
Cotton Bagging			402	203	27
Tarred Cables and Cordage		153			
Shoes, Boots, Slippers		5	29		89
Leather Gloves				446	1,354
Steel	259[2]	278	695	698	1,791
Sheet Iron					921
Hoop Iron			236	384	335
Chain Cables			106	137	308
Nails				61	127
Anvils			61	55	36
Anchors			10	13	63
Wire		80	49		
Iron Mfgs. General		173			
Saws			10		
Hammered Iron]	1,280[2]	1,823 {	} 1,727	904 {	} 10,430[5]
Rolled Iron }			} 1,442	2,176 {	
Bar Iron]					
Window Glass			91	80	565
Gunpowder		16	12		
Salt		622	730	924	1,412
Cigars		205	784	1,023	3,689
Rifles			34		
Copper, Nails, Bolts	23[2]	8			

[1] For purposes of derivation of class indexes starred semi-manufactures are classified as Raw Materials, unstarred as Manufactures.

[2] These several values are combined into an index which being weighted 2 is combined with textiles, weighted eight, to give index from Manufactures for 1815-21.

[3] Brackets indicate inclusion of several commodities as weights for the relative of one of them, in effect the use of an index.

[4] Excludes lead manufactures.

[5] Includes rails, 1854-60.

TABLE VII

IMPORTS INTO THE UNITED STATES BY ECONOMIC CLASS, 1821-1860

(in thousands of dollars)

Year	Crude Foods and Raw Materials	Manufactured Foodstuffs	Semi-manufactures and Manufactures
1821	10,089	9,229	35,203
1822	15,342	11,900	52,630
1823	17,209	9,134	46,057
1824	14,954	11,143	46,072
1825	18,493	10,852	60,844
1826	18,014	11,641	48,439
1827	13,844	10,807	46,682
1828	16,866	10,316	53,838
1829	14,851	8,276	43,962
1830	13,579	7,932	41,210
1831	16,808	10,256	68,821
1832	22,555	9,499	63,068
1833	25,900	11,745	63,403
1834	25,531	13,162	69,917
1835	28,237	15,650	92,877
1836	31,089	23,394	122,094
1837	32,269	16,560	81,644
1838	20,063	15,544	60,363
1839	25,595	20,495	110,407
1840	25,844	12,787	59,632
1841	27,189	15,655	80,144
1842	23,431	10,921	95,806
1843	15,080	4,433	22,920
1844	25,475	12,266	64,864
1845	26,726	11,064	75,396
1846	28,000	12,431	78,383
1847	23,997	17,259	81,168
1848	29,152	18,648	100,838
1849	26,004	16,499	96,703
1850	30,568	21,466	121,475
1851	36,468	29,261	145,042
1852	37,531	29,123	140,786
1853	44,330	32,857	186,590
1854	47,904	32,671	217,228
1855	59,991	34,138	163,679
1856	66,306	46,308	197,819
1857	74,994	71,671	201,763
1858	70,006	45,830	147,530
1859	82,466	57,339	191,475
1860	85,435	59,838	207,028

Class values 1821 through 1849 calculated from Annual Reports on Commerce and Navigation of the United States; 1850 through 1860 taken from Historical Statistics. The five classes given in HS are combined to give the 3 calculated from the original data. Comparison of values given in HS for 1821, 1830, and 1840 show slight differences due to differing bases of classification as described in notes in text on Exports by Economic Classes. Prior to 1821 no data is available to develop class value series.

TABLE VII (cont.)

COMMODITY LISTS USED IN IMPORT DIVISION

Raw Mat. and Foods	Manufactured Foods	Manufactures
Tea	Wines	Mfg. of
Coffee	Distilled Spirits	Cotton
Dye Wood and Wood	Beer	Wool
Barrels	Vinegar	Silk
Burr Stones	Molasses	Linen
Crude Brimstone	Chocolate	Hemp
Slates	Sugars	Grass
Wool	Cheese	Leather
Cork	Pork and Beef	Iron, etc.
Cocoa	Hams and Bacon	Paints
Fruits	Potatoes	Chemicals
Nuts	Fish	Glass
Spices	Articles paying Ad.V.	Earthenware
Ginger	Duties of from 6 to	Rags
Camphor	10 per cent	Mfg. of Tobacco
Bristles		Glue
Saltpeter		Gunpowder
Indigo		Bleaching Powder
Ivory		Soda Ash
Opium		Tanned and Dressed
Hemp		Skins
Manilla		Salt
Jute and grass		Books
Cordillat		Paper
Flax		Quicksilver
Coal		Lead
Hides		Smelter
Undressed furs		Watches
Articles paying Ad.V.		Saddlery
duties of from 1 to		Arms
5 per cent		All other Non-
		enumerated goods
Specie included		

TABLE VIII

YEARS IN EACH PERIOD OVER WHICH COMMODITY VALUES ARE AVERAGED FOR PURPOSES OF WEIGHTING
1821-1860

Period	Years Averaged	
	Exports	Imports
1820-1830	1821-1830	1821-1829
1830-1840	1831-1840	1830-1839
1840-1850	1841-1850	1840-1849
1850-1860	1851-1860	1850-1860

TABLE IX

WEIGHTING OF CLASS INDEXES BY PERIODS

Imports Period	Classes[1]				
	1	2	3	4	5
1790-1821	33.0			67.0	
1821-1830	21.0		13.9	65.1	
1830-1840	21.2		12.5	66.3	
1840-1850	21.0		12.0	67.0	
1850-1860	9.6	11.7	15.4	12.5	50.8
Exports					
1790-1815	65.0		20.0	15.0	
1815-1821[2]	62.1	5.4	15.6	6.2	10.7
1821-1831	60.1	4.8	17.1	8.0	10.0
1831-1841	69.3	3.3	11.4	6.4	9.6
1841-1851	56.9	6.9	18.6	6.2	11.4
1851-1860	61.9	6.6	15.5	4.1	11.9

[1] Class 1., Raw Materials
  Class 2., Raw Food Stuff
  Class 3., Processed Foods
  Class 4., Semi-manufactures
  Class 5., Manufactures
[2] Calculated as average of succeeding percentages for Classes.

TABLE X

SAMPLE COVERAGE BY CLASSES[1]

Imports

Period	Classes				
	1	2	3	4	5
1821-29	73.5		94.8		25.3	
1830-39	66.6		70.1		22.6	
1840-49	66.0		67.0		23.0	
1850-60	18.0	81.0	78.0	31.0	47.0

Exports

Period	1	2	3	4	5
1821-30	98.8	97.2	83.6	94.6	51.3
1831-40	98.4	93.9	88.7	93.5	50.4
1841-50	99.4	93.5	83.2	80.9	42.1
1851-60	96.5	87.7	82.3	95.2	31.4[2]

[1] Not calculated prior to 1821 because for imports it is impossible from existing data. For exports, though possible, the conclusions to be reached would be dubious because of the summary character of data.

[2] Full advantage was not taken of the index procedure explained in this paper: a fixed set of commodities was employed in the export index and new commodities entering trade, particularly manufactures, were not worked into the period indexes as they appeared in the statistical series.

Note: Though the data above is suggestive, the method of construction assumes complete coverage of all commodities in each class, i.e., the weighting procedures amount to treatment of each particular price relative as an index, and the class reweighting is an extension of this procedure.

BIBLIOGRAPHY

Books and Doctoral Dissertations

ALBION, ROBERT G., *Square Riggers on Schedule; the New York Sailing Packets to England, France and the Cotton Ports.* Princeton: Princeton University Press, 1938.

ALBION, ROBERT G., and JENNIE B. POPE, *Sea Lanes in Wartime: The American Experience, 1775–1942.* New York: W. W. Norton & Co., 1942.

BATES, WILLIAM W., *American Navigation; the Political History of its Rise and Ruin and the Proper Means for its Encouragement.* Boston and New York: Houghton Mifflin & Co., 1902.

BERRY, THOMAS S., *Western Prices Before 1861; a Study of the Cincinnati Market,* Harvard Economic Studies LXXIV. Cambridge: Harvard University Press, 1943.

BIGELOW, JOHN P., *Statistical Tables Exhibiting the Condition and Products of Certain Branches of Industry in Massachusetts, for the Year Ending April 1, 1837.* Boston: Dutton & Wentworth, 1838.

BLODGET, SAMUEL, *Economica: A Statistical Manual for the United States of America.* Washington: Printed for the author, 1806.

BUCK, NORMAN S., *The Development of the Organization of Anglo-American Trade, 1800–1850.* New Haven: Yale University Press, 1925.

BUCKINGHAM, JAMES S., *The Slave States of America,* 2 vols. London, Paris: Fisher, Son & Co., 1842.

CALLENDER, GUY S., *Selections from the Economic History of the United States, 1765–1860.* Boston: Ginn & Company, 1909.

CLARK, V. S., *History of Manufactures in the United States,* 3 vols. New York: McGraw-Hill Book Company, for the Carnegie Institution, 1929.

CLAUDER, ANNA C., *American Commerce as Affected by the Wars of the French Revolution and Napoleon, 1793–1812.* Philadelphia: University of Pennsylvania Ph.D. thesis, 1932.

COLE, ARTHUR H., *The American Wool Manufacture,* 2 vols. Cambridge: Harvard University Press, 1926.

COLE, ARTHUR H., ed. *Industrial and Commercial Correspondence of Alexander Hamilton, Anticipating his Report on Manufactures.* Chicago: A. W. Shaw & Co., 1928.

COXE, TENCH, *A View of the United States, in a Series of Papers . . .* Philadelphia: William Hall, Wrigley & Berryman, 1794.

COXE, TENCH, *A Statement of the Arts and Manufactures of the United States for the Year 1810.* Philadelphia: A. Cornman, 1814.

DEWITT, FRANCIS, *Statistical Information Relating to Certain Branches of Industry in Massachusetts for the Year Ending June 1, 1855.* Boston: William White, Printer for the State, 1856.

EVANS, GEORGE H., *Business Incorporations in the United States, 1800–1943.* New York: National Bureau of Economic Research, 1948.

FOLZ, W. E., *The Financial Crisis of 1819.* Urbana: University of Illinois Ph.D. thesis, 1935.

GIBB, GEORGE S., *The Saco-Lowell Shops, Textile Machinery Building in New*

293

England, 1813–1849, Harvard Studies in Business History 16. Cambridge: Harvard University Press, 1950.

GRAY, LEWIS C., *History of Agriculture in the Southern United States to 1860.* Washington: The Carnegie Institution, 1933.

HAMMOND, MATTHEW B., *The Cotton Industry, an Essay in American Economic History.* New York: Macmillan Book Company, published for the American Economic Association, 1897.

HAZARD, BLANCHE, *The Organization of the Boot and Shoe Industry in Massachusetts Before 1875,* Harvard Economic Studies XXIII. Cambridge: Harvard University Press, 1921.

HELPER, HINTON R., *Compendium of the Impending Crisis of the South.* New York: A. B. Burdick, 1860.

HIRSCHMAN, ALBERT O., *The Strategy of Economic Development.* New Haven: Yale University Press, 1958.

HOOVER, EDGAR M. JR., *Location Theory and the Shoe and Leather Industries,* Harvard Economic Studies LV. Cambridge: Harvard University Press, 1937.

INGLE, EDWARD, *Southern Sidelights, a Picture of Social and Economic Life in the South a Generation Before the War.* New York: Thomas Y. Crowell & Co., 1896.

JOHNSON, EMORY R., *et al., History of Domestic and Foreign Commerce of the United States.* Washington: The Carnegie Institution, 1915.

JONES, FRED M., *Middlemen in the Domestic Trade of the United States, 1800–1860,* Illinois Studies in the Social Sciences XXI, No. 3. Urbana: University of Illinois Press, 1937.

KETTELL, THOMAS P., *Southern Wealth and Northern Profits, as Exhibited in Statistical Facts and Official Figures . . .* New York: G. W. & J. A. Wood, 1860.

KOOPMANS, TJALLING, *Tanker Freight Rates and Tankship Building, an Analysis of Cyclical Fluctuations.* Haarlem: De erven F. Bohn, n.v., 1939.

LEIBENSTEIN, HARVEY, *Economic Backwardness and Economic Growth.* New York: Wiley & Sons, 1957.

McGRANE, REGINALD C., *The Panic of 1837; Some Financial Problems of the Jacksonian Era.* Chicago: University of Chicago Press, 1924.

MACESICH, GEORGE, *Monetary Disturbances in the United States, 1834–45.* Chicago: University of Chicago Ph.D. thesis, 1958.

MARTIN, ROBERT F., *National Income of the United States, 1799–1938.* New York: National Industrial Conference Board, 1939.

MATTHEWS, ROBERT C. O., *A Study in Trade Cycle History; Economic Fluctuations in Great Britain 1833–1842.* Cambridge: The University Press, 1954.

MORISON, SAMUEL E., *Maritime History of Massachussetts, 1783–1860.* Boston: Houghton Mifflin Co., 1921.

MYERS, MARGARET, *The New York Money Market,* 2 vols. New York: Columbia University Press, 1931.

Niles' National Register, 75 vols. Baltimore, Washington, Philadelphia: 1811–1849.

PITKIN, TIMOTHY, *A Statistical View of the Commerce of the United States: Including also an Account of Banks, Manufactures and Internal Trade.* New Haven: Durrie and Peck, 1835.

POOR, HENRY V., *Manual of Railroads of the United States, for 1869–1870.* New York: H. V. and H. W. Poor, 1869.

SEYBERT, ADAM, *Statistical Annals: Embracing Views of the Population, Com-*

merce, Navigation . . . of the United States of America. Philadelphia: Thomas Dobson & Son, 1818.

SMITH, ALFRED G. JR., *Economic Readjustment of an Old Cotton State, South Carolina 1820–1860.* Columbia: University of South Carolina Press, 1958.

SMITH, WALTER B., *Economic Aspects of the Second Bank,* Harvard Studies in Economic History. Cambridge: Harvard University Press, 1953.

SMITH, WALTER B. and ARTHUR H. COLE, *Fluctuations in American Business, 1790–1860,* Harvard Economic Studies L. Cambridge: Harvard University Press, 1935.

STORY, WILLIAM W., ed., *Life and Letters of Joseph Story, Associate Justice of the Supreme Court,* 2 vols. Boston: C. C. Little and J. Brown, 1851.

TAUSSIG, FRANK W., *The Tariff History of the United States,* 6th ed. New York: G. P. Putnam's Sons, 1914.

TAYLOR, GEORGE R., *The Transportation Revolution, 1815–1860,* Vol. IV of *Economic History of the United States.* New York: Rinehart, 1951.

THOMAS, BRINLEY, *Migration and Economic Growth, a Study of Great Britain and the Atlantic Economy.* Cambridge: The University Press, 1954.

THORP, WILLARD L., *Business Annals.* New York: National Bureau of Economic Research, 1926.

VAN VLECK, GEORGE, *The Panic of 1857.* New York: Columbia University Press, 1943.

WARE, CAROLINE, *The Early New England Cotton Manufacture, a Study in Industrial Beginnings.* Boston: Houghton Mifflin Company, 1931.

WARREN, G. F. and F. A. PEARSON, *Wholesale Prices for 213 Years, 1720 to 1932.* Ithaca: Cornell University Press, 1932.

WENDER, HERBERT, *Southern Commercial Conventions, 1837–1859,* Johns Hopkins University Studies in Historical and Political Science, Series XLVIII, No. 4. Baltimore: The Johns Hopkins Press, 1930.

WHITWORTH, JOSEPH and GEORGE WALLIS, *The Industry of the United States in Machinery, Manufactures, and Useful and Ornamental Arts.* London: George Routledge & Co., 1854.

YOUNGSON, A. J.: *Possibilities of Economic Progress.* Cambridge: The University Press, 1959.

Articles

ABRAMOVITZ, MOSES, "Long Swings in United States Economic Growth," *38th Annual Report* of the National Bureau of Economic Research. New York: National Bureau of Economic Research, 1958, pp. 47-56.

ALBION, ROBERT G., "New York Port and its Disappointed Rivals, 1815–1860," *Journal of Economic and Business History III* (1930–31), 602-29.

BALDWIN, R. E., "Patterns of Development in Newly Settled Regions," *The Manchester School of Economic and Social Studies XXIV,* No. 2 (May 1956), 161-79.

BURN, D. L., "The Genesis of American Engineering Competition," *Economic History,* Supplement to *Economic Journal II,* No. 6 (January 1931), 292-311.

CALLENDER, GUY S., "The Early Transportation and Banking Enterprises of the States in Relation to the Growth of the Corporation," *Quarterly Journal of Economics XVII* (1903), 111-62.

COLE, ARTHUR H., "Cyclical and Sectional Variations in the Sale of Public Lands, 1816–60," *Review of Economics and Statistics*, IX, No. 1 (January 1927), 50.

CONRAD, A. H., and JOHN R. MEYERS, "The Economics of Slavery in the Ante-Bellum South," *Journal of Political Economy* LXVI, No. 2 (April 1958), 95-130.

DAVIS, LANCE, "The New England Textile Mills and the Capital Markets: A Study of Industrial Borrowing, 1840–1860," *Journal of Economic History* XX, No. 1 (March 1960), 1-30.

DAVIS, LANCE, "Sources of Industrial Finance: The American Textile Industry, A Case Study," *Explorations in Entrepreneurial History* IX, No. 4 (April 1957), 189-203.

DAVIS, MARIAN, "Critique of Official United States Immigration Statistics," II, Appendix II of *International Migrations*, 2 vols., Walter F. Willcox, ed. New York: National Bureau of Economic Research, 1929-30.

DUSENBERRY, J. S., "Some Aspects of the Theory of Economic Development," *Explorations in Entrepreneurial History* III, No. 2 (December 1950), 63-102.

GALLMAN, ROBERT E., "Commodity Output, 1839–1899," *Trends in the American Economy in the Nineteenth Century*. Studies in Income and Wealth of the National Bureau of Economic Research, Vol. 24. Princeton: Princeton University Press, 1960.

KUZNETS, SIMON, "Current National Income Estimates for the Period Prior to 1870," International Association for Research in Income and Wealth, *Income and Wealth Series II: Trends and Structure in the United States*. Cambridge: Bowes and Bowes, 1952.

MORRIS, MORRIS D., "The Recruitment of an Industrial Labor Force in India, with British and American Comparisons," *Comparative Studies in Society and History*, II, No. 3 (April 1960), 315-20.

NICHOLLS, WILLIAM H., "Some Foundations of Economic Development in the Upper East Tennessee Valley, 1850–1900. II," *Journal of Political Economy* LXIV, No. 5 (October 1956), 400-415.

NORTH, DOUGLASS C., "Agriculture and Regional Economic Growth," paper delivered before American Farm Economics Association, Cornell University, August 1959, subsequently published in American Farm Economics Association *Proceedings*, XLI, No. 5 (December 1959), 943-51.

NORTH, DOUGLASS C., "International Capital Flows and the Development of the American West," *Journal of Economic History* XVI, No. 4 (December 1956), 493-505.

NORTH, DOUGLASS C., "Location Theory and Regional Economic Growth," *Journal of Political Economy* LXII, No. 3 (June 1955), 243-58.

NORTH, DOUGLASS C., "Ocean Freight Rates and Economic Development, 1750–1913," *Journal of Economic History* XVIII, No. 4 (December 1958), 537-55.

NORTH, DOUGLASS C., "Reply," to "Exports and Regional Economic Growth," by Charles M. Tiebout, in *Journal of Political Economy* LXIV, No. 2 (April 1956), 165-68.

NORTH, DOUGLASS C., "The United States Balance of Payments, 1790–1860," *Trends in the American Economy in the Nineteenth Century*. Studies in Income and Wealth of the National Bureau of Economic Research, Vol. 24. Princeton: Princeton University Press, 1960.

PAGE, THOMAS W., "Distribution of Immigrants in the United States Before 1870," *Journal of Political Economy* XX (1912), 676-94.

PARKER, WILLIAM N. and FRANKLEE WHARTENBY, "The Growth of Output Before 1840," *Trends in the American Economy in the Nineteenth Century.* Studies in Income and Wealth of the National Bureau of Economic Research, Vol. 24. Princeton: Princeton University Press, 1960.

SAWYER, JOHN E., "The Social Basis of the American System of Manufacturing," *Journal of Economic History* XIV, No. 4 (1954), 361-79.

SCHMIDT, LOUIS B., "Internal Commerce and the Development of National Economy Before 1860," *Journal of Political Economy* XLVII (December 1939), 798-822.

SCHMIDT, LOUIS B., "The Internal Grain Trade of the United States," *Iowa Journal of History and Politics* XVIII, No. 1 (January 1920), 103.

SCHMIDT, LOUIS B., "The Westward Movement of the Wheat Growing Industry in the United States," *Iowa Journal of History and Politics* XVIII, No. 3 (July 1920), 399-401.

SCHUR, LEON M., "The Second Bank of the United States and the Inflation After the War of 1812," *Journal of Political Economy* LXVIII (April 1960), 118-34.

SEARS, LOUIS M., "Philadelphia and the Embargo of 1808," *Quarterly Journal of Economics* XXXV (February 1921), 355-59.

SIMON, MATTHEW, "The United States Balance of Payments, 1861-1900," *Trends in the American Economy in the Nineteenth Century.* Studies in Income and Wealth of the National Bureau of Economic Research, Vol. 24. Princeton: Princeton University Press, 1960.

STIGLER, GEORGE J., "The Division of Labor is Limited by the Extent of the Market," *Journal of Political Economy* LIX, No. 3 (June 1951), 185-93.

TOWNE, MARVIN and WAYNE RASMUSSEN, "Farm Gross Product and Gross Investment During the Nineteenth Century," *Trends in the American Economy in the Nineteenth Century.* Studies in Income and Wealth of the National Bureau of Economic Research, Vol. 24. Princeton: Princeton University Press, 1960.

VINING, RUTLEDGE, "Location of Industry and Regional Patterns of Business Cycle Behavior," *Econometrica* XIV (January 1946), 37-68.

ZELLNER, ARNOLD and GEORGE G. S. MURPHY, "Sequential Growth, the Labor Safety Valve Doctrine, and the Development of American Unionism," *Journal of Economic History* XIX, No. 3 (September 1959), 402-21.

Government Documents

Great Britain

GREAT BRITAIN, PARLIAMENT. *Report of the Commission on the Machinery of the United States. Parliamentary Papers,* 1854–1855, L.

United States

U. S. CENSUS BUREAU, *A Century of Population Growth in the United States, 1790–1900.* Washington: Government Printing Office, 1909.

U. S. CENSUS BUREAU, *A Compendium of the Ninth Census, June 1, 1870,* by Francis A. Walker, Superintendent of Census. Washington: Government Printing Office, 1872.

U. S. CENSUS BUREAU, *A Compendium of the Seventh Census,* J. D. B. DeBow, Superintendent of Census. Washington: Senate Printer, 1854.

U. S. CENSUS BUREAU, *Eighth Census of the U. S., 1860, Agriculture.* Washington: Government Printing Office, 1865.

U. S. CENSUS BUREAU, *Eighth Census of the U. S., 1860, Manufactures.* Washington: Government Printing Office, 1865.

U. S. CENSUS BUREAU, *Foreign Commerce and Navigation.* Washington: Government Printing Office, 1906.

U. S. CENSUS BUREAU, *Historical Statistics of the United States, 1789–1945.* Washington: Government Printing Office, 1949.

U. S. CENSUS BUREAU, *Preliminary Report on the Eighth Census.* Washington: Government Printing Office, 1862.

U. S. CENSUS BUREAU, *Seventh Census of the U. S., 1850.* Washington: Government Printing Office, 1852.

U. S. CENSUS BUREAU, *Sixteenth Census of the U. S., Population,* Vol. I. Washington: Government Printing Office, 1942.

U. S. CENSUS BUREAU, *Sixth Census of the U. S., 1840.* Washington: Blair and Rives, 1841.

U. S. CENSUS BUREAU, *Twelfth Census of the U. S., Manufactures,* Part I, Vol. VII, IV. Washington: Government Printing Office, 1902.

U. S. CONGRESS, HOUSE, *Domestic Exports, 1789–1883.* House Miscellaneous Document No. 2236, compiled by C. H. Evans. 48th Congress, 1st Session, 1883–1884. Washington: Government Printing Office, 1884.

U. S. CONGRESS, HOUSE, *Miscellaneous Document No. 49,* Part 2, Tables 2 and 7. 48th Congress, 1st Session, 1884. Washington: Government Printing Office, 1884.

U. S. CONGRESS, HOUSE, *Report of the Secretary of the Treasury, on the State of the Finances, for the Year Ending June 30, 1863.* House Executive Document No. 3. 38th Congress, 1st Session, 1864, pp. 382-98. Washington: Government Printing Office, 1864.

U. S. CONGRESS, HOUSE, *Report on the Internal Commerce of the United States.* House Executive Document No. 6, Part 2. 50th Congress, 1st Session, 1888. Washington: Government Printing Office, 1888.

U. S. CONGRESS, HOUSE, *Treasury Department Technical Paper No. 10.* Executive Documents, 34th Congress, 1st Session, 1855–1856, Vol. 4. Washington: Government Printing Office, 1857. Criticism of census statistics prior to 1840 by Robert C. Morgan and W. A. Shannon.

U. S. CONGRESS, JOINT ECONOMIC COMMITTEE, *Hearings,* Part 2, "Historical and Comparative Rates of Production, Productivity and Prices." 86th Congress, 1st Session, 1959. Washington: Government Printing Office, 1959. Testimony of Moses Abramovitz, pp. 411-33.

U. S. CONGRESS, JOINT ECONOMIC COMMITTEE, *Hearings,* Part 2, "Historical and Comparative Rates of Production, Productivity and Prices." 86th Congress, 1st Session, 1959. Washington: Government Printing Office, 1959. Testimony of Raymond Goldsmith, pp. 230-79.

U. S. CONGRESS, SENATE, *Preliminary Report of the Inland Waterways Commission.* Senate Document No. 325. 60th Congress, 1st Session, 1908. Washington: Government Printing Office, 1908.

U. S. CONGRESS, SENATE, *Statistics of Foreign and Domestic Commerce.* Senate Executive Document No. 55. 38th Congress, 1st Session, 1864. Washington: Government Printing Office, 1865.

U. S. LABOR STATISTICS BUREAU, *Wholesale Prices, 1890-1923,* Bulletin No. 367, Appendix F, "Wholesale Prices in the United States, 1801-1840." Washington: Government Printing Office, 1925.

INDEX

299